D1548111

THE ILLUSTRATED
CULTURAL HISTORY
OF INDIA

The Oxford India Collection is a series which brings together
writings of enduring value published by OUP.

Other titles include

THE ILLUSTRATED
CULTURAL HISTORY
OF INDIA

edited by
A.L. BASHAM

OXFORD
UNIVERSITY PRESS

YMCA Library Building, Jai Singh Road, New Delhi 110001

Oxford University Press is a department of the University of Oxford. It furthers
the University's objective of excellence in research, scholarship, and education
by publishing worldwide in

Oxford   New York
Auckland   Cape Town   Dar es Salaam   Hong Kong   Karachi
Kuala Lumpur   Madrid   Melbourne   Mexico City   Nairobi
New Delhi   Shanghai   Taipei   Toronto

With offices in
Argentina   Austria   Brazil   Chile   Czech Republic   France   Greece
Guatemala   Hungary   Italy   Japan   Poland   Portugal   Singapore
South Korea   Switzerland   Thailand   Turkey   Ukraine   Vietnam

Oxford is a registered trade mark of Oxford University Press
in the UK and in certain other countries

Published in India by Oxford University Press, New Delhi

ISBN-13: 978-0-19-569192-4
ISBN-10: 0-19-569192-X

Illustrations by Kallol Majumder
Some illustrations from The Illustrated History of Sikhs by Khushwant Singh

Typeset in Bembo 11/15 by Eleven Arts, Keshav Puram, Delhi 110 035
Printed in India by Thomson Press (India) Ltd., New Delhi 110 020
Published by Oxford University Press
YMCA Library Building, Jai Singh Road, New Delhi 110 001

Contents

PART III: Challenge and Response—
The Coming of the West

Publisher's Note

The Illustrated Cultural History of India is an adapted version of the classic *A Cultural History of India* edited by A.L. Basham first published by OUP in 1975 and available to readers even today. This edition has been developed with the aim of bringing the knowledge of Indian history and culture to a much wider audience, including young readers. The book explores a vast, complex, and often controversial span of history imaginatively and accessibly. A part of the Oxford India Illustrated Collection that brings together writings of enduring value, this book combines the rich content of the original volume with complementary visuals to capture the interest of younger readers who may associate history with 'boring details about the past'. Teachers, parents, and general readers will find it a useful aid in understanding and explaining India's past.

Divided into three sections, the book covers all phases of India's cultural development from the ancient times to its rebirth as an independent nation. The first section traces 'The Ancient Heritage' of

the country, beginning with the Indus Valley Civilization and moves on to analyse the influence of the early Aryans and the Ashokan and Gupta periods. It traces the developments that took place in the fields of philosophy, literature, art and architecture, and music in this period. 'The Age of Muslim Dominance', the second section of the book, traces the rule of Muslim dynasties and their influence on Indian architecture. It also chronicles the rise of Islam and Sikhism, and the advent of medieval Indian miniature painting. The final section titled 'Challenge and Response—The Coming of the West' traces the period from the coming of the British to the Indian subcontinent to the ultimate demise of British supremacy.

Combining the best scholarship on the subject with lucid text, appealing visuals, and an easy-to-read format, this edition will, we hope, inform a wide range of readers.

The Publisher would like to thank the institutions and individuals who supported the idea of opening up the cultural wealth of India to a wider audience by providing visual material for the project.

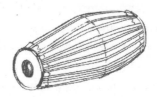

Introduction

A.L. BASHAM

THERE ARE FOUR MAIN CRADLES of civilization, from which elements of culture have spread to other parts of the world. These are, moving from east to west, China, the Indian subcontinent, the 'Fertile Crescent', and the Mediterranean, especially Greece and Italy. Of these four areas India deserves a larger share of the credit than she is usually given, because, on a minimal assessment, she has deeply affected the religious life of most of Asia and has provided very important elements in the culture of the whole of South East Asia, as well as extending her influence, directly and indirectly, to other parts of the world.

It has been commonly believed in the West that before the impact of European learning, science, and technology 'the East' changed little, if at all, over many centuries. The 'wisdom of the East', unchanging over the millennia, it was thought, preserved eternal verities which Western civilization had almost forgotten. On the other hand, 'the East' was not ready to enter into the rough and tumble of the modern world without the guidance for an indefinite period of more developed Western countries.

In fact India has always been steadily changing. The civilization of the Guptas was different from that of the Mauryas, and that of medieval times was different again. The Muslims altered conditions considerably, and the high flowering of Indian Muslim civilization under the four great Mughals brought yet more changes. The religious life of India, for all her 'ancient wisdom', has changed greatly over the centuries. Between the time of the early Greek philosophers and that of St Thomas Aquinas, Buddhism developed into a great religious movement in India, changed its outlook almost completely, declined, and finally sank back into the Hinduism from which it had emerged, but only after Buddhist missionaries had spread their message throughout half of Asia. The Athenian Acropolis was at least 500 years old before the first surviving Hindu stone temple was built. Some of the most popular gods of Hinduism, for instance Ganesha and Hanuman, are not attested until well after the time of Christ. Certain other features of Hinduism also, for instance the cult of the divine Rama and the complex and difficult system of physical training known as *hatha yoga*, are centuries later than Christianity.

Yet the older strata of India's cultural life go back far beyond anything we have in the West. The whole of the *Rig Veda* had been composed long before the *Iliad*, and there is hardly anything in the Old Testament in its present form which is as old even as the latest Rig Vedic hymns. Some practices and beliefs of popular Hinduism, for instance the cults of the sacred bull and the *pipal* tree, are as old as the prehistoric Harappa culture, and probably even older. In fact every generation in India, for over 4000 years, has bequeathed something, if only a very little, to posterity.

No land on earth has such a long cultural continuity as India, since, though there were more ancient civilizations, notably in Egypt and Iraq, these were virtually forgotten by the inhabitants of those lands, and were overlaid by new intrusive cultures, until nobody remembered the *Book of the Dead* or the *Epic of Gilgamesh*, and great kings such as Ramesses II or Hammurabi were not recorded in any living tradition. Only nineteenth-century scholarship resurrected them from oblivion, and if they are now national heroes, remembered by every schoolchild in their respective lands, this is not thanks either to the historical genius or to the retentive folk memory of the countries concerned.

On the other hand, in India the brahman still repeats in his daily worship Vedic hymns composed over 3000 years ago, and tradition recalls heroic chieftains and the great battles fought by them at about the same time. In respect of the length of continuous tradition China comes second to India and Greece makes a poor third.

The pre-Vedic Harappa culture bequeathed to later times sacred animals and trees, the Mother Goddess, and preoccupation with personal cleanliness, and, less certainly, other aspect of Indian culture. From the Vedic Aryans came many of the gods, the Vedic hymns, some of the most important personal rituals of Hinduism, the patriarchal and patrilineal family system, and the horse. Later Vedic times (c. 1000–600 BC) brought the passion for speculation on ultimate causes, the quest for the Absolute, the doctrine of transmigration, the search for release from the round of rebirth, and mystical gnosis. In social life and material culture the same period saw the crystallization of the four classes (varnas) of Hindu society, the introduction of iron from western Asia, the domestication of the elephant, and the development of kingdoms out of tribal chieftainships.

In the following 300 years coined money became common, and writing, known in the time of the Harappa culture and later apparently forgotten, became widespread. Heterodox teachers, chief of whom was the Buddha, spread new doctrines which bypassed the gods, the Vedas, and the brahmans, and the area of civilization steadily expanded into the remoter parts of the subcontinent.

Political developments over the preceding period led to the first great empire of India, that of the Mauryas, when for the first time most of the subcontinent was united under a single government. This period (c. 320–185 BC) produced the Machiavellian system of statecraft associated with the name of the minister Kautilya, the reputed author of the famous *Arthashastra*. From the Mauryas also come the earliest surviving stone sculpture of India, the oldest artificial caves, and the most ancient Buddhist *stupas*. Under Ashoka (*c.* 272–232 BC) Buddhism increased its influence, and was taken to Ceylon.

The 500 years between the Mauryas and the Guptas (*c.* 184 BC– AD 320) saw tremendous developments in Indian civilization, partly due to fresh influences brought in by various invaders and traders, and partly the result of internal developments. New forms of devotional religion emerged, centring on the gods Vishnu and Shiva, and these led to the composition of the Bhagavad Gita, now the most influential text of Hinduism. Buddhism developed a theology, the Mahayana, which was carried to China. Schools of law appeared, codifying in written form earlier traditions. The two great epics of India, the Mahabharata and the Ramayana, were edited in something like their present form. Courtly literature began developing out of vanished prototypes: drama, ranging from the heroic to the sentimental, and verse, wonderful in its polish and ingenuity yet often filled with deep and sincere feeling. Logically reasoned philosophical schools emerged, as distinct from the older religious teachers, most of whose arguments were analogical. Contact with South East Asia became closer with the spread of trade, and that region began to adopt many features of the religion and culture of India. These are only a few of the many innovations of this, perhaps the most formative period of Indian history before the nineteenth century.

The period from the rise of the Guptas to the death of Harshavardhana (320–647) can truly be called the classical period of Indian civilization. In this age the greatest sculpture of ancient India was produced, and the finest literature written, in the poems and plays of Kalidasa. This was the time of the best surviving ancient Indian mural painting, typified by Ajanta. Knowledge grew also in this period. India's most important practical contribution to the world, the system of place notation of numerals, with nine digits and a zero, was known by AD 500, and led to the great development of Indian mathematics and astronomy. The recording of ancient legends and traditions in the Puranas began. The Mother Goddess, after centuries of neglect, became an important object of worship again. Stone-built temples appeared throughout the land.

Between the death of Harshavardhana and the coming of Islam (647–*c.* 1200) the ecstatic devotional religion (*bhakti*), associated with the singing of hymns in the common tongue, appeared in Tamilnadu, later to spread all over the subcontinent. Temples became larger and grander, with spiring towers. The system of hatha yoga was developed, and tantrism, with its sacramentalization of sex, spread in both Hinduism and Buddhism. In Sankara and Ramanuja Hindu religious philosophy saw its greatest teachers. Some of the finest schools of bronze casting in the world appeared in Bengal and Tamilnadu. The former region also developed a fine school of miniature painting.

With the coming of Islam fresh cultural influences made themselves felt. The Sultanate period (1192–1526) saw the introduction of new styles of architecture, bringing the dome and arch. New schools of miniature painting, both Muslim and Hindu, emerged. Sufi teachers disseminated the doctrines of Islam and helped to make the religious climate of northern India favourable to the spread of popular devotional Hinduism from the south. Paper was introduced, slowly replacing the traditional Indian writing materials—palm-leaf and birch-bark. The Urdu language began to appear as the lingua franca of northern India, and poets began to compose in the everyday languages instead of classical Sanskrit.

The great days of the Mughal Empire (1526–1707) witnessed the perfection of the schools of Muslim architecture and miniature painting, with the production of such splendid buildings as the Taj Mahal at Agra. Cannon and smaller firearms began to be used in warfare. Europeans established trading stations at various ports, and through them, especially the Portuguese, new crops were introduced into India, among them the potato, tobacco, the pineapple, and, surprisingly, the spice which nowadays is commonly thought typical of India, the chilli pepper. The Sikh religion was born just as this period began, as a small devotional sect, and at about the time when the period concluded it was reborn as a martial brotherhood, to play an important part in the confused political life of the following century.

The eighteenth century saw the break-up of the Mughal Empire and the steady expansion of the power of the British East India Company. It was a time of general cultural decline in India, but the genius of the land was still at work. The Urdu language, little used hitherto as a medium of literary expression, became the vehicle of great poetry at the decadent courts of Delhi and Lucknow; while in the Himalayan foothills, at the end of the century at the petty courts of local maharajas, by some unexplainable miracle, there worked painters who produced works of unprecedented beauty and sensitivity. With the nineteenth century the subcontinent was exposed to the full force of Western influence, and innovations are too numerous to list.

As well as this great legacy of the human past, the people of the subcontinent have another inheritance from nature itself—the land and its climate. We cannot understand South Asia without knowing something about what its people have received from the primeval forces which shaped the surface of the earth millions of years before man existed. In this sense perhaps India's most important inheritance is the great chain of the Himalayas, without which the land would be little more than a desert.

As the plateau of Central Asia grows warmer in the spring, the warm air rises and winds bearing heavy masses of cloud are attracted towards the high tableland from the Indian Ocean. The movement of the clouds are interrupted by the mountains, and they shed their burden of rain upon the parched, overheated land. The monsoon, beginning in June, lasts for about three months, and brings water for the whole year. Except along the coast and in a few other specially favoured areas, there is little or no rain in other seasons, and thus the life of almost the whole subcontinent depends on the monsoon.

The conservation and just sharing out of the available water among the cultivators is a very important factor in the life of India. It has been one of the main concerns of Indian governments for over

2500 years and indeed the high civilization which is discussed in the pages of this book has depended, and still largely depends, on irrigation, promoted and supervised by government, for its very existence. In the past, whenever the rains have been inadequate, there has been famine; whenever a local government has lost grip and become ineffective, irrigation has been neglected, dams have broken, canals have been choked with mud and weed, and great hardship has resulted. Thus villagers have learnt to cooperate independently of their rulers, by forming their own village government, under a committee of locally respected leaders, the *panchayat*, to care for matters of common concern such as irrigation, and to settle disputes as far as possible outside the royal courts. On a large scale the climate has perhaps encouraged autocracy, but at the local level it has necessitated government by discussion.

South of the Himalayas lie the great plains of the subcontinent, the centres from which civilization expanded in ancient times. Composed of deep silt carried down by the rivers Indus (Sind, Sindhu) and Ganga (Ganges) these plains are naturally very fertile, but for centuries they have supported a dense population, whose peasants used the most easily available form of manure, cow dung, as fuel. Hence the fertility of the plains declined, until by the end of the last century many areas had reached a rock bottom of productivity, from which they have begun to emerge only recently, with the introduction of artificial fertilizers and the spread of knowledge of better agricultural methods. In ancient days, however, the fertility and the healthy well-fed peasantry of India were noticed by foreign travellers from the Greek Megasthenes (*c*. 300 BC) onwards.

South of the Ganga are the Vindhya mountains and the long and beautiful River Narmada, dividing the north from the plateau region of Maharashtra, generally called the Deccan (from Sanskrit *dakshina*, 'south'). The region, less naturally fertile than the great plains, has been for at least 2000 years the home of tough martial peasants who, whenever energetic leadership appeared to consolidate their clans, would take advantage of the political weakness of their neighbours to raid the wealthier lands to the north, south-east, and south.

The Deccan plateau becomes steadily less rugged and more fertile as one proceeds south and south-east. Along the eastern littoral of the peninsula are fertile riverine plains, the most important historically being that of Tamilnadu, reaching from Madras to Cape Comorin (Kanyakumari, the extreme southern tip of India). Here, over 2000 years ago, the Tamil people developed a fairly advanced civilization independently of the Aryan north; this region has throughout its history maintained a consciousness of its differences from the north, and has cherished its own language, while remaining part of the whole Indian cultural area; there may be an analogy between the Tamil attitude to the northern Aryans and that of the Welsh to the English, with the difference that, while many Welshmen have English as their mother tongue, few if any Tamils have a mother tongue other than Tamil.

Yet another inheritance of India from the distant past is her people. Despite the difficult mountain passes and the wide seas barring access to India, people have been finding their way there from the days of the Old Stone Age, when small hordes of primitive men drifted into the subcontinent. These are probably the ancestors of one of India's three main racial types—the Proto-Australoid, so called because of the resemblance to the Australian Aborigines. In India the most pure Proto-Australoid type is to be found among the tribal peoples of the wilder parts of the peninsula, but Proto-Australoid features can be traced almost everywhere in the subcontinent, especially among people of low caste. The ideal type is short, dark-skinned, broad-nosed, and large-mouthed.

The next main stratum in the population of India is the Plaeo-Mediterranean, often loosely called Dravidian, a term not now favoured by anthropologists. These people seem to have come to South Asia from the west, not very long before the dawn of civilization in the Indus valley, and they may have contributed to the foundation of the Harappa culture. Graceful and slender, with well-chiselled features and aquiline noses, the ideal type is particularly to be found among the better-class speakers of Dravidian languages, but also occurs everywhere in the subcontinent.

Then, in the second millennium BC, came the Aryans, speakers of an Indo-European language which was the cousin of those of classical Europe. Some have suggested that these people came in two or more waves, the earlier invaders being round-headed (brachycephalic) people of the type called Alpine or Armenoid, and the later long-headed folk, typical Caucasoids, similar in build to northern Europeans. Long before they entered India the people who called themselves Aryans had intermixed with other peoples, and their advent meant a severe cultural decline, which lasted for many centuries. Only when Aryan culture was fertilized by the indigenous culture did it begin to advance, to form the classical civilization of India. There are good arguments for the view that in the finished product non-Aryan elements are more numerous than Aryan. Nowadays the Caucasoid type is chiefly to be found in Pakistan, Kashmir, and the Panjab, but even here one rarely meets pure or nearly pure specimens. As one proceeds east and south, the type becomes progressively rarer.

These three, the Proto-Australoid, the Palaeo-Mediterranean, and the Caucasoid or Indo-European, are the most strongly represented racial types among the inhabitants of India; but they are by no means the only ones. Almost every race of Central Asia found its way to India. Turks provided the ruling families in much of what is now Pakistan long before the coming of the Muslims, who were also Turks. Mongolians of various races have been entering India over the Himalayan and north-eastern passes since long before history. The Muslim ruling classes imported numerous African slaves, who have long since merged with the general population. Persian and Arab traders settled along the west coast from before the Christian era. Some married Indian women, and the descendants have become indistinguishable from the rest of the population. Others, such as the small but vigorous Parsi community, have kept their stock pure. The various European traders and conquerors have left their mark also.

Along the west coast of India and Ceylon an appreciable quantity of Portuguese blood circulates in the veins of the general population, while elsewhere in India the so-called Anglo-Indian community is the result of many marriages and liaisons between European (not only British) soldiers and traders and Indian women.

Thus, in reading these chapters, we must also remember India's enduring inheritance of climate, land, and people, on the basis of which her high civilization has been built, and which will remain, more or less unchanging, to condition the lives of her people in all their triumphs and vicissitudes in future centuries.

PART ONE

The Ancient Heritage

The Indus Civilization

B.B. Lal

MORE THAN 4000 YEARS AGO there flourished in the north-western parts of the Indo-Pakistan subcontinent a civilization which, deriving its name from the main river of the region, is known as the Indus civilization. In fact, however, it extended far beyond the limits of that valley—from Sutkagen-dor, on the sea board of south Baluchistan, in the west to Alamgirpur, in the upper Ganga-Yamuna *doab* in Uttar Pradesh, in the east; and from Ropar, almost impinging upon the sub-Himalayan foothills, in the north of Bhagatrav, on the estuary of the Kim, a small river between the Narmada and Tapti, in the south. In other words, from west to east the Indus civilization covered an area of 1600 kilometres, and from north to south of 1100 kilometres, and it will not be surprising if future discoveries widen the horizons still further. This is an area much greater than that occupied jointly by the contemporary civilizations of Egypt and Mesopotamia. And throughout the region a notably high standard of living was reached, which is reflected in almost every walk of life.

The first thing that strikes a visitor to an Indus site—be it Harappa or Mohenjo-daro in Pakistan or Kalibangan, Lothal, or Surkotada in India—is the town planning. One finds the streets and lanes laid out according to a set plan: the main streets running from north to south and the cross-streets and lanes running at right angles to them. At Kalibangan, among the north–south streets there was a principal one, 7.20 metres wide, while the other north–south streets were three-quarters of its width. The cross-streets and lanes were, once again, half or a quarter of the width of the narrower streets from north to south. Such typical and minutely planned residential areas, often called the 'lower towns', were themselves only a part of the entire settlement complex. For at Harappa, Mohenjo-daro, Kalibangan, and Surkotada, there was a 'citadel', smaller in area than the 'lower town' and invariably located to the west of it. At Lothal, although no 'citadel' as such has been found, a similar conception seems to have existed, for the more important structures rested in a group on a high mud-brick platform. In marked contrast might be cited the contemporary example of Ur in Mesopotamia, where there was no rigorous planning of this kind, the main street wandering and curving as it wished.

Both at Harappa and Mohenjo-daro the houses were made of kiln-burnt bricks. At Kalibangan and Lothal too, although mud bricks were used for most of the residential houses, kiln-burnt bricks in large quantities were used for drains, wells, and bathing-platforms, and in particular for the dockyard at the latter site. Such bricks were rare in contemporary Mesopotamia or Egypt. At Mohenjo-daro and Kalibangan, where large areas have been excavated, an average house consisted of a courtyard around which were situated four to six living rooms, besides a bathroom and a kitchen. Larger houses, however, might have up to thirty rooms, and the presence of staircases in many of them indicates a second storey. For the supply of fresh water, most of the houses had their own wells, and in addition, there were public wells. Sullage-water was discharged through well-covered street-drains made of kiln-burnt bricks. At intervals they were provided with manholes for clearance.

The citadel at Mohenjo-daro contained many imposing buildings, all made of kiln-burnt bricks: for example, the great bath, the college, the granary, and the assembly hall. In the bath the actual tank measured 12 metres in length (north to south), 7 metres in width, and 2.5 metres

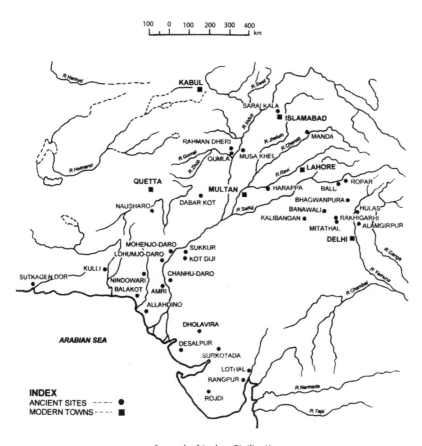

Spread of Indus Civilization

in depth. It was approached by two staircases, one each on the northern and southern sides. The floor and side walls of the tank were rendered watertight by the use of gypsum in the mortar, while the side walls were further backed by a damp-proof course of bitumen. Around the tank ran a pillared veranda from which there was access to a series of what might be called 'dressing-rooms'. The tank was fed with water from a large well situated in the complex, while, for the discharge of used water, there was corbelled drain in the south-west corner.

Whether the bath had a purely secular use or had a religious function as well is very difficult to say. However, it has been surmised that beneath the stupa of the Kushana period, situated hardly fifty metres to the east of the bath, there may be the remains of a temple. And this is not improbable, for a kind of worship place has indeed been identified within the citadel at Kalibangan, closely associated with a well and bathing-platforms.

Between the bath and the stupa lie the remains of a building 83 metres long and 24 metres wide, with a large number of rooms on three sides of a 10-metre square courtyard. The presence of staircases suggests the possibility of there having been some more rooms, besides terraces, on the first floor. From the general disposition of the building, the excavator was inclined to regard it as the residence of 'the high priest' or of a 'college of priests'.

Juxtaposed to the south-western wall of the bath was a granary covering an overall area of 55 by 37 metres. It consisted of a podium formed by 27 blocks of solid brickwork, arranged in three rows of nine each, and separated one from the other by passages about a metre wide. The latter were evidently provided for the circulation of air underneath the timbered floor of the storage hall that stood above the podium. Built on to the northern side of the podium was a platform, with a ramp going down to ground level outside. To this, one can imagine, were brought wagons full of wheat and barley for unloading.

There are many other buildings within the citadel, but one is particularly striking. Though not completely excavated, it covers an area of over 750 square metres. It has twenty massive piers of kiln-burnt bricks arranged in four rows of five each, with traces of corresponding pilasters at the ends. Thus there are six aisles from north to south and at least five from west to east, the further plan on the east being incomplete. The building was very probably an assembly hall, which would fit the general context of other specialized buildings in the citadel.

Harappa was regarded as another 'capital' of the 'Indus Empire'.[1] Here hardly any excavation has been done in the 'lower city' to the east

---

[1] This expression is rather loosely used, for there is no concrete evidence to prove that the system of government was that of an empire. The possibility of there having been city states, as in Mesopotamia, should not be overlooked.

of the 'citadel'. In fact, even within the citadel, the sporadic diggings have not helped very much to produce a coherent picture. Of the enclosing wall, however, many details are available. A section cut across it at about the middle of the western side showed that it was built of mud bricks, externally revetted with kiln-burnt bricks. The mud-brick wall measured over 13 metres in width at the base and tapered inwards on both the exterior and interior. At places it was found to rise to a height of about 15 metres above the surrounding plain. Behind it was a 7-metre-high mud-brick platform upon which stood the buildings inside the citadel. Externally, the citadel wall was punctuated at places by rectangular towers, and the one at the north-west corner shows that it was substantially rebuilt on three occasions.

The lack of data regarding the buildings inside the citadel is more than compensated for by what has been excavated to the north. In its shadow, there lay the workmen's quarters, their working-platforms, and a granary, the entire complex suggesting a high degree of regimentation of the working population. Enclosed by a boundary wall, of which only odd bits are now to be seen, the workmen's quarters stood in two rows, running from east to west. Each dwelling, covering an area of about 17 by 7 metres, comprised two rooms, and was entered through an oblique passage evidently so arranged for privacy. The remarkable uniformity of these reminds one of modern barracks and all that they imply.

Immediately to the north of these quarters have been identified five east–west rows of working-platforms, and although six is the maximum number excavated in any row, there were doubtlessly many more. Made of kiln-burnt bricks set on edge in circular rings, each platform measured about 3.5 metres in diameter. Excavation has revealed a central hole about 60 centimetres in diameter into which, it is surmised, was inserted a wooden mortar for pounding grain. Such a guess is supported, on the one hand, by the presence of straw or husk and wheat and barley in the hole and on the platform and, on the other, by the location of a granary barely 100 metres to the north.

Why the granary at Harappa, unlike that at Mohenjo-daro, was located outside the citadel is a matter for debate. The proximity of the river Ravi may be the answer, enabling the harvest from the neighbouring countryside to be transported by water direct to the granary. As to its safe control, which its location within the fortified citadel would have otherwise guaranteed, it may be assumed that an ever-vigilant eye was kept over the entire area, right from the coolie quarters through the workshops up to the granary. Comprising two blocks, the granary complex occupied an overall area of 55 by 43 metres. Each of the blocks contained six storage halls, each hall measuring 15 by 6 metres externally. As in the case of Mohenjo-daro, here also air-ducts were provided underneath the floor.

Pottery is found in very large quantities at all ancient sites and may well be regarded as the index to the economic and artistic standards of the population—standards which may also be reflected in the few sculptural or other artistic pieces that survive. The Indus people used a very characteristic sturdy red ware, made of well-levigated and very well-fired clay. Often it had a red slip and was painted over in black pigment with a variety of pleasing designs, floral as well as geometric. Sometimes birds, animals, and human figures were depicted.

The terracotta figurines, human as well as animal, show vigour, variety, and ingenuity. The often illustrated short-horned bull from

North Gate, Dholavira—an example of town planning

Mohenjo-daro and a similar one from Kalibangan are among the
most powerful portrayals of the animal from any ancient civilization.
The human head from Kalibangan, though only an inch in height, is a
keen competitor, from the point of view of expression and art, with
the head of the famous steatite figure from Mohenjo-daro. The female
figurines, with their pannier head-dresses and bedecked bodies,
though hand modelled, are indeed pleasing little things. And then
there are the terracotta toys, some of which are to be noted for their
ingenuity: for example, a bull with a mobile head or a monkey going
up and down a string.

    The Indus people had a highly developed art of making stone
sculptures in the round. There is a striking steatite figure of a bearded
man, supposed to be a priest, from Mohenjo-daro. The inward-looking
eyes and the serene expression induce a reflective, meditative mood. In
the art of metal sculpture too, great heights were achieved. The famous
bronze female figure from Mohenjo-daro, supposed to represent a
dancing girl, with her right hand poised on the hip, her bracelet-covered
left arm swung to rest on a bent left leg, a necklace dangling between her
breasts, and, above all, her well-braided head haughtily thrown back, is a
perfect piece of art. In this case the feet are missing, but one is tempted

to imagine that she wore anklets as shown in another fragmentary bronze sculpture, of which only the lower portion is preserved.

But the Indus artist was at his best when he dealt with his seals. Cut out of steatite, the seals are usually 20 to 30 millimetres square. On the obverse is an inscription, generally accompanied by an animal figure; on the reverse, a perforated knob, evidently for suspension. It is in the engraving of these seals that the great gifts of the Indus valley artists are especially reflected. Indeed, there can be no two opinions about the superb depiction on the seals of the brahmani bull, with its swinging dewlap, pronounced hump, and muscular body.

That the Indus people were literate is fully borne out by the inscriptions on the seals. The occurrence of inscriptions even on pottery and other household objects further shows that literacy was not confined to a select few. The script, seemingly pictographic and having nearly 400 signs, has not yet been deciphered. However, overlaps of the signs inscribed on some potsherds discovered at Kalibangan clearly show that the direction of writing was from right to left.

While reading and writing are duly attested to by these inscriptions, proficiency in the third R, arithmetic, is clearly shown by the cleverly organized system of weights and measures. Made usually of chert and cubical in shape, the weights fall in the progression of 1, 2 8/3, 8, 16, 32, etc. up to 12,800. The scales of ivory or shell indicate a 'foot' of about 13.0 to 13.2 and a 'cubit' of 20.3 to 20.8 inches Mention in this context may also be made of plumb-bobs and 'angle-measures' of shell.

The Indus civilization represented a perfect Bronze Age, though chert blades continued to be used for certain specific purposes. Bronze objects for domestic use included knife-blades, saws, sickles, chisels, celts, razors, pins, tweezers, fish-hooks, and the like. Those for defence or offence comprised spears, arrow-heads, and short swords. That bronze was used in plenty is shown by its employment for non-essential items like vessels.

However, as in most other contemporary civilizations of the world, agriculture was the backbone of the Indus economy. The extensive use of kiln-burnt bricks, for the firing of which plenty of wood was needed, and the frequent depiction of jungle fauna such as the tiger, bison, and rhinoceros on the seals, suggest the possibility of there having been more rainfall during the Indus period than there is now. Today it is news if Mohenjo-daro gets even 10 centimetres of rain during the whole year. Moreover, dry channels occurring close to the sites show that in ancient times the Indus, Ravi, Ghaggar, Satluj, and Bhogavo flowed respectively on the outskirts of Mohenjo-daro, Harappa, Kalibangan, Ropar, and Lothal. Thus there was an adequate water supply which, coupled with a rich alluvial soil, produced crops of wheat and barley, besides bananas, melons, and peas. However, perhaps the most remarkable agricultural achievement was the cultivation of cotton. Even Egypt did not produce it until several centuries after it was grown in the Indus valley.

The Indus population, particularly of the cities, was a cosmopolitan one. It included Mediterraneans, Proto-Australoids, Alpines, and Mongoloids. In keeping with such a mixed population, there was a wide variety of religious practices. The portrayal on several seals of a horned, three-faced figure, surrounded by various animals, wild and domesticated, brings to mind the conception of Shiva in the form of *Pashupati*, the Lord of Animals. There was also the worship of the Mother Goddess. The adoration of trees and streams, or perhaps of the spirits supposed to be residing in them, is also suggested by the relevant data. A belief in life hereafter is evident from the burial practice according to which along with the dead person were placed objects like mirrors, antimony rods, mother-of-pearl shells, and a large number of pots, some of which in life seem to have been used for eating and drinking. In one case a fowl was also placed in the gravepit. For some reason now unknown, the body is invariably to be found lying from north to south, the head being towards the north.

Contacts with western Asia are suggested on the one hand by the occurrence at the Indus sites of articles of known western origin, for example spiral- and animal-headed pins, mace heads, socketed adze axes of copper or bronze, and vases of chlorite schist with typical 'hut-and-window' decoration; and, on the other, by the find of seals and sealings of the Indus style at West Asian sites such as Ur, Susa, Umma, Lagash, and Tell Asmar. In more recent years, a seal has been found at Lothal, which is more or less of the same type as those found at contemporary sites on the Persian Gulf such as Barbar, Ras-al-Qala, and Failaka. This discovery, combined with that of the dockyard at the same site, proves beyond doubt that the trade with western Asia was, at least in part, maritime. Overland trade with Iraq, Iran, Afghanistan, and Central Asia, also seems to have taken place.

What brought the Indus cities to an end has long been a matter of debate. The occurrence in the habitation area at Mohenjo-daro of some human skeletons, including one of which the skull bears the mark of a cut, has been interpreted as evidence of a massacre at the hands of the invading Aryans. This view, however, now seems untenable. In the first place, the skeletons do not all belong to one and the same occupation level, which should also be the latest, marking the end of the Indus settlement. Second, at the site there is no evidence of an alien culture immediately overlying the Indus one. To save the situation, the post-Indus Cemetery H at Harappa has been brought into the picture. It has, however, been demonstrated elsewhere by the present writer that there was an appreciable time lag between the end of the Indus civilization and the beginning of Cemetery H. Thus the Cemetery H people can hardly be regarded as invaders if those invaded had ceased to exist at the time. And to regard the Cemetery H people as Aryans is fraught with still greater difficulties. In the present state of our knowledge, such people are conspicuously absent from the Ghaggar (ancient Sarasvati), Satluj, and upper Ganga valleys—regions where the early Aryans are known from their own literature to have resided.

Another theory ascribes the end of the Indus civilization to heavy flooding. This may, however, be only partly true. For, while some evidence of devastation by floods is to be found at Mohenjo-daro and Lothal, there is no such evidence in respect of other sites, for example Kalibangan. Here perhaps the drying up of the Ghaggar—gradual or sudden, owing either to climatic changes or to the diversion of the waters resulting from factors at or near their source—may have been the cause of the desertion of the site. Pestilence and the erosion of the surrounding landscape owing to overexploitation may also be reasons for the end of certain settlements.

Be that as it may, there is enough evidence to show that the great Indus civilization did not come to a sudden dead end. For example, at Lothal, from its Period A (Indus) to B (post-Indus), there is a gradual change in the pottery and the disappearance or replacement by others of certain kinds of antiquities. This devolution is further continued at the neighbouring site of Rangpur. Likewise a change of face is also indicated by the evidence from sites in eastern Panjab and north-western Uttar Pradesh. The Indus civilization no doubt fell; all the same it left many indelible imprints on the latter-day cultures of the subcontinent.

The Early Aryans

T. Burrow

THE CLASSICAL CIVILIZATION OF INDIA developed from the earlier Vedic civilization, and the Vedic civilization was the creation of the Aryans, an invading people, whose first arrival in the subcontinent is probably to be dated about 1500 BC. Perhaps some 200 years after this estimated date there began to come into being a collection of religious hymns which were eventually organized as the *Rig Veda*, the final redaction of which probably antedates 1000 BC. Our knowledge of the Aryans in India during this earliest period is based primarily on this work. From the *Rig Veda* emerges a fairly clear picture of the situation at that time. A series of related tribes, settled mainly in the Panjab and adjacent regions, speaking a common language, sharing a common religion, and designating themselves by the name *arya-*, are represented as being in a state of permanent conflict with a hostile group of peoples known variously as Dasa or Dasyu. From the frequent references to these conflicts it emerges that their result was the complete victory of the Aryans. During the period represented by the later *Samhitas* and the *Brahmana* texts the Aryans are seen to have extended their territory, principally in the direction of the east, down the Ganga valley, and references to conflicts with the Dasa are rare. Other terms, for example *mleccha-* and *nisada-* are used as designations of non-Aryan tribes, while the word dasa becomes the usual word for 'slave'. On the other hand, the term arya- is opposed not only to the external barbarian, but also to the lowest of the four castes, the *sudra*. In the latter context the word arya- naturally acquires the meaning 'noble, honourable', and the word continues in use in both senses down to the classical period. North India is referred to as Aryavarta, 'the country where the Aryans live', or, in Pali, as *ariyam ayatanam*. The Jaina texts have frequent references to the distinction between Arya and Mleccha. In Tamil literature the kings of north India are referred to as Aryan kings. On the other hand, the ethical use of the word is illustrated by the Buddhist 'Noble Eightfold Path' (*ariyam atthangikam maggam*) where the word has no ethnic significance.

The Aryans, whose presence in north-western India is documented by the *Rig Veda*, had reached the territory they then occupied through a migration, or rather, a succession of migrations, from outside the Indian subcontinent. The final stage of this migration cannot have been very far removed from the beginning of the composition of the *Rig Veda*, but, at the same time, a sufficient period of time must have elapsed for any clear recollection of it to have disappeared, since the hymns contain no certain references to such an event. The Aryan invasion of India is recorded in no written document, and it cannot yet be traced archaeologically, but it is nevertheless firmly established as a historical fact on the basis of comparative philology. The Indo-European languages, of which Sanskrit in its Vedic form is one of the oldest members, originated in Europe, and the only possible way by which a language belonging to this family could be carried all the way to India was a migration of the people speaking it.

It has been observed that the Aryan invasion of India seems to have taken place some considerable time before the composition of the Vedic hymns, since no clear recollection of this migration is to be found in them. On the other hand, references are frequent to the struggle with the previous inhabitants, the Dasas or Dasyus, and to the occupation of their land and the capture of their possessions. As to the identity of these people who were displaced or subjugated, the predominant and most likely view is that they were the authors of the Indus civilization. This civilization, which was quite unexpected when it was first discovered, was certainly earlier than the Vedic period, but there has been some argument as to whether its fall was brought about by the invading Aryans, or whether some period of time elapsed between the end of the Indus civilization and the appearance of the Aryans. The evidence of the Vedic texts themselves is decidedly in favour of the former view, notably on account of the frequent references to the destruction of cities, the war-god Indra being known as *purandara*, 'destroyer of cities'. Agni, the fire-god is also prominently mentioned in this capacity, understandably, since many of the Indus cities appear to have been destroyed by fire. In view of these repeated references the conclusion seems inescapable that the destruction of the Indus cities was the work of the Aryans.[1]

It is clear from the material remains that the Indus civilization was in certain respects superior to that of the Aryans. In particular it was a city civilization of a highly developed type, while by contrast city life was unfamiliar to the Aryans. The superiority of the Aryans lay in the military field, in which their use of the light horse-chariot played a prominent part. Their victory resulted in the almost complete

---

[1] This statement may not apply to Mohenja-daro in Sind, where strong evidence has been produced to show that the city decayed owing to frequent disastrous floods. Mohenjo-daro, however, was not in the main line of the Aryan advance. [ed.]

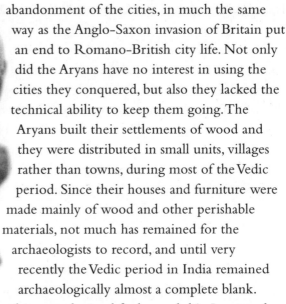

abandonment of the cities, in much the same way as the Anglo-Saxon invasion of Britain put an end to Romano-British city life. Not only did the Aryans have no interest in using the cities they conquered, but also they lacked the technical ability to keep them going. The Aryans built their settlements of wood and they were distributed in small units, villages rather than towns, during most of the Vedic period. Since their houses and furniture were made mainly of wood and other perishable materials, not much has remained for the archaeologists to record, and until very recently the Vedic period in India remained archaeologically almost a complete blank. Even now the position has not advanced far beyond this. It was only towards the end of the Vedic period that the development of cities was resumed. Whereas for the Indus civilization archaeology is the only source of our knowledge, information concerning the Vedic Aryans depends entirely on literary texts which were handed down by oral tradition. These do not provide any proper historical account, since that is not their concern, but a good deal of incidental information of a historical or semi-historical character emerges, and also a fairly clear and consistent picture of the life and civilization of the period.

It is a much-discussed question as to what extent the Indus civilization influenced the Aryans, and opinions on this matter have considerably diverged. On the whole the Vedic texts themselves give the impression that such influence, if it existed, was not of great importance.

The territory occupied by the Aryans at the time of the *Rig Veda* can be defined with reference to the river names mentioned in the text. These are, in the first place the Indus (Sindhu) and its main tributaries, the five rivers of the Panjab. To the west of this there is mention of the Krumu, Gomati, and Kubha (the Kurram, Gomal, and Kabul rivers) and of Suvastu (Swat), showing that the Aryans extended to within the boundaries of present Afghanistan. To the east the Sarasvati, Drsadvati, and Yamuna are in Aryan territory, and the Ganga is mentioned in one late hymn. Most of this territory had lain within the sphere of the Indus civilization. On the other hand little is heard of the regions of the lower Indus where that civilization had equally flourished.

The Aryans were divided into a large number of independent tribes, normally ruled by kings, who, when not fighting the Dasas or Dasyus, were frequently engaged in fighting each other. Nevertheless, the Aryans were highly conscious of their ethnic unity, based on a common language, a common religion, and a common way of life, and of the contrast between themselves and earlier inhabitants. The latter were partly absorbed into the Aryan community in the capacity of sudras, and partly they withdrew to regions temporarily out of the reach of the Aryans. The fact that the Aryans were able to retain their identity and maintain their culture so completely, in a country which had previously been both well populated and highly civilized, implies that they must have come in great numbers, not in one campaign of conquest, but in a series of waves lasting over a long period, sufficient to provide a numerous population which in turn could form the basis of further expansion. The situation was just the opposite of that which prevailed in the Near East, where conquests effected by small bands of warriors resulted in temporary domination, but where their numbers were too small to prevent their absorption after a few generations into the native population.

Terracotta figurines

The area occupied by the Aryans continued to expand in the period represented by the later Vedic texts, and there was a shift eastwards in the centre of gravity. By the time of the *Brahmanas* the centre of Aryan civilization had become the country of the Kurus and Pancalas, corresponding roughly to modern Uttar Pradesh, while the western settlements in the Panjab were less important. Further expansion to the east had taken place and the most important states in this region were Kosala, Kashi, and Videha. The main Aryan advance at this period was down the Ganga valley, keeping primarily to the north of the river. It is likely that the main route of migration followed the foothills of the Himalaya, avoiding in the first instance the densely forested country surrounding the river itself. By far the greater number of tribes and kingdoms mentioned in the texts of this period lay to the north of the Ganga. Those lying to the south, for example the Cedis, the Satvants, and the kingdom of Vidarbha, were much fewer, and more rarely mentioned. The Aryans were at this time surrounded by a variety of non-Aryan tribes, of which a list is provided by the *Aitareya Brahmana*: Andhras, Pundras, Mutibas, Pulindas, and Shabaras. The countries of Anga and Magadha appear from the sources to have been only partially Aryanized.

In the *Rig Veda* the conflict between Arya and Dasyu figured prominently, reflecting, as we have seen, a prolonged armed struggle in which the Aryans finally emerged as the undisputed victors. Such references cease in the later Vedic literature, and the term Dasyu, as applied to non-Aryan peoples, is comparatively rare. On the other hand, the term *Nisada*, applied to primitive forest dwellers, is comparatively frequent. The explanation is that the nature of the Aryan advance and settlement had changed. Once the Indus civilization had been overthrown, and the greater part of its territory occupied, there remained no advanced civilized states to contend with. The Ganga valley seems at this time to have been thinly populated by forest tribes, possessing no advanced civilization and unable to offer any coherent resistance to the Aryans. The colonization that took place down the valley, as first principally to the north of the river, was mainly a matter of clearing forests and founding agricultural settlements, a continuous and prolonged process extending over centuries. In the uncleared forest regions the primitive tribes of Nisadas continued to reside in the midst of Aryan territory, and relations between the two seem to have been established on a basis of mutual toleration. Naturally as the activity of forest clearing proceeded, the scope for the independent existence of the forest tribes became more limited, and sections of them, under such names as Pukkasa and Candala, attached themselves to the fringe of Aryan society, forming the nucleus of what were to become eventually the depressed classes.

The third stage in the Aryan occupation of India falls within the period 800–550 BC. It has been observed that at the beginning of this period, according to the evidence of the *Brahmanas*, the portion of India occupied by the Aryans was still comparatively limited, and that they were surrounded by a ring of non-Aryan peoples, some of whose names are mentioned. A very much wider extension of Aryan language and culture can be observed at the time of the rise of Buddhism and Jainism, towards the end of the sixth century BC. Obviously the intervening period had been one of extensive migration and colonization. The result was that the boundaries of Aryavarta, the country of the Aryans, were defined as the Himalaya and Vindhya mountains to the north and south, and the eastern and western oceans. One of the main lines of expansion at this time lay to the south-west, embracing Avanti and adjacent regions, and extending as far as Asmaka and Mulaka in the region of the upper Godavari. The advance to the east continued with the occupation of the greater part of Bengal (Pundra, Suhma, Vanga, etc.) and Orissa (Kalinga). The areas to the south of the Ganga connecting these two lines of advance were also progressively brought within the Aryan fold. References to these events can be found scattered throughout the epics and Puranas, of which it will be sufficient to mention and foundation of Dvaraka on the west coast ascribed to Krishna, and the activities of the Haihayas and allied tribes in Avanti. The overall result was that by the end of

the sixth century BC the portion of India occupied by Aryans was
vastly increased, and the currency of the Indo-Aryan language was
correspondingly extended. A map representing the extent of the
Aryan occuption at the end of this period would probably show a
general correspondence with the boundaries of Indo-Aryan in a
modern linguistic map. After this, Aryan influence further south, in
Dravidian India, was a matter of cultural penetration not, as
previously, of conquest and settlement.

During the *Brahmana* period the Aryans maintained in essentials
their ethnic identity and their Vedic culture. There was considerable
internal development, and, in particular, the brahmans increased their
status and strengthened their organization. The ritual was enormously
developed, and the texts on which we depend for a picture of the period
are mainly concerned with this. This state organization was stabilized and
developed, and a variety of offices are recorded, even though their
precise functions are not always clear. The political units became larger
and the state began to replace the tribe. There were considerable
advances in material culture, as attested by both literature and
archaeology. City life began again in a small way, since a
number of places mentioned, for example Kampilya,
Paricakra, Asandivant, appear to have been towns rather
than villages.

The rapid expansion during
the 800–550 BC period had the result that in the new
territories the Aryans were much more thinly spread
than in the old, and they were to a greater extent
mixed with the pre-existing population. This fact is
noted in some ancient texts. For instance the
Baudhayana Dharmasutra says that the peoples of
Avanti, Anga, Magadha, Surastra, Daksinapatha,
Upavrt, Sindhu, and Sauvira are of mixed origin
(*sankirna-yoni-*), and further lays down an offering of
atonement for those who visit the countries of the

Dancing girl

Arattas, the Karaskaras, the Pundras, the Sauviras,
the Vangas, the Kalingas, and the Pranunas.
These lists cover a large part of the territories
colonized during the period 800–550 BC, and
attest to the fact that these territories were
only imperfectly Aryanized in contrast to
what had happened in the earlier
periods. The lists also contain the
names of a number of non-Aryan
tribes, many of which still no doubt
retained their identity and language.

   The influence of the pre-Aryans
on Aryan culture should probably be
regarded as having begun to take effect during
this period, and it is associated with the
transition from the Vedic civilization to the
later Hindu civilization. This was probably also the time when the epic
traditions, later to culminate in the Mahabharata and the Ramayana,
began to take shape. New developments in religion which eventually
evolved into the later Hinduism, which contrasts in many ways with
the Vedic religion, also had their first beginnings in this period. The
great increase in the complexity of the caste system which characterizes
later Hindu civilization was also stimulated at this time by the necessity
of somehow fitting into the framework of Aryan society a large variety of
previously independent tribes, who in many parts of the newly
conquered area must have formed the majority of the population. The
Aryan culture, based on the Vedic culture, remained the centralizing
factor, but from now on it was more subject to non-Aryan influences.
The influence of Aryan civilization was felt latest in the Dravidian
south. The first Aryan colonization of Ceylon is supposed to have taken
place about the time of the Buddha, and the earliest Aryan penetration
in south India is likely to have occurred about the same time. Later the
Maurya Empire was in control of most of the Deccan, only the

Tamil princes of the extreme south remaining independent. The
Satavahana Empire which followed also represented Aryan
domination and penetration in this region, as can be seen from the
fact that the official language of this dynasty and of some of its
immediate successors was Middle Indo-Aryan. This political influence
was associated with the spread of religions from north India, both
Brahmanical and Buddhist or Jaina. In contrast, however, to the
previous states of expansion, the Aryan language was not permanently
imposed on this region, and after about AD 500 Kannada, and later
Telugu, began to be used in inscriptions. Gradually the native
Dravidian element gained the upper hand, and the boundaries
between Aryan and Dravidian India were restored to a line
representing the limit of Aryan conquests about 500 BC. At the same
time the whole subcontinent was united by a common culture, of
which the Aryans were the original founders, but to which Dravidians
and others also made their contributions.

Ashokan India and the Gupta Age

ROMILA THAPAR

ASHOKAN INDIA AND THE GUPTA Age are the terminal points of a span of
one thousand years, from the fourth century BC to the sixth century AD.
The span extends over a period of considerable historical change; yet it
is possible to perceive an underlying continuity. The origin of institutions
which were to mould Indian culture is frequently traceable to this
period. The Ashokan age saw the establishment of a centralized imperial
structure which embraced almost the entire subcontinent and rested on
a methodically organized and efficient bureaucracy. This was the first
time that the imperial idea found expression in India. In the subsequent

period the personality of India acquired new contours and delineations which were both the result of an imperial system and the foreshadowing of other patterns. The Gupta Age, for a brief period, came close in spirit to the government of the Mauryas, but it carried the seeds of a new political system—the early stages of a feudal-type organization—which was not conducive to empire building. The Gupta Age is better remembered as the age which saw the triumph of Sanskritic culture in many parts of the subcontinent.

Chandragupta Maurya conquered Magadha (south Bihar) and in 321 BC founded the Mauryan Dynasty with his capital at Pataliputra (in the vicinity of modern Patna). He proceeded to annex various parts of northern India and campaigned against the Greek, Seleucus Nicator, the former general of Alexander. The successful outcome of this campaign brought him the trans-Indus region and areas of Afghanistan. His son, Bindusara, continued the campaign into peninsular India. But it was his grandson Ashoka who, inheriting the subcontinent, established an all-India empire and discovered both the advantages and problems inherent in such a political structure.

The mechanics of a centralized empire came into existence after a lengthy germination involving the life and death of numerous kingdoms and republics in northern India from the sixth century BC onwards. Perhaps the earliest glimmerings of empire were visible to the Nandas, the dynasty which immediately preceded the Mauryas, though the actual birth of empire had to wait until the arrival of the latter. Ashoka inherited an efficiently running machine dominated by a central administration. The imperial structure was provided with a base through the spread and establishment of an agrarian economy. In later centuries, in spite of the contribution of other types of economic activity such as internal and overseas trade, agriculture remained the dominant factor in the economy, with these other activities providing substantial but subsidiary incomes.

Land revenue had been recognized as a major source of state income before the Mauryas. The proverbial wealth of the Nandas was doubtless due to their efficient collection of revenue from the fertile

Bull seal, Mohenjo-daro

middle Ganga plain. That the legitimacy of taxation had been established by the time of the Mauryas and its potentiality in terms of income recognized, is evident from the references to land revenue and taxes in Kautalya's *Arthashastra* and a significant reference in the inscriptions of Ashoka.[1] According to the *Arthashastra* every activity, from agriculture to gambling and prostitution, might be subjected to taxation by the state. No wasteland should be occupied nor a single tree cut down in the forest without permission from the state, since these were all ultimately sources of revenue. It was conceded that the main item of income was land revenue and this was dependent on correct assessment and proper collection. But other activities had also to be controlled and supervised by the state so that they would yield the maximum revenue.

All this necessitated a carefully worked out bureaucratic system, and from descriptions of administration in Mauryan sources this seems to have been achieved. Practically every professional and skilled person was

[1] Kautalya, alternatively known as Kautilya and Chanakya, was the chief minister of Chandragupta Maurya and a work on political economy, the *Arthashastra*, is attributed to him. In its present form the work has been dated by scholars to the second and third centuries AD. But parts of its appear to reflect notions which were current in the administrative system of the Mauryas. With regard to land revenue, it is significant that, on visiting Lumbini, Ashoka ordered a reduction in land revenue as a favour to the birthplace of the Buddha. This is a clear indication of the importance of such revenue to the Mauryan political and economic system.

registered and was under the ultimate control of a superintendent. The officers were very well paid, in the belief that a well-paid bureaucracy was likely to be more efficient. High salaries could be maintained only if taxes were rigorously collected. Thus the two factors of taxation and administration were interlinked.

These two factors had a bearing on yet another factor: the army and its role in the politics and economy of the Mauryan period. A large army was not only essential to vast conquests, it was equally important as a means of holding the empire together. Mauryan rulers were aware of this. The estimated strength of Chandragupta's army, according to near-contemporary classical sources, was 9000 elephants, 30,000 cavalry, and 600,000 infantry. Even allowing for a margin of exaggeration in these figures the Mauryan army was a large one by any standards. To maintain such an army would require a large state income, and this in turn would depend on taxation and the size of the kingdom. Thus it was the interdependence of taxation, administration, and armed strength which went into the making of a centralized empire.

Control over these factors lay with the king, who was regarded as the supreme source of power and authority. This enabled the king to adopt a paternalistic attitude towards his subjects, as is evident from Ashoka's edicts, where he says, 'All men are my children and just as I desire for my children that they should obtain welfare and happiness both in this world and the next, the same do I desire for all men...'[2] Or as, when referring to his officers in the rural areas, he writes, 'Just as one entrusts one's child to an experienced nurse, and is confident that the experienced nurse is able to care for the child satisfactorily, so my *rajukas* have been appointed for the welfare and happiness of the country people...'[3].

Paternalism demands a continued contact between king and subjects. The Mauryan kings, we are told, were always available for consulation. But the availability of the king was not sufficient. In a system as

[2] Second Separate Rock Edict.
[3] Fourth Pillar Edict.

centralized as that of the Mauryas it was essential that communication be maintained with all parts of the subcontinent and with every level of society. This was done in part by building a network of roads linking the entire empire with Pataliputra. Ashoka's justified pride in the excellence of the roads which he had constructed is corroborated by Pliny the Elder's enthusiasm in describing the Royal Highway which ran from Taxila to Pataliputra, a distance of over a thousand miles.

At another level, contact with the populace was maintained through the use of agents and informants. These were used both to propagate the ideas of the king and to bring him reports on public opinion.[4] Frequent tours and the appointment of specially trusted inspectors were other means of communication with the people.

Although agriculture provided the most substantial part of the state income it was not the sole source of revenue. An indirect source of income for the Mauryan state was the use of the sudras, the lowest of the four orders of Hindu society, as free labour when so required. The settlement of new areas, the opening of wasteland to agriculture, the working of the state-owned mines such as the salt mines of the Panjab and the iron ore deposits in Magadha, were some of the activities for which sudras, in addition to prisoners of war and criminals, provided labour power.

Among the more significant changes which had taken place by the middle of the first millennium BC was the development of towns and urban culture. The coming of Aryan culture, based on pastoralism and agrarian village communities, resulted in the entire process of development from village cultures to urban cultures being re-experienced in northern India. Towns evolved from trade centres and craft villages, and consequently the dominant institution of urban life was the guild. By the end of the fourth century BC artisan and merchant guilds were an established part of the urban pattern.

[4] A similar system was adopted by the Achaemenid kings of Persia, where the inspectors were called 'the king's eye' and 'the king's ear' and also by Charlemagne, in whose kingdom they were know as the *missi*.

The manufacture of goods and trade formed additional sources of income in a tax-oriented system. Not surprisingly the *Arthashastra* lists a number of taxes on goods at various stages of production and distribution. The existence of an all-India empire under a single political authority and the excellent communications developed within the subcontinent led to an expansion in internal trade which added to the growing profits of the guilds. Ventures in overseas trade were doubtlessly encouraged by the protection of diplomatic missions sent by the Mauryan emperors. The exchange of envoys between the Greek kings of western Asia and Egypt and the Mauryas is on record, as also the curious request for gifts such as sophists, singing boys, and wine. The close and friendly ties between Ashoka and Tissa, the king of Ceylon, must have resulted in greater communication between the two countries.

The improved economic status of the guilds introduced complications in the existing social pattern. Guild leaders became powerful citizens controlling large economic assets. But, in the caste-based society of this period, the trader or the artisan was not included among the most socially privileged citizens. The challenge which the mercantile community presented to the more established sections of society was yet to come, but the germinal tensions came into being at this stage. That there was an element of fear on the part of the authorities of the growing power of the guilds seems evident from the *Arthashastra*, which favours a rigid control of guild activities. For instance, every guild had to be registered with the local administration and no guild was allowed to move from its location without prior permission.

There was yet another factor which possibly aggravated social tensions. The two new religions, Buddhism and Jainism, had won the sympathy of the artisans and the merchants; and these religions were heterodox sects which challenged the established order. The association of the emergent urban groups with dissident thinking and practice would make them suspect in the eyes of the orthodox.

These new religions sprang from a considerable intellectual ferment which had begun earlier in the period, around 600 BC. A healthy rivalry was apparent among a number of sects, such as the Charvakas, Jainas, and Ajivikas, whose doctrines ranged from pure materialism to determinism. This intellectual liveliness was reflected in the eclectic interests of the Mauryan rulers, since it was claimed by the Jainas that Chandragupta was a supporter and there is evidence that Bindusara favoured the Ajivikas. Close contacts with western Asia must have provided yet another stream of unorthodox ideas.

For many centuries Ashoka remained almost unknown to the Indian historical traditional. The proclamations issued by Ashoka were engraved on rocks and pillars throughout the subcontinent and these remained visible, but unfortunately the Brahmi script in which they had been engraved had become archaic and the inscriptions could not be read.[5] However, in 1837 the Orientalist James Prinsep deciphered the script. Although the text was now known, the author of the inscriptions could not be identified, since he was generally referred to only by his titles—*Devanampiya Piyadassi*—The Beloved of the Gods, of Gracious Mien—and these were unknown to the Indian king lists. A tentative identification with Ashoka was made in the late nineteenth century on the evidence from the Buddhist chronicles of Ceylon. It was not until 1915 that this identification was confirmed, however, with the discovery of an inscription which referred to the author as *Devanampiya Ashoka.*[6]

The association of this name with Buddhist sources led to his edicts being interpreted almost as Buddhist documents. Undoubtedly Ashoka was a Buddhist and much of the ideology of *Dhamma*[7] which he enunciated was inspired by Buddhism. But to equate it totally with Buddhism and to suggest that Ashoka was propagating Buddhism as the state religion is to read more into the edicts than was intended by the

---

[5] One of the sultans of Delhi in the fourteenth century, Firoz Shah Tughluq, was both intrigued and impressed by an Ashokan pillar which he found near Delhi, and he had it removed to his capital. But no one could read the inscription on the pillar or explain its purpose.

[6] Minor Rock Edict at Maski: *devanampiyassa Asokassa.*

Ashokan pillar at Lewviya Nandangarh

monarch. A careful analysis of the inscriptions reveals that they were of two categories. Some were addressed specifically to the Buddhist Church or *Sangha* and were concerned entirely with matters relating to the Sangha. The majority of the inscriptions are, however, addressed to the public at large and deal with questions of wider interest. It is significant that it is in this second category of inscriptions that the king expounds his ideas on Dhamma.

It would appear that Ashoka aimed at creating an attitude of mind among his subjects in which social behaviour had the highest relevance. In the context of conditions during the Mauryan period, this ideology of Dhamma may have been viewed as a focus of loyalty and as a point of convergence for the existing diversities of people and activities. Dhamma stressed toleration, non-violence (where the emperor himself forswore violence and force as means to an end), respect for those in positions of authority, including both the brahmans and the Buddhist monks, consideration and kindness towards inferiors, and the general acceptance of ideals conducive to human dignity. The king instituted a special class of officers—the officers of Dhamma—who were responsible for the propagation of this ideology and who worked for the general welfare of the people.

Yet the ideology of Dhamma died with the death of the emperor. As an attempt to solve the problems of the time it was perhaps too idealistic. At the same time it can hardly be described as a revolutionary doctrine, since it was largely an emphatic reiteration of certain existing principles of ethics. But credit must be given to the man who had the vision to seek such a solution and the courage to attempt it.

Fifty years after the death of Ashoka the Mauryan Empire had declined. The divergences in the various parts of the subcontinent were too great to allow the formation of a national unit. The doctrine of Dhamma, which might have created a common factor of loyalty, failed

[7] The word *dhamma* is the Pali form of the Sanskrit *dharma* and is almost impossible to translate adequately into English. Generally accepted renderings are 'morality, piety, virtue, the social order'.

to do so. The subsequent fragmentation of the subcontinent was not entirely arbitrary, for it led to the identification of geographical areas as political entities. These (with some modification) were to remain the nuclei of political units in the Indian subcontinent for many centuries.

In 185 BC the Mauryan Empire ceased to exist. The immediate inheritors of the Mauryas in the Ganga heartland, Magadha, were the Sungas, a brahman family which had usurped the throne at Pataliputra. The Sungas were to give way to the Kanvas, to be followed by a series of minor dynasties until the rise of the Guptas in the fourth century AD. During these centuries Magadha tended to remain somewhat isolated, and few attempts were made by its rulers to participate in events elsewhere.

Kalinga (a part of modern Orissa) came to the forefront with the meteoric rise of King Kharavela, and then subsided into quietude. A biographical sketch of Kharavela is available from an inscription, where he asserts his dominion over the entire Mahanadi delta and claims many victories over south Indian kings. Such maritime kingdoms rose sporadically, their prosperity being due to sea trade and the fertility of their hinterland, generally a delta region.

Meanwhile the north-western part of the subcontinent—the Panjab and the Indus valley—was once again being sucked into the vortex of Iranian and Central Asian politics. Alexander, after his rapid campaign through Persia and north-western India, left behind a number of governors, who on his death in 323 BC declared themselves kings of the respective provinces which they governed. The house of Seleucus in western Asia and its erstwhile satraps, the Greek rulers of Bactria, came into conflict, and gradually the conflict spilled over into north-western India, involving the small and politically isolated Indian kingdoms which were unable to hold back the Bactrian Greeks. The latter established themselves in the north-west during the second century BC. Fortunately for us, these kings were enthusiastic minters of coins and their history has been partially reconstructed, largely on numismatic evidence.

Further south the Parthians made a brief thrust in the region of Sind, but could not maintain their power there for long. Events in Central Asia were now to influence north India politics. A nomadic

movement originating on the borders of China made the Yueh-chih
tribe migrate westwards to the neighbourhood of the Caspian Sea,
dislodging the existing inhabitants of this region, the Shakas (Scythians).
Further migrations brought both the Shakas and the Yueh-chih to India.
The early decades of the first century AD saw the Yueh-chih settled in
northern India and the Shakas concentrated in the region of Kutch and
Kathiawar in western India. The Shakas were now neighbours of the
Satavahana or Andhra kings, who had established a kingdom centred
around the north-western area of the Deccan plateau. In this the Shakas
found themselves sandwiched between two important powers, for in
the north the Yueh-chih or Kushana kingdom had been consolidated by
Kanishka, who not only extended its southern and eastern boundaries as
far as Mathura and Varanasi, but also participated in campaigns in Central
Asia.[8] To the south of the Shakas, the Satavahanas drew their strength
from the fact that they were a bridge between the northern and southern
parts of the subcontinent. This characteristic of the Deccan kingdoms,
deriving their power from their location, was to remain an important
geo-political factor in Indian history for many centuries.

The history of south India emerges in clearer perspective during
the period between 200 BC and AD 300, the evidence being that of
archaeology, epigraphy, and the *Sangam* literature of the early Tamils.
The extreme south of the peninsula, Mysore and beyond, had not been
under actual Mauryan control, though the relationship between the
imperial power and the southern kingdoms was a close and friendly
one. This is revealed by Ashoka's references to his neighbours in the
south, the kingdoms of the Cholas, Pandyas, Keralaputras, and
Satiyaputras, some of which are also mentioned in the Sangam
literature. Conflicts among the kingdoms were perpetual, because each
had two objectives—to control the fertile deltas, the only regions where
agriculture was possible on a large scale, and to have access to the

---

[8] In fact the prestige of Kanishka is such that the inauguration of the much-used
Saka era of AD 78 is frequently attributed to him. His date is very uncertain, however,
and recent estimates vary between this date and the third century AD.

The main stupa at Sanchi

important trading stations along the coasts which were lucrative sources of revenue, since many of them traded with the Yavanas, the peoples of western Asia.[9]

The fragmentation of the subcontinent which took place during this period may have been politically emasculating, but it was at this time that a new and vital interest came to be introduced into economic development. It was the age when India discovered the potential wealth inherent in trade. Despite the many political frontiers, internal trade increased very considerably. The woollen blankets of Gandhara and the linen of Bengal were familiar to all parts of the country, as were the precious stones from south India. But even more relevant to the economic prosperity of India was the overseas trade. Indian traders ventured out in all directions: to Central Asia and China, to western Asia, and in South East Asia as far as the kingdom of Funan in modern

[9] *Yavana*, a back formation from the Prakrit word *Yona*, is believed to refer originally to Ionian Greeks and came to be used for any of the trading peoples of western Asia—the Greeks, the Romans, and in later centuries the Arabs.

Vietnam. Indian merchants became the middlemen in the commerce between South East Asia and the Mediterranean. They were the entrepreneurs in the trade supplying the needs and luxuries of the Graeco-Roman world.

This increase in trade resulted quite naturally in the greater prosperity of the guilds. Guilds became not only the basis for the production and distribution of merchandise but also the financial centres of trade. The Satavahana rulers, for instance, often gave to religious charities donations which came from money invested with guilds. The intensification of the guild system influenced sub-caste relations within caste society, for each guild tended to become a sub-caste drawing on its own resources for manpower. Thus even in urban areas the economic basis of the organization of caste society became firmer. With the accumulation of wealth in the hands of guilds and merchants, patronage of learning and the arts was no longer limited to royalty. Not surprisingly, some of the most magnificent Buddhist monuments are of this period and many of them owe their existence to the donations of wealthy guilds and merchants. The stupas at Sanchi, Bharhut, and Amaravati stand witness to this.

Together with Indian traders went the brahmans and the Buddhist missionaries. Western Asia came into contact with them in the centuries before Christ. China received its first Buddhist mission in AD 68 at Loyang. In the early centuries after Christ, Buddhists were active in Funan and Champa. Meanwhile Buddhism itself had undergone a considerable change, with doctrinal differences creating a split which was formally recognized at the Fourth Buddhist Council, held according to tradition during the reign of Kanishka; and two groups of Buddhists were established, the *Mahayana* and the *Hinayana*. Missionaries of Mahayana sects established themselves in Central Asia, China, and Japan. Hinayana Buddhism was more popular in Ceylon, and later it ousted the Mahayana in South East Asia.

With increasing contact through commerce between the various parts of the known world, the communication of ideas between these regions improved. For instance, Indian astronomers discovered the

Ashokan pillar at Kolhua

existence of Graeco-Roman astronomy. Graeco-Roman art, particularly of the Alexandrian variety, not only found admirers in north-western India and Afghanistan but became the model for a hybrid local school which art historians have subsequently called Gandhara art. Yet another result was the arrival of Christian teaching in India, which according to the legends came in the mid-first century AD, brought by St Thomas.

The political fragmentation of the subcontinent did not put an end to the dream of an empire as vast as that of the Mauryas. An attempt was made by kings of the Gupta family to establish such an empire in the early part of the fourth century AD.

The Guptas were in origin probably a family of wealthy landowners who gradually attained both economic power and political status. Unlike the founder of the Mauryan Dynasty, who is described as an adventurous young man with no significant antecedents, the founder of the Gupta Dynasty, also called Chandra Gupta, belonged to a family which had established its power at a local level in Magadha. A judicious marriage with a Licchavi princess gave him additional prestige, the Licchavis claiming a long-established respectability. Following his coronation as king of Magadha in AD 319–20 Chandra Gupta took the title of *maharajadhiraja*—Great King of Kings.

In about AD 335 his son, Samudra Gupta, inherited the kingdom of Magadha. He issued a series of beautifully executed gold coins in which he is depicted both as a conqueror and as a musician, a strange combination of interests. Fortunately for later historians a lengthy panegyric on him was composed by one of his high officials and engraved on an Ashokan pillar which has since been brought to Allahabad. The inscription refers among other things to the martial exploits of Samudra Gupta; to the kings uprooted and the territory annexed in the northern part of the subcontinent. It mentions also the long march which Samudra Gupta undertook in the south, reaching as far as Kanchipuram. Nor are the tributes from foreign kingdoms omitted. Mention is made of the Shakas, Ceylon, various Iranian rulers of the north-west and the inhabitants of all the islands. The latter may

refer to Indian trading stations on the islands of South East Asia and in
the Indian ocean.

The nucleus of the Gupta kingdom, as of the Mauryan Empire,
was the Ganga heartland. This and the adjoining territory to the west
were the only regions over which Samudra Gupta has absolute and
unchallenged control. Gupta control of the Deccan was uncertain and
had to be propped up with a matrimonial alliance, a Gupta princess
marrying a prince of the Vakataka Dynasty of the Deccan, the successors
to the Satavahana power. This secured a friendly southern frontier for
the Guptas, which was necessary to Samudra Gupta's successor, Chandra
Gupta II, when he led a campaign against the Shakas in western India.

It was during the reign of Chandra Gupta II that Gupta
ascendancy was at its peak. His successful campaign against the Shakas,
resulting in the annexation of western India, was, however, not his
only achievement. Like his predecessor, he was a patron of poets,
philosophers, scientists, musicians, and sculptors. This period saw the
crystallization of what came to be the classical norm in ancient India
on both the political and the cultural levels.

The Gupta kings took exalted titles such as *maharajadhiraja
paramabhattaraka*—Great King of Kings, the Supreme Lord. This was
in striking contrast to the Mauryas who, though politically far more
powerful, never used such exalted titles. Superficially Gupta
administration was similar to that of the Mauryas. The king was the
highest authority and the kingdom was divided into a hierarchy of
administrative units—provinces, districts, and groups of villages—each
with its own range of officers responsible to the most senior officer in
the unit. Yet there was a significant difference between Gupta and
Mauryan administration: during the Gupta period there was far greater
stress on local administration and far less direct control from the centre.
Even in urban administration, the City Boards consisted of representatives
of local opinion and interest (such at the heads of guilds and artisan and
merchant bodies) rather than officers of state.

A parallel tendency was developing in the agrarian system,
particularly in the sphere of land revenue. The revenue was still collected

by the King's officers, but they retained a certain predetermined percentage in lieu of a regular cash salary. This procedure of payment to officers came to be adopted with increasing frequency. On occasion the king would even grant the revenue from an area of land or a village to non-officials, such as brahmans renowned for their learning. Inscriptions recording such grants are known from the early centuries AD onwards. Since a major part of the state revenue came from the land, grants of revenue were gradually to cause a radical change in the agrarian system. Although it was the revenue alone which was granted, it became customary to treat the land itself as part of the grant.

Patronage requires the easy availability of money, and the Gupta kings had the financial wherewithal to be patrons on a lavish scale. The steady stream of revenue from the land was augmented by income from commercial activity. Indian trading stations were dotted throughout the islands of South East Asia, Malaysia, Cambodia, and Thailand. The gradual acceptance of many features of Indian culture in these areas must doubtlessly have been facilitated by activities such as commerce. Indian merchants carried spices from Java to Socotra or were busy participating in the trade between China and the Mediterranean lands via the Central Asian 'Silk Route', not to mention the increasing trade within the subcontinent itself. Goods were transported by pack animals and ox-drawn carts, and by water when rivers were navigable. Spices, pepper, sandalwood, pearls, precious stones, perfume, indigo, herbs, and textiles were exported in large quantities. Amongst the more lucrative imports were silk from China and horses from Central Asia and Arabia.

Some of the wealth of merchants and princes was donated to religious causes. Large endowments had made the Buddhist Church extremely powerful, and provided comfortable, if not luxurious, living for many Buddhist monks in the more important monasteries. These endowments enabled the monasteries to own land and to employ labour to work it. The surplus income from such sources was invested in commercial enterprises which at times were so successful that monasteries could even act as bankers. Monastic establishments built in splendid isolation, like the one at Ajanta, were embellished with some of the most magnificent murals known to the ancient world. The growth of centres of Buddhist teaching led to devoted scholars spending many hours on theology and philosophical speculation, thus sharpening the intellectual challenge which the Buddhists presented to the brahmans.

Hindu institutions and personalities were also the recipients of enviably lavish patronage. There are references to donations of land or revenue from villages to learned brahmans and renowned priests, enabling them and their families to live in comfort for many generations. This was the age which saw attempts at building small stone temples to Hindu deities, temples which within half a millennium were to become the dominant focuses of society in many parts of the subcontinent. Together with the temples came the carving of images and the depiction of popular legends in stone.

Hinduism had by this time evolved from the beliefs of the Vedic period into a humane and sophisticated religion. Perhaps the most fundamental changes were the two features which arose partially out of the heterodox challenge to early Hinduism. The first of these was the tendency towards monotheism, which was stressed by the increasing worship of either of the two deities Vishnu and Shiva. In addition the ritual of worship was also changing in favour of personal devotion (bhakti) rather than sacrifice. Thus Hinduism revitalized itself and was able slowly to supplant the heterodox religions. The brahmans, who regarded themselves as the interpreters of Hinduism, were able to rewrite the older texts to conform to their own vision of society, as is evident from Puranic literature, and were able to convert popular secular material, such as the two epics, the Mahabharata and the Ramayana, into sacred literature.

It was from these cultural roots that the classical norm evolved. The language of brahmanism, Sanskrit, became the language of erudition and court literature. The works of Kalidasa exemplify the inspired literary craftsmanship of the period. The brahman genius for classification was given full vent, as is apparent from the careful

categorizing of the divergent philosophical schools. Compendia of
scientific writings were produced and the classification of scientific
knowledge led to many exciting results. Medical knowledge began to
travel west and aroused the interest of West Asian physicians.
Experienced metallurgists displayed their skill in minting beautiful
coins, in the use of iron of such excellence that it defies reproduction
(as in the famous Iron Pillar of Mehrauli), in metal sculpture, and in
copper-plate characters. Indian mathematical knowledge was probably
the most advanced of its time, with the use of place notation of
numerals and familiarity with the concept of the cipher. Astronomy saw
even more spectacular progress. In AD 499 Aryabhata calculated π as
3.1416 and the length of the solar year as 365.358 days. He also
postulated that the earth was a sphere rotating on its own axis and
revolving round the sun, and that the shadow of the earth falling on the
moon caused eclipses. The works on astronomy written by
Varahamihira show knowledge of Greek and Roman systems.

The advancement of knowledge lay in the hands of the brahmans.
This had the advantage of intensifying the intellectual tradition within
a small group of society. Unfortunately however, owing to the evolution
of the social pattern in ancient India, this also led to intellectual
constriction. Brahman superiority was in part sustained by the
maintenance of caste in Indian society. With the rewriting of early
literature, especially legal literature, the division of society into castes was
reiterated and the pre-eminent status of the brahman was emphasized.
The result was a fairly rigid ordering of society, in theory at least.

Despite the theoretical rigidity of the caste system, the sudras now
had a somewhat more advantageous position than in the Mauryan
period, doubtlessly due to the decreasing need for establishing new
settlements and clearing wasteland. But the position of the
untouchables—those beyond the pale of caste society—had declined
considerably. Even accidental contact with an untouchable by a high-
caste person was a source of great pollution and required ritual
ablutions, a custom which mystified the Chinese Buddhist pilgrim

Hsuan Tsang when he visited India in the early seventh century. The untouchables lived on the outskirts of towns and villages and theirs were the lowlier and unclean occupations such as scavenging, keeping the cremation grounds clean, and making leather goods. Fa-hsien, who was in India between AD 400 and 411, was favourably impressed by the prosperity of the people, more particularly the town-dwellers, an impression which is borne out by archaeological evidence.

One of the most interesting of the documents throwing light on the social mores of the well-to-do citizens is the *Kamasutra*. Better known as a manual on the art of love, it incidentally also depicts the young dilettante in his daily routine: a life given over to a certain relaxed comfort; devoted to poetry, music, painting, and sculpture; and embellished with flowers, delicate perfumes, well-seasoned food, and other refinements of gracious living. An even more graphic documentation of life in the Gupta Age is available from the vast number of terracotta figurines and models of this period, ranging from toys and representations of ladies and gentlemen of fashion, to cult images relating to the more popular manifestations of religion.

The supremacy of Gupta power in northern India did not remain unchallenged. The challenge came from the unexpected invasion of north-western India by a distinctly barbaric people, the *Hunas*. The name is etymologically related to the late classical *Hunni* or Huns, but they were probably only remotely connected, if at all, with the barbarian hordes of Attila. The threat was felt during the reign of Chandra Gupta's son and successor Kumara Gupta (AD 415–54) when a tribe of Hunas, branching away from the main Central Asian hordes, had settled in Bactria, and gradually moved over the mountains into north-western India. Slowly the trickles became streams as the Hunas thrust further into India. The successor of Kumara Gupta, Skanda Gupta (AD 454–67), had to bear the brunt of the Huna attacks, which were by now regular invasions. Gupta power weakened rapidly. By the early sixth century the Huna rulers Toramana and Mihirakula claimed the Panjab and Kashmir as part of their kingdom.

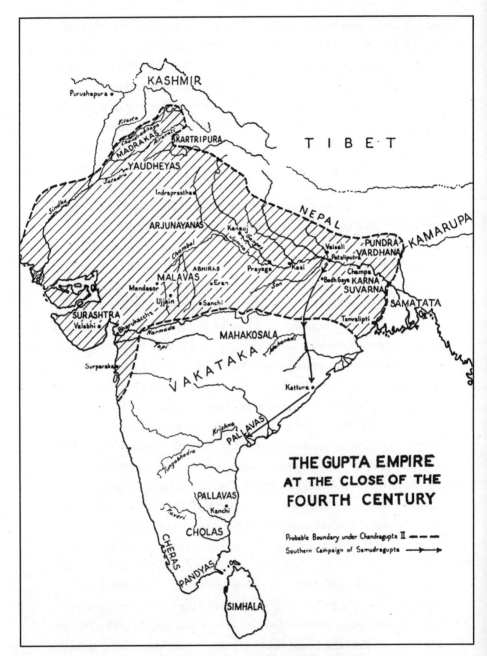

Gupta Empire at the close of the 4th century

The migration of the Hunas and other Central Asian tribes accompanying them and their settling in northern India resulted in displacements of population. This disturbance led in turn to changes in the caste structure, with the emergence of new sub-castes. The rise of many small kingdoms was also due to the general confusion prevalent during this period.

With the decline of the Guptas the northern half of the subcontinent splintered into warring kingdoms, each seeking to establish itself as a sovereign power. But, unlike the picture at the end of the Mauryan period, this sovereignty was to be based on a distinct regionalism which, though blurred and confused at first, achieved clarity in later centuries. The successors of the Guptas attempted to recreate an empire, but the political fabric was such that an empire was no longer feasible, a possible exception being the Pratihara kingdom in limited periods. The ability to create large kingdoms and empires moved south to the powers of the peninsula—the kingdoms of the Deccan and the Tamil country. In the centuries that followed the Gupta period it was in the kingdoms of the Chalukyas, Rashtrakutas, Pallavas, and Cholas that Indian civilization showed its greatest vitality.

Medieval Hindu India

A.L. BASHAM

THE GUPTA EMPIRE BROKE UP and disappeared. By the middle of the sixth century a line of rulers with the same surname, but not connected in their official genealogy with the imperial line, ruled in Bihar and parts of Uttar Pradesh. The great emperors of the fourth and fifth centuries were soon forgotten, with the exception of Chandra Gupta II, who was remembered by his title Vikramaditya (in colloquial Hindi Raja Bikram) and the palmy days of whose reign passed into folk tradition.

In the second half of the sixth century a city on the Upper Ganga, before its confluence with the Jamuna, Kanyakubja (later known as Kanauj), rose to prominence as the capital of the Maukhari kings. The city of Sthanvisvara, now Thanesar, in the watershed between the Ganga and the Indus, became the capital of a rising family of rulers descended from a certain Pushyanhuti. Gujarat and Malwa were in the power of the Maitraka Dynasty, founded by a general of the Guptas. In the Deccan the Chalukya Dynasty was gaining in strength, while in Tamilnadu the dynasty of the Pallavas was also enlarging its boundaries.

This is the pattern of India politics until the Muslim invasion. There were generally five or six main focuses of power throughout the subcontinent, with numerous lesser kingdoms, sometimes independent, sometimes tributary to one of the greater rulers. Those corners of the subcontinent with well-defined natural frontiers, such as Kashmir, Nepal, Assam, Orissa, and Kerala, were less involved in the constant struggles for power, and their political life, though also often marked by local conflict, was rarely much affected by the constant strife in the great plains.

The usual system of government bore some resemblance to the feudal system of medieval western Europe. As the previous chapter has shown, the Mauryas established a bureaucracy, and the Guptas revived some features of Mauryan administration, though they allowed greater devolution of power. As the Guptas declined, provincial governors, whose posts were already often hereditary, took to calling themselves maharajas, and increasingly assumed the status of kings. The typical larger kingdom of medieval times consisted of an area controlled directly from the capital city, and a number of provinces under hereditary *samantas*, a term loosely translated as 'vassal'. The more powerful samantas took regal titles and had subordinate chiefs who paid them homage and tribute.

A temporarily successful effort at empire building was made by Harsha or Harshavardhana (606–47), of the Pushyabhuti line of

Sthanvisvara, who gained control of Kanyakubja and made it his capital. His reign is comparatively well documented, thanks to his court poet Bana and the Chinese pilgrim Hsuan Tsang. The former composed an account of his rise to power, *The Career of Harsha (Harshacharita)*, in ornate poetic prose, while the latter left a lengthy account of his travels, *Records of Western Countries (His-yu chi)*, which tells us much about Harsha and the general condition of India at the time. Harsha appears to have governed his empire according to the system which was by now traditional, through vassal kings and henchmen, resembling the barons of medieval Europe, who might hold high offices at court or act as district or provincial governors, but who were also great landowners, and were virtually kings in their own domains. Harsha succeeded in maintaining their loyalty and holding his loose empire together through the strength of his personality and his untiring energy. When he died, apparently without heirs, his empire died with him.

The succeeding period is very obscure and badly documented, but it marks the culmination of a process which had begun with the invasion of the Hunas in the last years of the Gupta Empire. The sixth and seventh centuries saw the rise of many new dynasties, small and great, in the northern part of the subcontinent. Few of these ruling families are to be found mentioned in sources from periods before the Guptas, and many of their genealogies began with names which do not seem Sanskritic. These people appear to have been newcomers. Some of them may have been related to the Hunas. A new people, who began to make their presence felt towards the end of the sixth century, the Gurjaras, gave their name to the present Gujarat and founded several important ruling dynasties. Since place-names containing a similar element can be found as far to the north-west at Pakistan and Afghanistan, it is commonly suggested that the Gurjaras entered India in the wake of the Hunas. Their name had been linked with that of the ancient people of the south Russian steppes called Khazars, and with the Georgians (*Gruz*) of the Caucasus. In any case, new ruling houses arose in the post-Gupta period and many of their names survive to the present day as those of the Rajput clans.

Towards the end of the eighth century three of the recently arisen dynasties contended for Kanyakubja, by now the acknowledged metropolis of northern India. These were the Palas of Bihar and Bengal, the Rashtrakutas of the Deccan, and the Gurjara-Pratiharas, who controlled parts of Malwa and Rajasthan. The great city was for a time occupied by the Palas, whose Buddhist king Dharmapala drove up the Ganga valley and exacted tribute from many kings of the area. The Rashtrakuta Govinda III, whose policy of raiding the north, continued by his successors, was to have many repercussions, drove Dharmapala out, but was forced to return to his base owing to trouble at home. The vaccum was filled, very early in the ninth century, by Nagabhata II of the Gurjara-Pratiharas.

For about a hundred years the Gurjara-Pratiharas of Kanyakubja restored a little of the glory of the earlier empires. Under their greatest kings, Mihira Bhoja (c. 836–90) and Mahendrapala (c. 890–910), they received tribute from rulers from Gujarat to the borders of Bengal, and Muslim travellers were much impressed by the peacefulness and prosperity of their quasi-feudal empire. But their old enemies, the fierce Rashtrakutas from the Deccan, were constantly worrying them, and in about 916 Kanyakubja was again temporarily occupied by Indra III of the Rashtrakutas, whose lightning raids provided a foretaste of the similar attacks of the Marathas 800 years later.

Indra III soon returned to the south; but his effects were longer lasting than those of previous Rashtrakuta raiders. Though the Pratiharas returned to their capital, they were humiliated and weakened, and their vassals ceased to respect them. Within a generation or two the greater vassals had thrown aside their allegiance, and were fighting with their former masters and among themselves. It was in these circumstances that Mahmud of Ghazni, in the early years of the eleventh century, carried out his seventeen raids on India; but though the Turkish raiders ransacked and destroyed palaces and temples and returned to their headquarters in Afghanistan with immense caravans of riches and slaves, India resumed her traditional political ways as if nothing had happened.

Rathas, Mahabalipuram, Gupta Period

The Turks overwhelmed the Sahi kingdom, which had controlled a large area of the north-west, from Kabul to Lahore. The rulers of this realm had also been Turks, but Turks who had adopted Hindu traditions, and who offered no serious threat to their neighbours to the east. The Ghaznavids also conquered the Muslim kingdoms of Sind, occupied by the Arabs early in the eighth century, whose chiefs had long ceased to trouble the Hindu kingdoms on their frontiers. Thus the Hindu states of the Gangetic basin and Rajasthan now had on their borders a young aggressive kingdom with new methods of warfare and with a religious ideology which might be expected to encourage aggression.

The most remarkable feature of the situation was that, as far as surviving records show, nobody whosoever in Hindu India recognized the menace of the Turks. The Ghaznavids made a few further raids, but these were far less impressive than those of Mahmud. The Turks were soon torn by internal strife and, though they continued to hold the Panjab, it must have seemed to the Hindu politicians of the time that, like the Arabs before them, they would be contained indefinitely. Having no real historical tradition, the Indian memory of earlier conquerors coming from the north-west—Greeks, Shakas, Kushanas, and Hunas—was so vague that it was quite ineffectual as a warning to the rulers of the time.

In the involved situation arising from Mahmud's raids, five larger kingdoms shared most of northern India between them, the Chahamanas (Chauhans) of Rajasthan, the Gahadavalas (Gahrwals) of

Kanyakubja (Kanauj) and Varanasi (Banaras), the Chaulukyas or Solankis of Gujarat, the Paramaras (Parmars) of Malwa, and the Chandellas (Chandels) of Bundelkhand, to the south of the Ganga. These dynasties bore names which are among the best-known of the thirty-six Rajput clans. Their kings had already acquired something of the traditional Rajput character—gallant, extremely sensitive to points of honour, glorifying war, but of a gentlemanly kind, intensely devoted to tradition, and quite incapable of serious cooperation with one another. The Palas, who governed Bihar and Bengal, had been quite untouched by Mahmud's invasions. Early in the twelfth century they were replaced by the Sena Dynasty, which reversed the Palas' traditional support of Buddhism and encouraged Hindu orthodoxy. They seem to have played little or no parts in the politics of the western part of India, where the five major kingdoms and numerous lesser tributary realms fought honourably among themselves, basing their strategy and tactics on principles inherited from the epics.

In 1173 Ghazni was captured by Ghiyas-ud-din, whose headquarters were Ghur in Afghanistan. From his new capital Ghiyas-ud-din turned his attention to India. His brother, Muhammad bin Sam, occupied the Panjab and deposed the last ruler of the line of Mahmud. Then in 1191 Muhammad bin Sam attacked Prithviraja, king of the Chahamanas, the Hindu ruler on his eastern frontier. Prithviraja, fighting on his ground with a larger army, defeated Muhammad at Tarain, and he retreated. In the following year, 1192, Muhammad came again with stronger forces, and on the same field of Tarain Prithviraja lost the day, and the Ganga valley was open to the invaders. Before the century was over Turkish control was established along the whole length of the sacred river.

These were not by any means the last attacks from the north-west, however. Soon after the Turkish occupation, Mongol hordes swept into India and occupied much of the territory west of the Indus. In 1938 Timur, the great Mongol conqueror, sacked Delhi and raged through western India, causing tremendous carnage and destruction. In 1526 Babur, the Mughal, defeated the Afghan rulers of

Delhi and occupied the country. In 1555 his son, Humayun, reconquered it from his base in Afghanistan. During the eighteenth century Persians and Afghans raided India in turn, both sacking Delhi before returning to their homelands.

If we examine all these conquests together it becomes clear that many frequently heard explanations of the failure of the defenders of India to resist invasion are facile generalizations, based on too few instances. Indian Muslims were hardly more successful at defending themselves against invasion than Hindus, and the weakness of Indian armies in these circumstances cannot therefore to be due to the fact that the pacific Hindu is essentially a less competent soldier than the Muslim.

Some modern Indian historians are inclined to blame the caste system for the Hindu debacle, which, they suggest, was brought about by the fact that most Hindus were non-combatants, who felt no real sense of national patriotism but only loyalty to their caste brotherhoods. But Hindu armies never consisted only of *kshatriya*s and all classes, including brahmans, could take part in war. Moreover to deplore the fact that the Hindus did not adopt a scorched-earth policy against their attackers is tantamount to regretting that they did not share the nationalist values of the nineteenth and twentieth centuries. The same is probably true of nearly every people of the period which we are considering.

In all the invasions which we have listed there seems to be at least one common factor. The Indian armies were less mobile and more cumbrous, archaic in their equipment, and outmoded in their strategy when compared with those of their attackers. The invaders generally had better horses and better-trained cavalry. They were not burdened by enormous bodies of camp followers and supernumeraries, nor did they make use of the fighting elephant, the courage of which in the face of the enemy was unpredictable, but which Indian commanders, whether Hindu or Muslim, seem to have found fatally fascinating. Often the invaders had new weapons which added greatly to their effectiveness. The Aryans had the horse-drawn chariot, the Achaemenians siege engines, Alexander *ballistae*. The Central Asian nomads were equipped with small composite bows, carried by mounted archers, who could hit their mark while they were in full gallop. Babur made effective use of a small park of field guns. In fact one of the main reasons for the repeated ineptitude of Indian armies in the defence of the natural frontiers of India was their outdated and ineffective military technique.

Another important factor in the weak defence of India was the failure of her rulers to recognize the very existence of the threat from the north-west. Where this threat was recognized, the defence was more successful. The three great empires of the Mauryas, the Guptas, and the Mughals were able to maintain their frontiers because they were united. Even the Hunas, who invaded India towards the end of the period of the Gupta Empire, were expelled in the end, though the empire disintegrated in the process. The great Mughals were well aware of the potential danger from the north-west and tried to maintain their hold on Kabul and Kandahar, beyond the natural frontiers of India, in order to keep out invaders. Only when their empire was already disintegrating after the death of Aurangzeb did the Iranians and Afghans mount their great raids into Mughal territory. The early Turkish sultans managed to hold off the Mongols because, though their henchmen were far from united and not always loyal to their leaders, they were well aware of the common danger and took what steps they could to ward it off.

The Hindu kings at the time of the Turkish invasions were hopelessly divided. We have seen that, when Mahmud of Ghazni defeated the Sahis of the north-west and occupied the Panjab, no Hindu king seems to have been aware of the danger to the rest of India. When, nearly 200 years later, Muhammad bin Sam threatened a further attack, the main kingdoms of northern India were in a state of constant friction, frequently erupting into warfare, but warfare of the inconclusive type traditional to Hinduism, which never pushed a victory home and thus inhibited both the building up of stable empires and the establishment of firm alliances. If Prithviraja had some help from his neighbours to the east, as certain Muslim accounts assert, it was half-hearted and ineffectual.

Nara-Narayana, Deogarh, Gupta Period

The period from AD 550 to 1200 saw the rapid development of
Aryanized culture in the peninsula. Two main focuses of power emerged,
one in the Deccan and the other in the Tamil plain, and their rulers
contended constantly and indecisively for mastery for more than 600
years. The events of this region throw an interesting light on the
workings of the Hindu political system. For instance, in the Deccan the
Chalukya Dynasty held power from the middle of the sixth to the
middle of the eighth century. A sudden revolt by an important vassal,
Dantidurga of the line of Rashtrakutas, brought about the overthrow of
the Chalukyas. They were not completely eradicated, however, but were
allowed to continue as the Rashtrakutas' vassals. Thus the Chalukyas
persisted for 200 years, until in the tenth century the Rashtrakutas grew
weak. Then the Chalukyas seized their chance and regained supremacy,
only for their empire to be partitioned among three of their own vassals
after a further 200 years.

The first great dynasty to control the Tamil plain was that of the
Pallavas, whose rulers introduced many features of northern civilization
into the south. Between the Pallavas and the Chalukyas were several
minor kingdoms, usually tributary to one of the greater powers, but
always ready to become independent whenever they found an
opportunity. Among these the Kadambas are worth mentioning because
of their origin. The line was founded in the fourth century by a young
brahman, Mayurasarman, who gave up his studies and became leader of
a troop of bandits, and levied protection money from villages in the
hilly western part of the Pallava kingdom. In the end the Pallava king
recognized Mayurasarman as a vassal; he established his capital at
Vanavasi in Mysore and his descendants were classed as kshatriyas,
though they remembered their brahman ancestry with pride.

In the ninth century the Pallavas gave way to the Cholas, who
claimed descent from the early Tamil kings of the same surname who
had disappeared from history over 500 years earlier. The Cholas are
noteworthy for their patronage of art and architecture—splendid
temples with majestic towers and fine sculpture, especially in bronze,
were produced during their rule. To some extent they revived the
tradition of bureaucracy, and developed a more centralized form of

government than that of most other Indian kingdoms, finding a place in the system for village councils, usually chosen by lot, the records of whose deliberations are still to be seen engraved on the walls of village temples in various part of Tamilnadu.

The Cholas are also noteworthy as the one dynasty of India which, if only for a while, adopted a maritime policy, expanding their power by sea. Under the great Chola emperors Rajaraja I (985–1014) and Rajendra I (1012–44), first Ceylon was conquered and then the whole eastern seaboard of India as far as the Ganga. Finally, under Rajendra, a great naval expedition sailed across the Bay of Bengal and occupied strategic points in Sumatra, Malaya, and Burma. This Chola maritime empire, the only certain instance of Indian overseas expansion by force of arms, was not an enduring one. Later Chola rulers became once more involved in the endemic wars with the Chalukyas and lost interest in their overseas possessions. Within fifty years of the expedition all the Chola troops had been withdrawn to the mainland. Later the Cholas weakened, and were replaced as the dominant power in Tamilnadu by the Pandyas, whose capital was the sacred city of Madurai, in the extreme south.

The whole of the peninsula was shaken to its foundations by the invasions of the troops of Sultan 'Ala'u'd-Din Khalji of Delhi (1296–1316), led by his general Malik Kafur. As a result the Deccan came under Muslim domination for 400 years, but the south remained under Hindu control, after a brief interlude when a short-lived Muslim sultanate ruled from Madurai. The hegemony of the Dravidian south fell to the Empire of Vijayanagara, founded in 1336 and surviving until 1565, when its forces were defeated by a coalition of Deccan sultans. This was the last of the great empires on the old Hindu model, and by the time of its fall the Portuguese were already controlling the seas around India.

The long period whose history we have outlined above is sometimes thought of as one of decline, when compared with the stable and urbane days of the Guptas. This judgement is true in some particulars. The literature of the period, though it includes many important works, has nothing as near perfection as the main works of Kalidasa. There is much excellent sculpture from this period, but nothing as fine as the best Gupta productions. Yet in architecture there was an immense advance over Gupta times, and, only a century or two before the Muslims occupied northern India, there arose such splendid temples as those at Khajuraho, Bhubaneshwar, Kanchipuram, and Thanjavur, among many others.

In the religious life of India, after the Gupta period, the greatest vitality seems to have been found in the peninsula. Here certain south India brahmans developed Hindu philosophy and theology as never before, and, basing their work on the Upanishads, the Bhagavad Gita, and the *Brahma Sutras*, produced commentaries of great length and subtlety, to defend their own systematic interpretations of the texts. Chief of these was Sankaracharya, a Keralite brahman of the ninth century, who has with some justification been called the St Thomas Aquinas of Hinduism. Sankaracharya was only one of many teachers nearly as great as he, such as Ramanuja (died 1137) and Madhav (?1197–1276), who founded sub-sects of the Vedanta philosophical school.

Perhaps even more important was the growth of simple popular devotionalism (bhakti), which began among the Tamils near the beginning of this period with the production of the beautiful Tamil hymns of the *Nayanars* and *Alvars*. Other products of the same movement were the Sanskrit *Bhagavata Purana*, which, composed in the Tamil country, soon spread all over India and was later translated into the everyday languages, to diffuse the cult of Krishna as the divine lover. Before the Muslim conquest of the Deccan, this movement had begun to spread northwards and left its traces in the earliest important Marathi literature, such as the *Jnanesvari* of Jnanesvar.

Meanwhile Buddhism steadily lost ground, though it was still very much alive in Bengal and Bihar when the Muslims occupied these regions. Both Buddhism and Hinduism had become affected by what is generally known as Tantricism or Tantrism, emphasizing the worship of

A temple at Khajuraho

goddesses, especially the Mother Goddess, the spouse of Shiva, known by many names. With this came sexual mysticism, and the sacramentalization of the sexual act, which was performed ritually by circles of initiates. Other socio-religious practices, looked on as reprehensible by most modern Hindus, became more common in this period. Among these were the burning of widows on their husbands' funeral pyres, wrongly called sati (suttee), child marriage, animal sacrifice, female infanticide, and the religious prostitution of the *devadasi*. One feels that there was a definite lowering in the value of human life in comparison with the days of the Guptas, when, according to Chinese accounts, even the death penalty was not inflicted.

Ancient Indian Religions

Hinduism

S. RADHAKRISHNAN

The Spirit of Hinduism

IF WE LOOK AT THE various and sometimes conflicting creeds which it contains, we may wonder whether Hinduism is not just a name which covers a multitude of different faiths, but when we turn our attention to the spiritual life, devotion, and endeavour which lie behind the creeds, we realize the unity, the indefinable self-identity, which, however, is by no means static or absolute. Throughout the history of Hindu civilization there has been a certain inspiring ideal, a certain motive power, a certain way of looking at life, which cannot be identified with any stage or cross-section of the process. The whole movement and life of the institution, its entire history, is necessary in order to disclose to us this idea, and it cannot therefore be expressed in a simple formula. It requires centuries for ideas to utter themselves, and at any stage the institution has always an element that is yet to be expressed. No idea is fully expressed at any one point of its historical unfolding.

What is this Idea of Hinduism, this continuous element that runs through all its stages from the earliest to the latest, from the lowest to the highest, this fundamental spirit which is more fully and richly expressed in the highest though it is present in the very lowest? Life is present in every stage of a plant's growth and it is always the same life, though it is more fully expressed in the developed tree than in the first push of the tender blade. In the Hindu religion there must be a common element that makes every stage and every movement an expression of the religion. The different phases and stages have proper content and meaning only in so far as this common element exists. With the perception of the unity which runs through error and failure up the long ascent towards the ideal, the whole achievement of Hinduism falls into coherent perspective.

Historical Outline

The spirit is not a dead abstraction but a living force. Because it is active and dynamic the Hindu civilization has endured so long and proved so capable of adaptation to the growing complexity of life. The great river of Hindu life, usually serene but not without its rapids, reaches back so far that only a long view can do justice to its nature. From prehistoric times influences have been at work moulding the faith. As a result of the excavations in Harappa and Mohenjo-daro we have evidence of the presence in India of a highly developed culture that 'must have had a long antecedent history on the soil of India, taking us back to an age that can only be dimly surmised'.[1] In age and achievement the Indus valley civilization is comparable to that of Egypt or Sumeria. The noteworthy feature of this civilization is its continuity, not as a political power but as a cultural influence. The religion of the Indus people is hardly distinguishable, according to Sir John Marshall, from 'that aspect

[1] Sir John Marshall, *Mohenjo-Daro and the Indus Civilization*, 1931, Vol. I, p. 106.

of Hinduism which is bound up with animism and the cults of Shiva and the Mother Goddess'.[2] These latter do not seem to be indigenous to the vedic religion.

Though the Shakti cult was later accepted by the Vedic people, their original opposition to it is not altogether suppressed. To the sacrifice of Daksha, all the vedic deities are said to have been invited except Shiva, who soon gained authority as the successor of the vedic Rudra. Even so late as the *Bhagavata Purana* the opposition to Shiva worship is present. 'Those who worship Shiva and those who follow them are the opponents to holy scriptures and may be ranked with *pashandins*. Let the feeble-minded who, with matted locks, ashes, and bones, have lost their purity, be initiated into the worship of Shiva in which wine and brewage are regarded as gods.'[3]

It is a matter for conjecture whether the Indus people had any relation to the Dravidians. Nor can we say whether the Dravidians were natives of the soil or came from outside. Besides the Aryans and the Dravidians there a was also a flat-nosed, black-skinned people who were commonly known as Dasas. The religion, in the first literary records that have come down to us, is that of the Aryans, though it was much influenced by the Indus people, the Dravidians, and the aborigines. The simple hymns of the *Rig Veda* reveal to us an age when Pan was still alive, when the trees in the forest could speak and the waters of the river could sing and man could listen and understand. The spells and the charms to be found in part of the tenth book of the *Rig Veda* and in most of the *Atharva Veda* suggest a type of religious practice based on fear and associated with the spirits of the dark. A religious synthesis of the different views and practices on the basis of monistic idealism is set forth in the early Upanishads. Soon after, a composite culture, springing

[2] Ibid., Vol. I, p. viii.

[3] *Bhagavata Purana*, iv. 2. In the *Padma Purana, pashandins* are said to be 'those who wear skulls, ashes, and bones, the symbols contrary to the Vedas, put on matted locks and the barks of trees, even without entering into the third order of life and engage in rites which are not sanctioned by the Vedas'. *Uttara-khanda*, Ch. 235.

from a union of Greek with Persian and Bactrian influences, dominated north-western India. Successive descents of Muslim conquerors from about AD 1000 affected Hindu life and thought. The Parsi fugitives who were expelled from Persia by Muslim invaders found a welcome shelter in India. St Thomas brought the Christian faith from Syria to south India and for over a thousand years this remained the only Christian centre of influence. In the sixteenth century St Francis Xavier introduced Latin Christianity. The modern Christian missionary movement started over a century ago. The cultural invasion of the West has been vigorous, thanks to its political superiority and industrial efficiency.

Jainism, Buddhism, and Sikhism are creations of the Indian mind and may be interpreted as reform movements from within the fold of Hinduism put forth to meet the special demands of the various stages of the Hindu faith. Zoroastrianism, Islam, and Christianity have been so long in the country that they have become native to the soil and are deeply influenced by the atmosphere of Hinduism.

India was a thorough 'melting-pot' long before the term was invented for America. In spite of attacks, Hellenic, Muslim, and European among others, Hindu culture has maintained its tradition unbroken to the present day. The spiritual life of the Hindus at the present time has not precisely the same proportion or orientation as that of either the Indus people or the Vedic Aryans or even the great teachers, Sankara and Ramanuja. Its changes in emphasis reflect individual temperaments, social conditions, and the changing intellectual environment, but the same persistent idea reappears in different forms. Hinduism grows in the proper sense of the word, not by accretion, but like an organism, undergoing from time to time transformation as a whole. It has carried within it much of its early possessions. It has cast aside a good deal and often it has found treasures which it has made its own. The history of Hinduism is chequered by tragic failures and wonderful victories, by opportunities missed and taken. New truth has been denied and persecuted occasionally. The unity of its body, realized at the cost of centuries of effort and labour, now and then came near being shattered by self-seeking and ignorance.

Yet the religion itself is not destroyed. It is alive and vigorous and has withstood attacks from within and without. It seems to be possessed of unlimited powers of renewal. Its historic vitality, the abounding energy which it reveals, would alone be evidence of its spiritual genius.

Postscript by the Editor

The most important religious heritage of India from her ancient past is no doubt the doctrine of transmigration (*samsara*) which is characteristic of all Indian religions and sharply distinguishes them from those with a Semitic ancestry, such as Judaism, Christianity, and Islam.

Transmigration must also have encouraged the doctrine of *ahimsa* (non-injury), which was specially supported by Buddhism and Jainism in their campaign against animal sacrifice, for this doctrine linked all living things together in a single complex system—gods, demi-gods, human beings, demons, ghosts, souls in torment, warm-blodded animals, even humble insects and worms, all possessed souls, essentially the same.

The great majority of Indians still believe in this doctrine, and the concomitant doctrine of *karma*, that man is reborn in happy or unhappy conditions according to his works, and these doctrines, in their Buddhist form, have affected more than half of Asia. They provide a potent sanction against evil-doing, or at least against a man's infringing the ethical norms of his society, for this leads to inevitable suffering, while righteous conduct brings happiness to the next life.

Moreover the afflicted can learn to accept suffering with the thought that it is not sent at the whim of fate or chance, and is not the visitation of a capricious god, but is the just recompense for one's own evil deeds in past lives. This doctrine is not fatalism, and does not imply that the sufferer should not try to better his lot but it makes suffering of all kinds intelligible, and gives hope to the sufferer who bears affliction patiently. Thus, as a source of consolation, it has done much to mould the Indian character and to shape the Indian way of life.

A further potent factor in the moulding of the Indian mind is the concept of endless cyclic time in a cosmos so immense that the mind boggles at conceiving its size. The simple and comparatively small universe of Ptolemy, which provided the traditional worldview of later Judaism, Christianity, and Islam, is intelligible and homely by comparison; and the traditional Semitic and Christian doctrine of linear time—commencing at a period some 4000 years BC and likely to come to an end and give way to eternity in the comparatively near future— was equally intelligible, giving an urgency to man's life which might not be felt in a society which believed that time was infinite, with an infinite number of opportunities for the individual to rise or fall in the scale of being. The Hindu universe is closer to that of modern science than the Ptolemaic one, and for this reason among others Hindus, even orthodox ones of the old school, have little difficulty in accepting scientific theories on the nature of the cosmos or of man.

The forbidding universe of science differs from that of the Hindus in one particular, however. The Hindu world, in all its immense length and breadth, is completely and fully underlain by the Divine. There is no corner of the cosmos where God, or the impersonal *Brahman* for the monistic Vedantin, is not. Facets of the personality of the one Lord behind the many appear in all aspects of life on earth, and the immense

Nataraja

empty spaces of the universe are full of deities, all aspects or partial manifestations of the One.

If the intellectual Hindu prefers to think of the One spirit as impersonal and to equate that One with the *Atman*, the innermost kernel of his own being, the ordinary Indian of all times has thought of the One as personal—a High God who created for himself all the lesser gods and the whole cosmos. Complicated theories evolved in the period following the composition of vedic literature, and continued to develop throughout the pre-Muslim period and even after. New gods appeared and old gods faded away and almost vanished, in response to the needs of the times. They formed two broad groups, crystallizing round the two High Gods, Vishnu and Shiva respectively; and the fantasy and inventiveness of the whole folk, not merely of the learned brahmans, expressed itself in the richest collection of mythology and legend in the world—ranging in quality from the sublime to the grotesque and occasionally even to the repulsive.

For the Vaishnavites, the worshippers of Vishnu, the god has in the past taken material form, in order to save the world from impending disaster. His incarnations (*avataras*), especially those as Rama and Krishna, have given the Hindus their most exuberant and vital mythology, legend, and folklore. Rama and his faithful wife Sita combine the ideals of heroism, long-suffering, righteousness, loyalty, and justice in a story so full of exciting incidents that it has become part of the tradition not only of India, but also of most of South East Asia. And Rama's henchman, the gigantic monkey Hanuman, the archetype of the loyal helper, striding out with his mighty club, is still among the most popular of the lesser gods of Hinduism. He figures as the divinity of countless minor shrines throughout the length and breadth of India, and is the personification of the strong arm of the Lord, ever ready to help the righteous in the hour of need.

Krishna, probably even more popular than Rama, is a divinity of a rare completeness and catholicity, meeting almost every human need. As the divine child he satisfies the warm maternal drives of Indian womanhood. As the divine lover, he provides romantic wish fulfilment in a society still tightly controlled by ancient norms of behaviour which give little scope for freedom of expression in sexual relations. As charioteer of the hero Arjuna on the battlefield of Kurukshetra, he is the helper of all those who turn to him, even saving the sinner from evil rebirths, if he has sufficient faith in the Lord.

Shiva, the divine dancer and the divine ascetic, has a less vivid body of mythology and legend associated with him. He dwells in the heights of Mt. Kailasha with his beautiful wife Parvati, his bull Nandi, and his two sons, the elephant-headed Ganesha and the six-headed Karttikeya. Despite its superficial forbiddingness and its bizarre elements, this group of divinities forms a sort of paradigm of family life. Often worshipped in the *lingam*, a much-formalized phallic symbol, Shiva represents the eternal power through which the universe evolves. As the divine dancer, subject of some of the most wonderful bronze sculpture in the world, Shiva dances new steps in never-ending variety until at length, in a very fierce and wild dance (*tandava*), he will dance the universe out of existence, later to create a new one by yet another dance.

Stories and legends like these have provided the raw material for most of India's early art and literature, and they have given courage and consolation in face of adversity to countless millions through the centuries. Moreover they have provided India with her main source of entertainment.

Buddhism

Bhikshu Sangharakshita

The Buddha

From the traditional point of view Buddhism begins with the believer going for refuge to the Three Jewels (*triratna*), the Buddha, the Doctrine (*Dharma*), and the Community of monks (*Sangha*). In all probability the Buddha lived between 563 and 483 BC.

Born at Lumbini, in the territory of the Sakya republic, of wealthy patrician stock, the Buddha went forth 'from home into the homeless life' at the age of twenty-nine, attained Supreme Enlightenment at

Bodh Gaya at the age of thirty-five, and passed away at Kusinagara at the age of eighty. During his lifetime his teachings spread throughout the kingdoms of Magadha and Kosala (corresponding to the modern south Bihar and eastern Uttar Pradesh), as well as in the circumjacent principalities and republics. His disciples were recruited from all classes of society, and included both men and women. Besides instructing an extensive circle of lay adherents, he trained a smaller, more select band of monks and nuns who constituted the Sangha proper and upon whom, after the Parinirvana, the responsibility for carrying on his mission mainly devolved. His personality, as it emerges from the ancient records, was a unique combination of dignity and affability, wisdom and kindliness.

The Dharma

The word Dharma probably has more meanings than any other term in the entire vocabulary of Buddhism. As the second of the three Refuges it has been variously translated as Law, Truth, Doctrine, Gospel, Teaching, Norm, and True Idea, all of which express some aspect of its total significance.

The Dharma consists of various doctrines or teachings. According to the most ancient canonical accounts of a crucial episode, the truth, law, or principle which the Buddha perceived at the time of his Enlightenment— in the perception of which, indeed, that Enlightenment consisted—and which, on account of its abstruseness, he was at first reluctant to disclose to a passion-ridden generation, was that of the 'conditionally co-producedness' (*paticca-samup-panna*) of things. The doctrine of Conditioned Co-production represents an all-inclusive reality that admits of two different trends of things in the whole

Kathakali

of existence. In one of them the reaction takes place in a cyclical order between two opposites, such as pleasure and pain, virtue and vice, good and evil. In the other the reaction takes place in a progressive order between two counterparts or complements, or between two things of the same genus, the succeeding factor augmenting the effect of the preceding one. The *Samsara* or Round of Conditioned Existence represents the first trend. Herein, as depicted by the 'Wheel of Life', sentient beings under the influence of craving, hatred, and bewilderment revolve as gods, men, demons (*asuras*), animals, ghosts (*pretas*), and denizens of hell in accordance with the law of karma, and experience pleasure and pain.

The Path to Deliverance and Nirvana together represent the second trend. The Path is essentially a sequence of progressively higher mental and spiritual states, and the practice of the Dharma consists above all in the cultivation of these states.

The Sangha

The last of the three Refuges is the Sangha. This great institution, which with the possible exception of its Jain counterpart is the oldest surviving religious order in the world, came into existence within a few months of the Buddha's Enlightenment. It consisted—and ideally still consists— of those of the Buddha's followers who, having renounced the household life, devote the whole of their time and all their energies to the realization of Nirvana.

In a more general sense the Sangha comprises the entire Buddhist community, sanctified and unsanctified, the professed *religieux* and the lay devotees, men and women. As such it is sometimes known as the *Mahasangha* or 'Great Assembly'. Lay devotees (*upasakas* and *upasikas*) are those who go for refuge to the Three Jewels, worship the relics of the Buddha, observe the Five Precepts of ethical behaviour, and support the monks (*bhikshus*).

The Oral Tradition

It is well known that the Buddha himself wrote nothing. Spiritual influence and personal example apart, his teachings were communicated entirely by oral means, through discourses to, and discussions with, his disciples and members of the public, as well as through inspired spontaneous utterances. While we do not definitely know what language he spoke, it would appear that he rejected the more 'classical' Sanskrit in favour of the vernacular, especially the dialects of Kosala and Magadha.

The Canonical Literature

Even during the period of oral tradition the complete words of the Buddha were referred to as the *Tripitaka*, the three 'baskets' or collections of the Buddha's words. These three are the *Vinaya Pitaka*, the *Sutra Pitaka*, and the *Abhidharma Pitaka*. Together with the *Tantras* they make up the four chief divisions of the canonical writings.

The word *vinaya*, meaning 'that which leads away from (evil)', stands for the practical or disciplinary aspect of Buddhism, and the Vinaya Pitaka comprises the Collection of (Monastic) Discipline.

The *sutra*, literally a thread, and hence by extension of meaning the 'thread' of discourse connecting a number of topics, is perhaps the most important and characteristic of all Buddhist literary genres. The Sutra Pitaka is the Collection of Discourses, and constitutes the principal source of our knowledge of the Dharma. Some discourses are either partly or wholly in dialogue form. Others are delivered not by the Buddha but by disciples speaking either with his approval or under his inspiration.

Abhidharma means 'about Dharma', though traditionally the term was often interpreted as 'higher Dharma'. The Abhidharma Pitaka is a collection of highly scholastic treatises which annotate and explain the texts of the Sutra Pitaka, define technical terms, arrange numerically classified doctrines in order, give a systematic philosophical exposition of the teachings, and establish a consistent method of spiritual practice.

The Tantras are the most esoteric of the canonical texts. The word itself, derived from a root meaning 'to spread', is applied to a variety of treatises, and affords no clue to the contents of these works. While resembling the sutras in literary form, they differ from them in dealing with ritual and yoga rather than with ethics and philosophy and in being unintelligible without the traditional commentary.

The greater part of this enormous literature is now available only in translation, the principal collections being the Imperial Chinese *Tripitaka* and the Tibetan *Kanjur* or 'Translated Word [of the Buddha]'. Within the last hundred years, however, a number of Sanskrit Buddhist texts, both canonical and non-canonical, have come to light in Gilgit (Pakistan) and been recovered from the sands of Central Asia.

Phases of Development

From the Parinirvana of the Buddha to the sack of Nalanda (*c.* 1197) Indian Buddhism passed through three great phases of development, traditionally known as the Hinayana, the Mahayana, and the Vajrayana, each with its own characteristics and its own spiritual ideals. These phases were not mutually exclusive. The earlier *yanas*, besides continuing to exist as independent schools, were also incorporated in the later ones and regarded as constituting, with modifications, their indispensable theoretical and practical foundation.

The Hinayana, 'Little Vehicle' or 'Lower Way', was so called by the Mahayanists because it teaches the attainment of salvation for oneself alone. It is predominantly ethico-psychological in character and its spiritual ideal is embodied in the austere figure of the *Arhant*, a person in whom all craving is extinct, and who will no more be reborn. The Hinayana insists upon the necessity of the monastic life, with which, indeed, it tends to identify

Yakshagana

the spiritual life altogether. The laity simply observe the more elementary precepts, worship the relics of the Buddha, and support the monks, by which means merit (*punya*) is accumulated and rebirth in heaven assured.

The Mahayana, literally 'Great Vehicle' or 'Great Way', is so called because it teaches the salvation of all. Predominantly devotional and metaphysical in character, its ideal is the Bodhisattva, the heroic being who, practising the six or ten Perfections (paramita) throughout thousands of lives, aspires to the attainment of Buddhahood for the sake of all sentient beings. Perspectives infinitely vaster than those of the Hinayana are here disclosed. The earlier vehicle is regarded by the Mahayanists not as wrong but only as inadequate, the provisional rather than the final teaching, given out by the Buddha to disciples of inferior calibre whom a sudden revelation of the transcendent glories of the Mahayana might have stupefied rather than enlightened. In the Mahayana Arhantship, far from being the highest achievement, is only a stage of the path; the true goal is Supreme Buddhahood.

The Vajrayana, the 'Diamond Vehicle' or 'Adamantine Way', is so called because, like the irresistible *vajra*, meaning both thunderbolt and diamond, it immediately annihilates all obstacles to the attainment of Buddhahood. It is predominantly yogic and magical in character, and its ideal is the *Siddha*, 'a man who is so much in harmony with the cosmos that he is under no constraint whatsoever, and as a free agent is able to manipulate the cosmic forces both inside and outside himself'.

Nirvana

Although the state of perfection attained by following the Path is said to be ineffable, it is referred to in the Scriptures by a bewilderingly rich variety of names. The best known of these in the West is Nirvana (Pali, *Nibbana*), from the root *va*, meaning to blow, and the prefix *nir*, out or off. Hence the traditional explanations of Nirvana as the 'blowing out' of the fires of greed, hatred, and delusion and as the state wherein the thirst for sensuous experience, for continued existence, and even for non-existence, is altogether absent.

However, the goal of Buddhism is far from being a purely negative state. Nirvana is a state of absolute illumination, supreme bliss, infinite love and compassion, unshakeable serenity, and unrestricted spiritual freedom. It is for the Hinayana an eternal, unchanging, extra-mental spiritual entity, wholly unconnected with the cosmic process, and for the Mahayana the Absolute Reality transcending all oppositions including that between itself and Samsara. As the supreme object of the spiritual consciousness, or *Dharmakaya*, it is the embodiment of Great Wisdom and Great Compassion and embraces all possible virtues and perfections. It is the Infinite Light (*Amitabha*) and Boundless Life (*Amitayus*), which has nothing to do with personal immortality.

Decline and Revival

The reason for the decline and alleged disappearance of Buddhism in the land of its birth is a problem that has perplexed historians ever since it became the object of scientific study and research. The key to the solution lies in the relation of the religion to what is now popularly known as Hinduism. Both systems were tolerant to a degree which to the exclusive monotheisms of the West and the Middle East seems incredible, and neither hesitated to borrow from the other what was required for its own development. Poetic genius needs a language as its medium of expression; but by being used in this way the character of the language itself is modified.

After fifteen centuries of mutual interaction the existence of a Sangha in large centres of monastic learning remained the chief discernible difference between the two religions. When these centres—Nalanda, Vikramashila, Odantapuri, and others—were destroyed by the fury of the Muslim invader, and the native kings who might have sponsored their restoration were replaced by rulers with an uncompromising and alien faith, Buddhism quietly disappeared.

Modern Buddhist revival in India began about a hundred years ago. After being awakened by the pioneer work of Western Orientalists, historians, and archaeologists, interest in the cultural and religious achievements of the long-forgotten faith was stimulated by the resurgence of national feeling and reinforced by the missionary endeavours of Buddhists from other Asian countries. The year 1959 saw the flight of the Dalai Lama from Tibet to India and the influx of about 50,000 Tibetan refugees, among them more than a thousand monks. From the point of view of Buddhist revival, however, the most decisive and far-reaching event of modern times occurred when the late Dr B.R. Ambedkar, the Untouchable leader, embraced Buddhism at Nagpur on 14 October 1966 along with half a million followers. Despite his untimely death a few weeks later, the movement of mass conversion among the Untouchables snowballed to such an extent that whereas the Census of 1951 returned 181,000 Buddhists for India, that of 1961 recorded 3,250,000, the greatest gains having been made in Maharashtra.

Jainism

A.N. Upadhye

Jainism is essentially an Indian religion and it is still a living faith in some parts of the country. The number of its followers is just over two million. Its contribution to the Indian heritage is more significant than might be expected from its numerical strength. As an institutionalized religion, it has held its ground all along. It has sometimes enjoyed royal patronage, and it has produced worthy monks and laymen of whom any society could be proud. The Jaina contributions to Indian art and architecture, to the preservation and enrichment of Indian literature, and to the cultivation of languages, both Aryan and Dravidian, are praiseworthy. Lastly, the religious instincts inculcated by Jainism have left an abiding impression on many aspects of Indian life.

Scene from *Mrichchakatika*, Mathura, Kushan, Second Century AD

According to Jainism there have flourished in this age twenty-four *Tirthankaras*, or leaders of their religion. The first of them was Rishabha, the twenty-second Nemi or Neminatha, the twenty-third Parsva, and the last Mahavira. Rishabha figures as a great saint of antiquity; and, in later Hindu literature, he is noted for his queer practices and credited with propagating heretic doctrines which are common to Jainism. He is said to have laid the foundations for orderly human society. Neminatha is associated in Jainism with Krishna of the Yadava clan, whom the Hindus adopted as an avatara of Vishnu. The other Tirthankaras are prehistoric in character. It is now accepted on all hands that Parsvanatha, who according to Jaina tradition flourished two centuries before Mahavira, was a historical person. His followers lived in the time of Mahavira, with whose disciples they held discussions. The parents of Mahavira followed the creed of Parsva.

Mahavira was a senior contemporary of the Buddha. He was born at Kundagrama near Vaishali to the north of Patna in Bihar. He belonged to the Naya (Jnata) clan; and he is called Nataputta in the Pali cannon. His father was Siddhartha, a ruler of that area. His mother, Trishala alias Priyakarini, hailed from the royal family of the tribe of the Licchavis. Tradition is not unanimous about Mahavira's marriage. He left home at the age of thirty and started practising penances in search of knowledge. Unlike the Buddha, he had no need to wander in search of a teacher, because he belonged already to the well-established religious order of his predecessor, Parsvanatha. While wandering as an ascetic he endured a number of hardships. After twelve years of rigorous penance and meditation he attained enlightenment: the knowledge he is said to have attained was free from the limitations of time and space. He preached what he lived. His was a career of supreme detachment, and he was called *Nirgrantha*, one without any ties, whether internal or external.

All living beings want to live, and therefore he conceded to every being the right to live: thus the sanctity of life in all its forms constituted the basis of his moral values. Everyone is responsible for his own karmas; and when karmas are annihilated there is an end to transmigration, followed by the attainment of supreme spiritual bliss. The age Mahavira lived in was marked by great philosophical speculation, in which a number of eminent teachers participated, both brahmanas and sramanas. The seeds of the *atma* doctrine of the Upanishads and the further flowering of religious systems like Ajivikism, Jainism, and Buddhism are to be assigned to this period. Mahavira had family connections with the ruling dynasties of eastern India. He preached ahimsa or universal love; and his metaphysics was based on common-sense realism and intellectual reconciliation. His followers consisted of monks, nuns, householders and their women-folk; and a well-knit Sangha, or socio-religious organization, was formed in his own times. He travelled for thirty years preaching his doctrines, only halting from any length of time at one place during the rainy season. He died at the age of 72, traditionally in 527 BC, at Pava in Bihar. This occasion was celebrated with a lamp festival by the two ruling families of the region, the Mallakis and the Licchavis; and the present-day Dipavali, one of the most widespread and popular of Hindu festivals, is said in Jaina tradition to be a continuation of this.

Unlike Buddhism, which soon spread far and wide, with numerous monasteries in India and elsewhere, the Jaina Church has shown quite a modest yet steady progress. After Mahavira eminent teachers such as Gautama, Jambu, and others led the Church, which received patronage from such kings as Shrenika Bimbisara of Magadha, Chandragupta Maurya, India's first great emperor, Kharavela, the Orissan conqueror, and others. The influence of Jainism gradually spread to the western parts of India. Under the leadership of Bhadrabahu a number of monks also went to the south owing to adverse conditions caused by famine in the north. Possibly it was the subsequent differences in ascetic practices which led to a split in the Church, dividing it into its two main sections, the Digambara and the Shvetambara. This division affected both the monks and laity. The basic religious principles remained the same for both, but they differed among themselves on minor dogmas, mythological details, and ascetic practices.

The ruling classes and the mercantile community were often attracted by the rigorous asceticism and religious life of the Jaina monks and adopted the Jaina way of life. In the south, during the early medieval period, royal dynasties such as the Gangas, Kadambas,

Buddha, Mathura, 200 BC to AD 200

Chalukyas, and Rashtrakutas patronized Jainism.

In Gujarat patronage came from wealthy merchants rather than from the rulers. Under the Chaulukya King Kumarapala (1142–73), however, Jainism saw glorious days in Gujarat. A new era of literary activity started under the leadership of the Jaina scholar Hemachandra and other teachers and scholars. Ministers such as Vastupala constructed magnificent temples in marble. Later, Akbar highly honoured the Jaina teacher, Hiravijaya; and some of the Mughal rulers issued *firmans* prohibiting the slaughter of animals during the Jaina festival of *Pajjusana* in all those places where the Jainas lived. Prominent Jaina families in Delhi and Ahmedabad built excellent Jaina temples and had influence in the Mughal Court. Jaina laymen also played an important part in the political activities of Rajasthan during the Mughal period. Even during the period of the East India Company Jaina families like the Jagatseths and Singhis acted as state bankers, and naturally wielded great influence in society.

Jainism has all along instilled a religious zeal among its votaries, the concrete expression of which is seen all over the country in works of art and architecture: statues, free-standing pillars (*manastambha*), caves, and temples. The 57-foot-high statue of Gommateshvara at Sravana Belgola in Mysore, erected in about 983 or 984 by the Ganga minister Chamundaraya, is a marvel of its kind; and it is imitated in many places even to this day. The temples at Mount Abu and those at Palithana in Gujarat and Moodbidri and Karkal in the south make a rich contribution to the Indian heritage.

The soul has been in association with karmic matter from time immemorial, and the object of the Jaina religion is to free the soul from karma. The activities of mind, speech, and body lead to the constant influx of karmas which form the *karmana-sarira*, or karmic body, for the soul, whereby it moves in Samsara. Everyone is responsible for his own karmas, and there is no escape from them unless one experiences their fruits, good or bad. Jainism admits no God to bestow favour or frown: the law of karma works automatically in shaping one's lot.

As the influx and destruction of karmas entirely depend on man's activities, Jainism lays special stress on the ethical code. This takes two forms, one intended for the householder and the other for the monk. Both are complementary; and if they differ, it is only in the degree of the rigour of practice. The basic vows are five: (1) abstention from injury to living beings (ahimsa); (2) speaking the truth (*satya*); (3) not stealing (*asteya*); (4) chastity (*brahmacharya*); and (5) limiting one's possessions (*aparigraha*). The principle of ahimsa is the logical outcome of the Jaina metaphysical theory that all souls are potentially equal. No one likes pain. Naturally, therefore, one should not do to others what one does not want others to do to oneself. The social implications of this principle of reciprocity are profoundly beneficial.

What apparently distinguishes a Jaina monk from a layman is his itinerant way of life, with no abode of his own and no possessions or paraphernalia beyond those required for his religious observances. In outward form and equipment there are different schools among the Jaina monks. The Digambara monk, who goes about naked if of the highest grade, has a water pot made from a gourd (*kamandalu*) for the calls of nature and a bunch of peacock feathers to clean the place where he sits, etc. But if he belongs to the lower stage, he has a minimum of clothing to cover his private parts. A Shvetambara monk is clad in white robes, and he is equipped with a staff, a bunch of wool, and wooden pots. These sects differ somewhat in their rules of outward behaviour, which affect their mode of travelling, eating, etc. The inner religious life, however, is fundamentally the same for the various schools.

The five *anuvratas* (lesser rows) of layman, not to kill, not to lie, not to steal, to abstain from sex, and to renounce property, are called *mahavratas* (great vows) in the case of a monk, who has to observe them with maximum rigour and thoroughness. These sins lead to the influx of karmas; therefore the monk must abstain from them in thought, word, and deed, and neither commit, commission, nor consent to them. The rigidity with which he is expected to observe the rules and the

Details of a Sanchi Gateway

elaborate details of conduct only show how minutely the whole system of ascetic morality is worked out.

Numerous traces of Jaina influence on Indian life can be detected. The worship of idols in a refined form, the building of temples, the founding of charitable lodges for men and animals, the preservation of rich libraries of manuscripts, and the distribution of food and other necessities to the poor; these are some of the outstanding features of Jaina society, and to a large extent they have been imitated by other Indian religious groups. Jainism and Buddhism have been foremost in upholding the doctrine of ahimsa, and Jainism has held firm to its original ideology much more closely than Buddhism.

Philosophy

S.N. Das Gupta

ONE MAY DIVIDE THE PHILOSOPHICAL development of India into three stages: pre-logical up to the beginning of the Christian era, logical up to the Muhammadan domination of India, AD 1000 or 1100, and ultra-logical, AD 1100–1700. The contribution of the first period is to be found in the philosophical hymns of the Vedas; in the more mature Upanishads; in the Gita, which is something like a metrical commentary on the Upanishads, working out their ideals in their practical bearing to life; and in the rise and growth of Buddhism and the *Sankhya* and the *Vaisheshika* philosophy. From about the beginning of the first or second century BC we have the various systems of Indian philosophy, the *Yoga-sutras*, the Sankhya treatises, the *Mimamsa-sutras*, the *Brahma-sutras*, and the *Nyaya-sutras*, and their numerous commentaries and sub-commentaries. In the third period we have keen discussions

The Ajanta caves

and dialectics of an extremely subtle character such as had never developed in Europe at that time, and which are in part so difficult that few Occidental scholars have been able to master them.

In the philosophical hymns of the Vedas we come across men who were weary of seeking mere economic welfare through religious rituals of a magical character. They wished to know something greater than their ordinary religion and sought to delve into the mystery of the Universe— the highest and the greatest truth. They formed the conception of a being who is the depository and the source of all powers and forces of nature, from whom nature with its manifold living creatures has emanated and by whom it is sustained and maintained. In spite of all the diversity

in the world there is one fundamental reality in
which all duality ceases. The highest truth is thus
the highest being, who is both immanent in the
world and transcendent. He holds the world
within him and yet does not exhaust himself in
the world. The ordinary polytheism and
henotheism of Vedic worship thus slowly pass
away, sometimes into monotheism and
sometimes into pantheism; and in this way
some of the Vedic hymns declare the spirituality
of the world and denounce the common-sense
view of things.

This view is developed in the Upanishads,
which may be regarded as a continuation of
the philosophical hymns of the *Rig Veda* and
the *Atharva Veda*. The Upanishads do not merely
speculate on the nature of Brahman externally
as both the immanent and the transcendent
cause of the world, but they also try to
demonstrate its reality in experience. Neither
the Upanishads, nor the philosophical hymns of
the Vedas, give us any reasons in demonstration of their conception of
the ultimate being.

The Upanishads are driven by their inner thought to give some
grounds for such assertions. Yet there is no attempt at logical speculation
and demonstrative reasoning. The intuitive affirmations surge forth with
the reality of the living faith of one describing an experience which he
himself has had. They affirm that this ultimate reality cannot be grasped
by learning or reasoning. It reveals itself only in our heart through
sublime purity, absolute self-control, self-abnegation, and cessation of
mundane desires. Man not only becomes moral in his relations to his
fellow beings, but becomes super-moral, as it were, by an easy control
of the conflicts of his lower instincts and desires, and by superior

excellence of character. It becomes possible for him to merge himself in an intuitive contact with the transcendental spiritual essence with which he can immediately identify himself.

The Upanishads again and again reiterate the fact that this spiritual essence is incognizable by any of the sense-organs—by eye or by touch—that it is beyond the reasoning faculties of man and is therefore unattainable by logic, and that it is indescribable in speech and unthinkable by thought. The apperception of it is not of an ordinary cognitive nature, but is an apperception of the essence of our beings; and, just as external nature was regarded as being held and maintained in Brahman, so the totality of our being, our sense-functions, and thought-functions were regarded as having come out, being held and sustained in this inner being. It was also regarded as the *antar-yamin* or the inner controller of our personality—the spiritual entity which is its root and in which lie sustained and controlled all our vital activities and cognitive and conative functions. We can have an apperception of it only when we transcend the outer spheres of ordinary life and penetrate into the cavern on which neither the physical luminaries nor the luminaries of thought and sense shed any light. Yet it is a light in itself, from which all other lights draw their illumination. It is subtle and deep, and reveals itself only to those who attain that high spiritual perfection by which they transcend the limits of ordinary personality.

We find anticipations of doubt as to the possibility of such a subtle essence, which was our inmost being, becoming identical with the highest reality of the universe from which everything else emanated. Various parables are related, in which attempts are made to prove the existence of a subtle essence which is unperceived by the eye. In the parable of the banyan tree we are told how the big tree can reside inside a grain-like seed. In the dialogue between Yama and Nachiketas, when the latter seeks instruction regarding the fate of men at death, he is told that when inquiry is earnestly made the true self in man is discovered to be eternally abiding, and can be grasped only through spiritual contact and spiritual union. Taken in this sense, death is a mere illusion which appears to those who cannot grasp the one absolute reality.

There are other passages in which this absolute reality is regarded as one which is undetermined in itself, but from which all our faculties and experiences emanate in concrete determinations. We have thus in ourselves an epitome of the emergence of the world from Brahman. From the subtle state of indifference in deep dreamless sleep one suddenly awakes to the varied experiences of ordinary life. Similarly, concrete varieties of objects have emerged into being from the pure subtle being of Brahman, in which they existed in an undivided and undifferentiated state. Since that which emerges into manifold variety ultimately loses itself in the being of the transcendent cause, and since the transcendent cause alone remains unchanged through all the processes of emergence and dissolution, that alone is the truth. The multiplicity of things is false, for the truth in them is the one abiding essence.

The Upanishads are not philosophy, if we mean by the word philosophy a reasoned account or a rationalization of experiences; yet they contain suggestions of rationalization as to the nature of reality from concrete experience of dreamless sleep and from ineffable mystical experience. Though ineffable, the mystical experience is not regarded as an ecstatic communion with the divine; it is a revelation of the subtlest essence of our being, which lies far below the depth of the common animal man. It is only when we transcend the limits of the ordinary biological man that we can come in contact with the pure personality which the Upanishads call the Atman or the self. This pure self is one in all and is identical with the highest reality of the universe. It is pure spirituality and pure experience (Jnana) and, as such, the absolute concrete truth which is immanent and transcendent at the same time in all our experiences and in all objects denoted by it. It is infinite reality, limitless and illimitable. The Upanisahds thus lay the foundation of all later Hindu philosophy. All Hindu thinkers accept in more or less modified form the fundamental tenet of the Upanishads that self is the ultimate reality, and all experiences are extraneous to it.

By the beginning of the Christian era six philosophical schools or systems had emerged in Hinduism. Though differing very widely, they were all looked on as orthodox, since they all accepted the inspiration of the Vedas and the claim of the brahmans to ritual supremacy. They were linked together in pairs, as complementing one another or otherwise showing close relations. The three pairs were: (i) Sankhya and (ii) Yoga; (iii) Nyaya and (iv) Vaiseshika; and (v) Mimamsa and (vi) Vedanta or *Uttara-mimamsa*.

The Sankhya is probably the earliest Indian attempt at systematic philosophy. Its foundation is attributed to Kapila, who is said to have written the original textbook of the school, the *Shashti-tantra* in sixty chapters. This work is now lost, and we know only the names of those chapters. We find elements of Sankhya even in the earliest Upanishads, and we have reason to believe that the system was probably not originally written, but underwent a course of development at different stages and under different influences; though it is possible that at some particular stage Kapila may have contributed so much towards its systematization as to be generally regarded as the original expounder of the system. It is generally accepted that the Sankhya has two principal schools—the atheistic and the theistic. The theistic Sankhya is now associated with *Patanjali* and is otherwise called the Yoga system. The Sankhya and Yoga, in their various forms, have profoundly influenced Hindu culture and religion in all their varied aspects.

According to Sankhya, the word *prakriti* means the original substance, which consists of three classes of neutral entities called *gunas*—*Sattva*, representing truth and virtue, *Rajas*, present in all that is active, fiery, or aggressive, and *Tamas*, the principle of darkness, dullness, and inactivity. These are continually associating with one another for the fullest expression of their inner potentialities. They form themselves into groups, and not only are the inner constituents of each of the groups working in union with one another for the manifestation of the groups as wholes, but the wholes themselves are also working in union with one another for the self-expression of the individual whole and of the community of wholes for the manifestation of more and more developed forms. Causation is thus viewed as the actualization of the potentials. The order of all cosmic operations is deduced from the inherent inner order and relations of the neutral reals. Relations are conceived as the functions of these reals, with which they are metaphysically identical. Prakriti is regarded as the hypothetical state of the pure potential conditions of these reals. It is supposed that this pure potential state breaks up into a state which may be regarded as the stuff of cosmic mind. This partly individuates itself as individual minds, and partly develops itself into space, from that into potential matter, and later on into actual gross matter as atoms. The individuated minds evolve out of themselves the various sensory and conative functions and the synthetic and analytic functions called *manas*. They also reveal themselves in the psychical planes or personalities of individuals.

It is evident that the complexes formed from the neutral reals derive their meaning and functioning through a reference to the other or the others, for the manifestation of which they are cooperating together. This other-reference of the reals (gunas) is their inherent teleology.

Boddhisattva Gandhara (Graeco-Buddhist), 2nd–5th Century AD

But such other-references must have a limit, if an infinite regression is to be avoided. In a general manner it may be said that the two broad groups, the psychical and the physical, are working together in mutual reference. It is therefore assumed that there is an unrelational element, called *purusha*, a pure consciousness which presides over every individuated mind. By reference to this the non-conscious psychic phenomena attain their final meaning as conscious phenomena. The whole history of conscious phenomena attains its last metaphysical purpose in self-annulment, by an ultimate retroversion of reference from purusha towards the ultimate principle of consciousness, by which the final other-reference to the purusha ceases. There must be a stage in which the positive other-references end themselves in self-reference, whereby the ultimate bond of the psychic manifestation or the personality with the purusha will cease. This cessation in the history of any individual psychic plane marks its culmination and is regarded as a final metaphysical liberation of the purusha associated with that individual psychic plane. There are as many purushas as there are psychic planes. The purusha is regarded as the principle of consciousness unrelated to its fellow purusha and also to any of the complexes of the neutral reals.

It has already been said that space is derived as a modification of the reals. Time is to be regarded as having a transcendental and a phenomenal aspect. Under the former, time is identical with the movement inherent in the guna reals and as such it is even prior to space. In the latter aspect, that is time as measurable, and as before and after, it is mental construction in which the ultimate unit of measure is regarded as the time taken by an atom to traverse its own dimension of space. Since all conceivable objects in the world are products of the guna reals, and since there is no other agent, the guna reals hold within themselves in a potential manner all things of the world, which are manifested first in the emergent categories of cosmic personality, ego, the eleven senses, five kinds of potential matter, and five kinds of actual matter. These together form the twenty-five categories from the enumeration of which the Sankhya system is supposed to have drawn its name, meaning numeration or counting.

The Yoga, which is in general agreement with the entire metaphysical position of the Sankhya, thinks that the elements leading to a positive misconception or mis-identification of the purusha as being of the same nature as the guna complexes are responsible for the possibility of the *nisus* and the resulting experience. This is technically called ignorance or *avidya*. Yoga further holds that this avidya manifests itself or grows into the various cementing principles of the mind, emotional and volitional, such as ego consciousness, attachment, antipathy, and the self-preservative tendency. As a result of the operation of these principles, as grounded in the avidya, the mind behaves as a whole and acquires experience and determines itself in the objective environment. According to both Sankhya and Yoga, the individuated mind has a beginning-less history of emotional and volitional tendencies integrated or inwoven, as it were, in its very structure as it passes from one cycle of life to another. The determination of the mind in pursuance of its end as desire, will, or action is called *karma*. It is further held that all such determinations create potential energies which must fructify as diverse kinds of pleasurable or painful experiences, environments, conditions, and the periods of particular lives in which these experiences are realized.

The self-determining movement of the mind for the attainment of liberation can only start when one begins to discover that all experiences are painful. As a result thereof, the young saint becomes disinclined towards all the so-called joys of the world and ceases to have any interest in the propagation of the life-cycle. Such a cessation cannot be by death. For death means further rebirth. The cessation of the life-cycles must necessarily be sought in the extinction of the conditions determining the mind-structure. For this, he adopts means by which he can invert the process of operation of the mind-structure, which consists of the integrated content of images, concepts, and their emotional and volitional associates, of various kinds, below the surface. These are immediately absorbed below the conscious levels as the subconscious, semi-conscious, and unconscious. The various elements of the psychic structure in the different levels are held together to a great extent by ties of emotion and volition referring to the enjoyment of worldly objects. It is these that are continually attracting our minds.

The followers of Yoga should in the first instance practise a definite system of moral and religious restraints, such as non-injury, truthfulness, purity, sincerity, sex-control, self-contentment, and the like, called *yamas* and *niyamas*, for the external purification of mind. Ordinarily all activities associated with mental life are of the nature of continual relationing and movement. The Yogin who wishes to invert the processes underlying the maintenance of psychic structure arrests his mind statically on a particular object to the exclusion of all others, so that on the focal point of consciousness there may be only one state, which does not move, and all relationing process of the mind is at complete arrest.

Yoga is defined as a partial or complete arrest or cessation of the mental states. As an accessory process the Yogin learns to steady himself in a particular posture (*asana*) and gradually to arrest the processes of breathing (*pranayama*). His efforts to exclude other objects and to intensify the selected mental state which is to be kept steady on the focal point are called *dharana* and *dhyana* respectively. As a result of his progressive success in arresting the mental states, there arise new types of wisdom (*prajna*) and the subconscious potencies gradually wear out; ultimately all the subconscious and unconscious potencies of the structural relations are destroyed, and, as a result thereof, the avidya which was determining the nisus of the mind is destroyed, and the whole fabric of the mind is disintegrated, leaving the pure purusha in his transcendent loneliness (*kaivalya*), which is regarded as the ultimate aspiration of the human mind.

The Yoga believes in the existence of God, who is associated with an absolutely pure mind. With such a mind he exerts a will such that the evolution of the prakriti or the guna reals may take the course that it has actually taken in consonance with the possible fruition of the mundane and supra-mundane or spiritual needs of the individual persons. The Yoga thinks that, had it not been for the will of God, the potentialities of the gunas might not have manifested themselves in the present order. The Sankhya, however, thinks that the necessity inherent in the potentialities is sufficient to explain the present order, and the existence of God is both unwarrantable and unnecessary.

The Yoga School of philosophy, of which Patanjali was the traditional founder, must not be confused with what is commonly called yoga in the Western world. This, the system of training known as hatha-yoga, is of much later origin, as far as can be gathered from the sources, and is based on physiological theories related to the 'serpent-power' (*kundalini*), which from its seat in the base of the spine may be raised by breathing and other exercises to rise through a vein or channel in the spine to reach 'the thousand petalled lotus' (*sahasrara*) at the top of the skull. This is scarcely a philosophy at all, but is rather a magico-religious system of training, with its roots probably to be found in primitive Shamanism.

The Nyaya School was essentially a school of logic, maintaining the view that clear thinking was an essential preliminary to salvation. This school evolved, about the beginning of the Christian era, a system of syllogistic logic which seems to have been quite independent of the Aristotelian system which conditioned the thought of Europe. The usual formula of the Indian syllogism was as follows:

(i)   There is a fire on the mountain,

(ii) because there is smoke on it,

(iii) and where there is smoke there is fire, as, for example, in a kitchen.

(iv) This is the case with the mountain,

(v)   and therefore there is a fire on it.

We may compare this with the Aristotelian formula:

(i)   Where there is smoke there is fire.

Stupa Site III, Nalanda, Gupta Period

(ii) There is smoke on the mountain.

(iii) Therefore there is fire on it.

The Indian syllogism is more cumbrous than the Greek one, but it might be more effective in debate, since the point is driven home by repetition, the first proposition being virtually the same as the fifth and the second the same as the fourth. The example (here the kitchen) was looked on as an essential element of the syllogism, and also seems to derive from debating technique.

On this basis the Nyaya logicians developed the very subtle and difficult doctrines referred to at the beginning of this chapter as ultra-logical, which have been little studied outside circles of specially trained pandits until quite recently. They are too recondite for consideration here, but it should be noted that in some respects they prefigure the new logic of the twentieth-century West, and represent a significant element in the intellectual heritage of India.

The Vaisheshika School was based on a system of atomism, explaining the cosmic process in which the soul was involved. The

Vaisheshikas, like the Sankhyas, held that the soul was wholly different from the cosmos, and that its salvation lay in fully realizing this difference. The first stage in this process was the recognition of the world's atomic character. The universe was an infinitely complex and endlessly changing pattern of atoms (*anu*) combining and dissolving according to regular principles. At the end of the cosmic cycle the atoms reverted to a state of complete equilibrium from which they only emerged at the beginning of the next cycle, as the raw material of a new cosmos.

The Indian atomic system, in many respects anticipating the theories of modern physics, was the result not of experiment and observation but rather of logical thought. Since an endless regress was logically and psychologically unsatisfactory, it was believed that there must be a final stage in the subdivision of any piece of matter, beyond which further subdivision was impossible. Hence the universe must be atomic in structure. Further developments of the theory led to a doctrine of molecules to account for the multifarious variety of the world. The Vaisheshika philosophers agreed thus far with modern scientific physics; they did not, however, hit on a realistic theory of elements, which would have demanded practical investigation and experiment. Like most other Indian philosophers, they maintained the existence of five atomic elements—earth, water, fire, air, and *akasha*, which filled all space; *akasha* is generally translated 'ether', in the sense in which this term was used in Western pre-relativity physics.

The Mimamsa School was primarily one of Vedic exegesis, and set out to prove the complete truth and accuracy of the sacred texts, in much the same manner as did the doctors of the medieval Catholic Church or such Protestant reformers as Calvin. The world-view of this school was not distinctive, but its teachers produced interesting and original theories of semantics, and some of them made contributions in the field of law.

Out of the Mimamsa School emerged the most important of the six systems, the Uttara-Mimamsa ('Later Mimamsa'), more commonly known as Vedanta, 'The End of the Vedas'. This term was apt because, unlike the Mimamsakas, who placed equal emphasis on all the Vedic literature, the Vedantins stressed the significance of the Upanishads, which for them formed a sort of New Testament, not a mere appendix to the earlier Vedic literature. The main task, as they conceived it, was to harmonize the teachings of these texts into a consistent body of doctrine.

The basic text of the Vedanta School is the *Brahma Sutras* of Badarayana, composed perhaps 2000 years ago. These are a series of very terse aphorisms, perhaps originally intended as lecture notes, to be filled out extempore by the teacher. Since they are so elliptical and ambiguous they were commented on and differently interpreted by numerous great doctors of medieval Hinduism to produce a wide range of philosophical and theological systems.

Undoubtedly the most influential and probably the most subtle of these teachers was Sankara, a south Indian Saivite brahman who, early in the ninth century, composed lengthy commentaries on the *Brahma Sutras*, the chief Upanishads, and the Bhagavad Gita. In these he put forward his famous doctrine of *Advaita* ('No second', that is monism), maintaining that the phenomenal universe with all its multifariousness, and the whole hierarchy of being from the greatest of the gods downwards, were not absolutely real, but were *maya*, the secondary emanations of the one ultimate absolute being, the impersonal neuter entity known as Brahman, characterized by the three attributes of being (*sat*), consciousness (*chit*), and bliss (*ananda*). Brahman was unchanging and eternally stable, while everything else, being finally unreal, was subject to change, which, in the case of the individual being, manifested itself in the form of samsara, the process of transmigration.

The eternal quest of the Indian mystic was to be fulfilled by the complete and final realization of the identity of his soul or inmost self (atma) with Brahman. This was to be achieved by spiritual training and meditation. Sankara did not reject the gods, but taught that they were the primary manifestations of the impersonal Absolute, sharing up to a point in the unreality of all things. Their worship might help humble souls, but the spiritual athlete strove to pass beyond them, to direct knowledge of final reality, which was to be found in his own self. Thus Sankara's system is sometimes referred to as 'The Way of Knowledge' (*jnana-marga*). It is wrong, however, to look on this system as fundamentally an intellectual one. The knowledge referred to is not comparable with that acquired by learning, but rather with the knowledge gained from intensely close acquaintance—the knowledge of the man who declares 'I know my wife', rather than that of the one who says 'I know the theory of prime numbers'.

The Upanishads contain a very wide range of doctrines and Sankara's reduction of their contents to a single consistent system was only achieved by brilliant exegesis, in no way inspired by the modern open-minded attempt to think the thoughts of the authors of the texts. Like most medieval Christian schoolmen faced with similar exegetical problems, Sankara approached his texts with the full conviction that he already knew what they meant. His task was to convince his readers and hearers that this was what they really did mean. His brilliant dialectic was on the whole successful with later generations, and his system even today is the most important one in intellectual Hinduism. It has influenced modern scholarship, and many students of the Upanishads have been inclined to ignore the wide range of speculation in these texts and have followed Sanakra's lead, reading almost everywhere the identity of the soul (atma) and the Absolute (Brahman).

Ramanuja, a Tamil brahman who flourished about AD 1100, gave the rising piety of the times a firm philosophical basis, with a philosophy of 'The Way of Devotion' (*bhakti-marga*). He interpreted the same texts as Sankara had commented on in a different light, to produce the system known as *Vishishtadvaita* ('Qualified Monism'). Ramanuja rejected Sankara's impersonal Brahman, which he interpreted as an inadequate and partial realization of 'The Supreme Person' (*Purushottama*), the god Vishnu, who was ultimate, eternal, and Absolute. Vishnu, inspired by a sort of cosmic loneliness, had diversified himself at the beginning of time, and hence had produced the cosmos, which, being the work of the wholly real creator, could not be ultimately unreal, but shared in God's reality. In the same way the individual soul, created by God who was also an individual, could never wholly lose its individuality, and even in the highest state of bliss was always conscious of itself as being part of God and the recipient of God's grace and love.

Ramanuja may not have been as brilliant a dialectician as Sankara, but his theology has probably as much justification in the Upanishads as that of Sankara. It provided a philosophy for the bhakti movements of the medieval period, and thus ramified into many sub-schools, whose doctors debated learnedly and earnestly on problems of faith and grace. The most remarkable of these later schools was that of Madhva, a Canarese theologian of the thirteenth century. Madhva's doctrine, also theoretically based on the *Brahma Sutras* and the Upanishads, was one of unqualified dualism (*Dvaita*). According to his system the individual soul was created by God, but never was and never would become one with him or part of him. In the state of highest bliss the individual soul drew infinitely close to transcendent godhead, and remained thus

Khajuraho temple carvings

forever, but it was always aware of its difference from God. Several features of Madhva's system, as well as this one, suggest Christian influence, and he may have gathered some of his ideas from the Syrian Christians of Kerala.

There was a heretical school of thought which was associated with the name of Charvaka, supposed to be its founder. It was also known by the name *Lokayata* ('popular'). The literature of the system is now practically lost, and we have to depend on the accounts of others to learn its main contents. The system had many schools, but the fundamental tenets seem to be the same. This school denied the existence of any soul or pure consciousness, which admitted by all schools of Hindu thought. It also denied the possibility of liberation in any form, the infallible nature of the Vedas, and the doctrine of karma and rebirth. All Hindu schools of thought assume as their fundamental postulates the above doctrines, and it is on account of their denial that this system was regarded as heretical (*nastika*). It held that consciousness was an emergent function of matter complexes, just as the mixture of white and yellow may produce red, or fermented starch become an intoxicant. Consciousness being thus an epiphenomenon, nothing remained of the man after death.

The system of thought that began with the Buddha and was developed by his followers was also regarded by the Hindus as heretical, as it did not accept the infallibility of the Vedas and the existence of an eternal and immortal soul. This, and the system known as Jainism, are both very important products of the Indian philosophical genius, but as they are treated in other chapters of this volume they are not considered here.

Ethical Philosophy

The Bhagavad Gita is a metrical interpretation of the instructions of the Upanishads in their bearing on social life. The Gita accepts the four types of duties fixed for the four classes, brahmana, kshatriya, vaishya and sudra, respectively, as study and sacrifice; fighting and the royal task of protecting subjects; looking after economic welfare, agriculture, and trade; and service and the menial duties. It also accepts the final instruction of the Upanishads regarding the nature of the self as the ultimate reality, and the means of the highest moral perfection as leading to it. But at the same time it enjoins on all persons that the moral and social duties should be strictly followed. It argues, therefore, that, having attained the highest moral perfection by cleansing himself of all impurities of passion, such as greed, antipathy, self-love, and the like, having filled the mind with a spirit of universal friendship, compassion, and charity, and having attained perfect stability of mind, so as to be entirely unaffected by pleasures and afflictions of any kind, and being attached to God through bonds of love which also unite man with his fellow beings, the true seer should continue to perform the normal duties that are allotted to his station of life in society. Even if he has no self-interest in the performance of his duties, no end to realize, no purpose to fulfil, no fruition of desire to be attained, he must yet continue to perform all normal duties, just as an ordinary man in his station of life would. The difference between the seer and the ordinary man in the sphere of performance of actions is that the former, through the attainment of wisdom, the conquest of passions, the wasting away of all inner impurities, through the bonds of love with God and fellow beings, and through the philosophical knowledge of the ultimate nature of the self, though dissociated and detached from everything else, yet takes his stand in the common place of humanity as represented in society and continues to perform his duties from a pure sense of duty in an absolutely unflinching manner. The ordinary man, however, being engrossed with passions and bound down with ties of all kinds, cannot take a true perspective of life, and while performing his duties can only do them from motives of self-interest. His performance of duties is thus bound to be imperfect, and vitiated by self-seeking tendencies and the promptings of lower passions.

The aim of transcendent philosophy is thus not merely theoretical, but is intensely practical. However high a man may soar, to whatsoever higher perspective of things he may open his eyes, he is ultimately bound in ties of social duties to his fellow beings on earth in every station of life. A high and transcendent philosophy, which can only open itself through the attainment of the highest moral perfection and which leads one through the region beyond good and evil, again draws him down to the sharing of common duties with the other members of society. The attainment of the highest wisdom, which makes one transcend all others, is only half of the circle. The other half must be completed by his being on an equal footing with his fellow beings. The philosophy of 'beyond good and evil' does not leave a man in the air, but makes him efficient in the highest degree in the discharge of duties within 'good and evil'. The illusoriness of good and evil has to be perceived only for the purpose of more adequately obeying the demands of duties in the common social sphere. Almost all systems of Indian philosophy, excepting the followers of the Sankara School of Vedanta, agree in enjoining the perfect performance of normal duties on the part of a seer.

Classical Literature

A.K. WARDER

THE CLASSICAL TRADITION IN INDIAN literature is essentially secular. Religious scripture (*agama*) and scholarly treatises (*shastra*) are usually distinguished from 'literature' (*kavya*), the latter being both human and an art. 'Tradition' (*itihasa*), including 'antiquity' (*purana*) and 'epic' (*akhyana*), is distinguished from all three as the inspired words of ancient sages. In fact its simple heroic verse, lacking the style and figurativeness of kavya, represents the narrative poetry of an age before the institutionalization of literature as an art according to the conscious principles of criticism elaborated in the *Natyashastra* (Treatise on Drama) and elsewhere.

Tradition as extant is mostly not as antique as it purports to be, but it follows the archaic narrative style and continues to be a source of classical themes for 'literature'. On account of its aesthetic power, some critics allowed the great epic Mahabharata to be 'literature' as well as 'tradition'. For our present purpose we too are interested in this 'true' epic derived from the bards (*sutas*) of antiquity as well as in the 'artificial' epics of individual authors.

The lay of the *Jaya* ('Victory') was handed down orally for at least a thousand years after the battle it celebrates (*c.* 900 BC) before becoming relatively fixed in writing as the Mahabharata, 'Great Bharata (Battle)'. A shadowy Dvaipayana or Vyasa is recorded first to have sung of this terrible struggle of his own time. Vaishampayana later elaborated the epic in 24,000 verses and *c.* 750 BC Lomaharsana and Ugrashravas are supposed to have recited the complete Mahabharata in 100,000 verses. On metrical and other grounds, however, the text constituted in the Critical (Poorna) Edition, which may approximate to the manuscripts of the fourth century AD, includes additions down to that century, with a balancing nucleus of archaic verses producing an average date of composition not earlier than *c.* 100 BC.

The theme of the Mahabharata has been well summed up, by Rajashekhara, as the anger of the Pandavas, sons of Pandu. Pandu had been consecrated Emperor, in the Bharata Dynasty, because his elder brother Dhrtarastra was blind and so legally disqualified from ruling. But Pandu died first and Dhrtarastra seized power, though claiming to act as regent for Pandu's son Yudhisthira, who was made crown prince and later given a fief to rule. Yudhisthira formed a marriage alliance with Krishna, leader of the Satvants, and then assumed imperial prerogatives. Dhrtarastra's son Duryodhana, ambitious and envying Yudhisthira's prosperity, challenged him to a gambling match, sure of victory through the trickery of an uncle. Yudhisthira loses everything, his kingdom, and finally his Queen Draupadi, who is publicly stripped as a slave by Duryodhana's brother, a humiliation she will never forgive. The elders intervene and arrange terms: Draupadi is

restored but Yudhisthira and his brothers are condemned to twelve
years' exile and a further year incognito. After enduring this, they
enter the service of King Virata of Matsya. From this base, Yudhisthira
sends Krishna as envoy to negotiate the restoration of a kingdom, but
Duryodhana will not give up even one village and war becomes
inevitable. Yudhisthira marshals his allies against a huge enemy army
and the battle lasts eighteen days. The main events are single combats:
finally, through the stratagems of Krishna (deceit and foul blows
contrary to the warriors' code), the Pandavas destroy their enemies
and Yudhisthira becomes Emperor.

In contrast to the simple style of the Mahabharata, with its refrains
and repetitions and verse-filling epithets, kavya, or literature as it
developed gradually from about the fifth century BC, becomes highly
organized in form, richly adorned with figures of speech, taut in style,
profuse in metres, and above all aimed at producing methodically a
defined aesthetic experience in an audience, hearer, or reader. This
trend, especially in metres, can be traced back to some of the lyrics of
the Buddhist *agama*, the *Tripitaka*, available in Pali, which appear to
reflect secular lyrics in the Magadhi language of the Buddha's time. The
Tripitaka was enriched by the art of certain poets and actors who,
becoming Buddhist monks, applied it in praise of the Buddha (notably
Vagisha), in describing mountains suitable for meditation (notably
Kashyapa), and in other unworldly themes. From about 400 BC onwards
we find also dramatic dialogues in the *Tripitaka*, in verse with prose stage
directions, showing the same new metrical art apparently extended to
the stage.

Apart from some incidental discussions on genres, figures of speech,
etc., in the *Tripitaka* and in grammatical and other works, the *Natyashastra*
of 'Bharata' (the mythical first 'Actor') is the oldest work of Indian
literary criticism now available. It is the outcome of several centuries of
theatrical practice by hereditary actors, from the fifth century BC or
earlier down to about the second century AD, no doubt at first handed
down by oral tradition like the Mahabharata. The purpose of drama is

the amusement of the audience, but the 'joy' (*harsa*) and solace given
them is not left to chance by the actors but induced through a special
technique or method of acting. The drama is an imitation of all the
actions of the world, but the essential part of this is the emotions (*bhavas*)
which the characters are represented as experiencing during their action.
There are eight basic emotions: love, humour, energy, anger, fear, grief,
disgust, and astonishment. These are not conveyed directly but by playing
their causes and effects, the latter including other, transient, emotions.
The audience, imagining the basic emotions in the characters through
this acting, enjoys eight corresponding tastes (*rasas*), in other words the
perception of them, the aesthetic experience (not the emotional
experience itself) correspondingly divided into sensitive (perception of
love), comic, heroic, furious, apprehensive, compassionate, horrific, and
marvellous. Besides being essentially enjoyable, the drama is incidentally
instructive because it represents all kinds of actions, good and bad, and
the ends or motives which inspire them.

According to the *Natyashastra*, drama originated because of the
conflicts which arose in society when the world declined from the
Golden Age (Krta Yuga) of harmony. Thus a drama always presents a
conflict and its resolution, and in construction, the conversion of a story
into a 'plot', with its elements and conjunctions, is based on the single
main action which ends the conflict. Each of the five 'conjunctions'
(opening, re-opening, embryo, obstacle, and conclusion) of a full-scale
play is bodied out with up to a dozen dramatic incidents and situations
(its 'limbs' or parts), showing the characters in action; and a large
number of other dramatic devices were available to express the causes
and effects of emotion through incidents related to the ultimate action.
Among these devices, the discussion of the 'characteristics' of dramatic
expression leads into the figures of speech and qualities of style in the
language of drama. The *Natyashastra* describes ten types of play,
distinguished as history or fiction if full scale (five or more acts,
implying as many nights' performance since the Indian theatre, though
highly organized, is not rapid in movement). The remaining eight types,

with from one to four acts only, are heroic, tragic, or comic plays, together with the satirical monologue, the street play, and three kinds of archaic play about the gods and demons. Secondary to all these is the four-act 'light play' as a fictitious sensitive comedy about a real character, whilst the solo tandava dance of Shiva and the delicate *lasya* invented by Parvati, as well as group dances (*pindibandhas*), may be introduced in drama where appropriate. The lasya represents a story, or part of a story, and is regarded as the prototype of the profusion of independent popular ballets which has always accompanied the more serious and classical theatre of India.

Bhamaha (fifth century AD?), the earliest individual critic whose work is available, extended the *Natyashastra* analysis (rasa aesthetics, construction) to literature as a whole, setting out the genres as drama, epic, lyric, prose biography, and the (usually prose) novel. Then he takes up as his main problem literary expression and what makes it beautiful, which the Treatise on Drama barely touched on. The 'ornament' (*alankara*) or beauty, which distinguishes literature from ordinary communication, consists in a kind of 'curvature' (*vakrata*), that is artistic distortion, indirectness, figurativeness. Both the meaning and the language (derivation of words) must be 'ornament' and hence the definition of literature is '(beautiful) language and meaning combined' (this is urged against earlier writers who advocated one or the other only). The beauty of meaning is analysed into some three dozen 'figures' (alankaras), simile, metaphor, etc., taken up from earlier writers but accepted by Bhamaha only to the extent that each embodies 'curvature'. Bhamaha, however, favours realism and rationalism in literature, though transmuted into art in this 'curved' way, and he devotes a chapter to epistemology and logic as applied to literature. Dandin (seventh century) adds to the genres *campu* or narration in mixed prose and verse, which became extremely popular later. His main contention is that ten qualities of style (developed from the *Natyashastra*) are essential in literature, the combination of the ten giving the excellent *vaidarbha* or 'southern' style.

In the evolution of the very numerous and ever-changing popular theatrical genres of India, finally, Kohala (second century?—known only from quotations) early noticed various musical plays, ballets, and *ragakavyas*, from the last of which such modern forms as *kathakali* eventually developed. Abhinavagupta noted a series of solo performances probably evolved from the lasya, among which the *dombika* was most characteristic. The modern so-called *bharatanatyam* is evidently descended from this, in which the dancer does not wear costume but impersonates in mime various characters in a story. Meanwhile the street play gave rise to *yaksagana* with its eastern (Andhra) and western (Karnataka) variants as well as the Tamil street play. We may recall here the social milieu of kavya as described in the *Natyashastra* and the *Kamasutra*, for 'classical' literature is not opposed to 'popular' and has usually sought a mass audience. The drama was contrasted with the Veda as being for the whole of society, sudras (helots) included, and wealthy amateurs were responsible for patronizing regular public festivals in the villages as well as the cities, with plays and other performances (modern yaksagana in the villages has substituted the box officer and sale of tickets for the vanished patrons).

The Ramayana, in Sanskrit, is traditionally ascribed to Valmiki, whom Bhavabhuti and others call the 'First *Kavi*' (kavi meaning the 'author' of a kavya). Although this epic, as we have it, is not as old as the first Pali kavyas, it is formally on the border line between itihasa (such as the Mahabharata) and kavya. Its average data of composition seems to fall in the first century BC.

If kavya is defined by its power to produce aesthetic experience (rasa), however, the Ramayana, with its unforgettable story of the conflicts of human passions, is certainly a kavya. This story was reworked by 'Valmiki' (if we apply the name to the author of the present text) from old traditions containing two or three probably separate legends in several versions (one is found in the Pali Cannon). In the Ramayana we thus find: (1) the palace intrigue at Ayodhya by Queen Kaikeyi resulting in her stepson Rama's exclusion from the succession to his father's throne and sentence to twelve years' exile and (2) Rama, exiled in the south,

finds its inhabitants oppressed by the raids of demons (*raksasas*) from
Lanka (Ceylon), the island fortress of the demon king Ravana, and
himself suffers the abduction of his wife Sita by Ravana; he raises an
army (mostly of 'monkeys'), gaining allies, invades Lanka, kills Ravana,
frees Sita, and returns home in triumph, the period of exile having
elapsed and his noble stepbrother Bharata generously surrendering the
throne to him. The legend or myth of Ravana itself, with his victorious
wars against the gods, may have been a separate source, as perhaps was
that of the great 'monkey' hero Hanuman, son of the Wind God.
Valmiki's finest cantos are surely those of the palace intrigue, with the
psychological study of the characters of Kaikeyi and her confidante. The
apocryphal last book of the Ramayana adds a tragic ending: Sita's new
exile on suspicion of unchastity, when a captive, and final disappearance.
This changes the main rasa to the 'compassionate', whereas originally the
poem would be 'heroic', though with a considerable compassionate
element resulting from Rama's sufferings.

Prose story telling in the Buddhist Canon is a little less heavy and
abrupt than in the Veda but still full of repetitions and rarely
ornamented except by the occasional insertion of a verse to emphasize
a point. Humour and satire, however, abound. The novel, as an extensive
prose fiction (running to hundreds of pages), seems to us to begin with
Gunadhya's *Brhatkatha* ('Great Story') about 100 BC (the lost *Carumati*
of Vararuci may have been an earlier novel). Gunadhya's language was
Paisaci, closely related to the Pali of the Buddhists, and both the
milieu and the matter of the *Brhatkatha* were akin to those of the old
Buddhist story telling. The novel moves between the intrigues and
struggles of the real world and the realization of wild dreams largely
in the realm of 'science fiction' (strange sciences and the construction
of 'space machines'). The rasa is thus the 'marvellous' (Dandin) rather
than the 'sensitive'.

Ashvaghosa's (first century AD) are the earliest epics now available
(Panini's *Jambavatijaya* is known only from quotations) to show the fully
fledged kavya technique: concentration of the matter in about twenty
cantos only (about 1500 quatrains) in many metres; perception of

discrete moments through the separate quatrains instead of a continuity of flowing narrative; numerous figures of speech. Each 'moment' may suggest the theme of the whole story, but we are to dwell on its significance before pressing on to know what happens next. Ashvaghosa was an earnest Buddhist, so that the ultimate significance he wishes to convey, through the delights of poetry, is the shallowness of the world and the true happiness of renunciation and peace of mind. Yet he appears far from indifferent to the pleasures of the world, describing most realistically just what he holds to be most ephemeral. This ambiguity and tension, which seems to reflect personal experience, inspires all the elaborate art, or 'ornament' of language and meaning, carrying Ashvaghosa's philosophy. Two epics are available, the Life of the Buddha (*Buddhacarita*) and the Handsome Nanda (*Saundarananda*, who was most unwilling to become a monk). It is a heavy loss that only fragments are now available of a series of dramas by Ashvaghosa, whose powers of characterization are so well displayed in the epics. The *Shariputra* and *Rastrapala* are again well-known stories of renunciation.

Bhasa (second century AD?), perhaps the greatest Indian dramatist, brings us at last a comprehensive view of the classical theatre. His masterpiece is the 'Dream of Vasavadatta', a fully-scale history (*nataka*) in which the heroine sacrifices all her happiness in order to save her husband's (Udayana) kingdom from a powerful enemy. Her courageous action, part of a subtle plan of a minister, bears fruit after great mental suffering, which Bhasa finely depicts, and she is reunited with Udayana restored to his throne.

The *Panchatantra* seems to have been written in the fourth century. The author was perhaps the narrator Vishnusarman and his country the Vakataka Empire of the south (Deccan). Its popularity was such that new versions were made, with additions from which it has been difficult to recover the original work (Edgerton's reconstruction seems a good approximation.) The genre is the 'illustrating novel' (*nidarshanakatha*), which is satirical and aims to teach by example. Here the subject is 'policy' (*niti*), public and private. The frame story is the instruction of

Kailash Temple Complex, Ellora

three young princes averse to formal education. Within this, five stories present five 'systems' (tantras) of policy: (1) splitting an alliance (or friendship) which obstructs one's interests, (2) forming an alliance oneself, (3) making war, (4) outwitting a strong but foolish enemy, and (5) a warning on the folly of action without reflection. Four of these are beast fables, which enhances the sharpness of the satire. Some further stories are emboxed, narrated by the characters to illustrate their own discussions of policy.

Kalidasa is associated with 'Vikramaditya' in tradition, but this may refer to Skanda Gupta, who used that title, whilst the poet is also supposed to have met the Vakataka Pravarasena II (c. 410–40). Essentially a lyric poet, he wrote epics and dramas too, taking advantage of the lyric tendency which had always pervaded kavya. He is appreciated for the *vaidarbha* style and especially for 'sweetness', whilst his waywardness sometimes puzzled the critics, sometimes pleased them (Kuntaka found in it the natural play of genius). Kalidasa's most quoted work is the lyric poem *Megha Sandesa*, 'Cloud Message', in which a distracted lover far from his beloved attempts to send her a message by a passing cloud at the beginning of the rains. The description of the route to be taken affords opportunity for the utmost fancy in that the landmarks are such as would be thought to appeal to a cloud: beautiful rivers who will return his love, high palaces, mountains. The short epic *Kumarasambhava*, 'Origin of Kumara', includes Indra's humourous plot to make a father of Shiva, the gods having been defeated (as usual) by a demon, whom only a son of Shiva can kill. The longer epic *Raghuvamsha* is a portrait gallery of the kings of Rama's line, illustrating the four ends, virtue, wealth, pleasure, and release, pursued by the different rulers. Only in relation to this discussion of ends can we see any thematic unity and development in the poem, which otherwise is a series of detached episodes. At the conclusion the dissolute Agnivarna carries pleasure to a ruinous extreme, but dies leaving his pregnant queen with 'royal fortune' and hope for the future of the dynasty under the guidance of the ministers.

Of Kalidasa's three plays, the *Malavikagnimitra* is dramatically the best and the least lyrical; it is probably the earliest. The story is a love intrigue at the Shunga court, the comic rasa perhaps predominating. The *Vikramorvasiya* is a musical play (*totaka*, a variety of nataka) on the Vedic story of Pururavas and the nymph Urvashi. The main interest is the character study of Urvashi, who is purely human. Lyric and lasya elements appear, especially in the pathetic scene where the hero has lost her. The *Abhijñanashakuntala*, 'Token *Shakuntala*', is admired for its lyricism, but its hero does nothing, things happen to him through fate, a curse or divine intervention, his character is a blank. The heroine is better characterized but also the helpless plaything of supernatural powers. Thus there is no real action but only a certain depth of helpless feeling. The story is changed from the more realistic history in the Mahabharata of an ancestor of the Bharatas. Kalidasa is a poet of love, of women sharply portrayed, and for Anandavardhana one of the great exponents of suggestion.

Vishakhadatta's *Mudraraksasa*, 'Signet Raksasa', is a play of political intrigue and secret agents, in which the famous minister Chanakya (Kautalya) destroys the remaining enemies of Chandragupta Maurya after the death of Nanda, winning over the best man among them, Nanda's minister Raksasa, to the new king's cause. This is one of the rare works in which anything like a 'national' or 'Indian' sentiment is suggested in place of the usual universalistic outlook, most of the enemies being 'barbarians' (mlecchas).

From the Emperor Harsa (seventh century) we have three plays which have stood the test of time in the theatre, as well as two Buddhist hymns. The *Nagananda*, a bodhisattva play like Chandragomin's, has held the stage down to the present day in Kerala, though the audiences there are not Buddhist. The rasa has always been a matter of philosophical controversy and practical interpretation; the excellent commentator Shivarama concludes that it may be either the calmed or the heroic, besides which all the others are developed too in a harmonious whole. The other two are 'light plays' on invented stories about Udayana, *Ratnavali* and *Priyadarshika*.

Bana at Harsa's court is universally regarded as the greatest master of Sanskrit prose. His style varies according to the content and the genre (biography bold and studied, novel delicate and flowing), but with more of what Kuntaka calls 'cultivated' ('beautiful' through art). The *Harsacarita* is a biography of the young Harsa, explaining how he found royal fortune. *Kadambari* is a psychological novel of the timidities and missed opportunities of youth, leading to tragedy; but no tragedy is final in Indian literature, since transmigration may bring the lovers together again.

Bhavabhuti, the favourite poet and dramatist of some connoisseurs, from Maharastra settled at Yashovarman's court in Kanyakubja. His *Malatimadhava* is a 'fiction' of the triumph of love over obstacles, especially over political convenience. A king proposes to have the daughter of one of his ministers offered to a court favourite, as part of a political alliance. The girl loves another and the lovers resist the plan, aided by sympathetic Buddhist nuns in the role of go-betweens. In an unsuccessful attempt at elopement the hero shows his mettle, attracts popular support, and thus so impresses the king that he changes his plans, preferring to have a brave young man under his patronage. The *Uttararamacarita* takes up the apocryphal last book of the Ramayana, the grievous renewed exile of Sita. Public opinion held her unfit to be queen after being the prisoner of Ravana. Here Bhavabhuti brings out most fully the pathos of human experience, bitter yet touched by the sweetness of association with happy moments in the past, the contrast intensifying both the pain and the sweetness. Bhavabhuti's plays are in the best dramatic tradition of conflict and passion, but on a scale giving the fullest scope to lyrics evoking the feelings of his characters, in relation to society and even more to nature. His lyrics are perhaps unequalled in expressiveness and in the beauty of their sound.

Apabhramsa epic, its conventions established by Chaturmukha whose works have not yet been found, comes into its own with two examples by Svayambhu, the *Padmacarita* on Rama and the *Aristanemicarita* on the twenty-second *jina* and the Jaina version of the events of the Mahabharata with the life of Krishna. Svayambhu takes his narratives from earlier Jaina works; he is praised for the beauty of his language and figurative expressions and is remarkable for his tolerant and syncretistic outlook.

The philosopher Jayanta wrote a play on the religious situation in Kashmira, the *Agamadambara*, 'Pomp of Scriptures'. His aim is to show the superior knowledge and humanity of the brahmans and satirize the Buddhists, Jainas, Lokayatikas, and Kapalikas. Though some unworthy sects should be proscribed, the better schools share the high moral purpose of the Vedic tradition and among these there should be toleration; their scriptures are different entrances to the same house.

King Kulashekhara (*c.* AD 900) wrote two plays, which have remained popular, to inaugurate new techniques of production on the Kerala stage, claiming to apply Anandavardhana's doctrine of 'revealed' meaning. It is supposed that all the reforms of the Kerala actors stem from him, including the repetition of the speeches in gesture language and the extemporized 'Tamil' (now Malayalam) patter of the 'fool', equivocally making fun of present-day personalities along with other characters in the play, but this seems unlikely.

Puspadanta's *Mahapurana* is generally acclaimed as the best Apabhramsa epic. A modest and disillusioned wanderer who finally accepted patronage with reluctance, his poetry is deeply felt and his wit pungent. The subject is the vast universal history of the Jainas, dominated by the 'sixty-three great men' (including Rama, Ravana, Krishna, and the *jina*s).

The Turkish conquests of more than half of India between 900 and 1300 were perhaps the most destructive in human history. As Muslims, the conquerors aimed not only to destroy all other religions but also to abolish secular culture. Their burning of libraries explains the large gaps in our knowledge of earlier literature. Our view now depends mainly on what has been preserved in the far south, in Kerala, supplemented by some Jaina libraries which miraculously escaped and by such outlying collections as those of Nepal. Though the Indian tradition was thus cut off over wide areas, it developed vigorously where Indian rule continued, including Rajasthan, Orissa, etc., as well as the south. In fact about 90 per cent of the extant Sanskrit literature, even, belongs to the period since AD 1200 and was written in the regions remaining under Indian rule. If we now devote little space to it, compared with the classics above, that should not be regarded as an adverse judgement (we reject the prejudiced opinion about 'decadence') but as due partly to lack of space and partly to the general neglect and lack of printed editions. What follows is a small selection among the noteworthy kavyas.

Amarachandra's *Balabharata* has been popular in Rajasthan as distilling the essence of the whole Mahabharata in a kavya epic. The author belonged to the literary circle of the minister Vastupala of Gujarat in the thirteenth century, from which more than ten epics and six dramas survive to show the work of such a group. Among these, the works of Someshvara and Balachandra are outstanding and the play 'Crushing of the Arrogance of the Amir' by Jayasimha is remarkable as presenting the contemporary history of Vastupala's victory over the Turks. In this age of perpetual Turkish wars there is a strong turn towards heroic themes. In Orissa, Jayadeva's *Prasannaraghava*, though widely studied for its difficulty and word music, is a variation on Murari's Rama play. Sakalavidyachakravartin's *Gadyakarnamrta* is a biography of a Hoysala emperor of Karnataka. The lyrics of Utpreksavallabha and Laksmidasa are admired. Of dramas in the south, we may note Kavivallabha's fiction and Ravivarman's *Pradyumnabhyudaya*.

The greatest fifteenth-century writer was probably Dindima (Kavisarvabhauma), praised by later authors, but his works, including an epic *Ramabhyudaya* and a comedy, are not yet printed. Kamaksi, apparently his daughter-in-law, modestly praises him in her own 'New' *Ramabhyudaya*, called 'exquisite' by a modern critic. Other members of the Dindima family wrote historical epics on the Vijayanagara emperors. The circle of the Eighteen and a Half in Kerala is famous and marks a peak of activity in the theatre and in poetry (Uddanda, Damodarabhatta, etc.).

The 'classical' literature in fact everywhere developed in the closest interaction with the 'modern', that is with the vernacular. In the north it is arbitrary to draw a line between 'Hindi' (Braj, Rajasthani, Maithili, etc.) and Apabhramsa, for they are the same language, using the same genres and metres. Tulsidas's epic has the same form as Puspadanta's. In the south, Sanskrit and Dravidian writers share ideas. The Oriya Mahabharata, Ramayana, and *Bhagavata*, assimilating antiquity into the life of the fifteenth and sixteenth centuries, influenced the Sanskrit epics of Divakara, Markandeya, and Jivadeva. The last also wrote plays and belongs to the Vaisnava movement of the sixteenth century, for which Rupa produced his theory of devotional drama on Krishna and plays exemplifying it. Many such plays were written and performed in Orissa, then circulated elsewhere, and popular forms such as the *ragakavya* and one-act *gosthi* (for example Jayadeva's *Vaisnavamrta*) were revived for the purpose. The Kerala variety of Vaisnavism is expressed in Narayana's lyric *Narayaniya* on the whole life of Krishna, probably the finest devotional poem in Sanskrit. This Narayana is among the greatest and most prolific Sanskrit writers of recent centuries. He wrote a long series of *campu*s on Puranic and Vedic themes for performance as *kuttu* monologues by comic actors. The Emperor Krisnadevaraya of Vijayanagara wrote a Krishna play. Queen Tirumala's *Varadambikaparinaya* is a beautiful biographical campu of her husband Acyutaraya, concluding remarkably with his marriage to another queen and consecration of the latter's son as heir apparent. Equal in style and much richer in content is the long biography *Vyasayogicarita* of a contemporary logician by Somanatha.

In the seventeenth century Jagannatha, moving between Andhra, Assam, and the Mughal Empire, reflects the brief flickering of Indian culture within that Empire in the wake of Akbar. His Sanskrit lyrics are popular with the pandits.

Under the British, the Indian tradition was submerged by the imposition of English as medium of administration and education, except in the 'Native States' such as Travancore and Cochin. The modern vernaculars under this domination partly copied European

Brihadiswara Temple, Thanjavur (Tanjore)

models and developed a hybrid literature which is neither European nor Indian. With political independence the cultural scene has hardly changed as yet and the unity of India is threatened by the centrifugal force of the vernaculars. Vernacular writers often seek European orbits, considered 'modern', lacking the national character and relationship among themselves which only the common Indian tradition could give them. Sanskrit is the only truly national language India has ever had, linking all regions and all classes with the immortal springs of Indian thought. If it disappears, with its cultural heritage, India will never be a nation and will surely break up into a series of European-type states. The decision still lies in the future; meanwhile the semi-underground classical tradition conserves its vigour and the twentieth century produced several hundred Sanskrit plays, whilst the theatre of Bhasa is being revived in Kerala. India's cultural unity may yet be saved and through it her political unity.

Early Art and Architecture

P. S. RAWSON

VERY FEW PEOPLE YET REALIZE how great a debt the art of the world—especially that of the Eastern world—owes to India. It is true to say that without the example of Indian forms and ideas the arts of the whole of South East Asia, of China, Korea, Mongolia, Tibet, and Japan would all have been radically different, and would have lost by that difference. So, too, would modern Western art, especially architecture and painting. Buddhism, a merchant's religion par excellence, was the chief vehicle for this artistic influence, though Hinduism did penetrate South East Asia and the islands; and Buddhist art, at home in India, owed a good deal to the Hindu art that flourished alongside it.

The earliest art of India, that produced in the great cities of the Indus valley civilization (*c.* 2000 BC), could not have had much direct impact on the art of the rest of the world. There can, however, be little doubt that this art shared a common heritage of ideas with other regions of the ancient Middle East.

Most important of all is the fact that certain symbols and images which appear in later historical art first showed themselves in the miniature sculptures, in the seals and the sealings of the Indus valley. Examples are the ithyphallic deity seated with knees akimbo as 'lord of the beasts', the naked girl, the dancing figure with one leg lifted diagonally across the other, the sacred bull, the stout masculine torso, the 'tree of life', and innumerable modest types of monkeys, females, cattle, and carts modelled in terracotta.

After the end of the Indus valley civilization there is the first of many gaps in our knowledge of Indian art history. During the third century BC the first major works of architecture and stone carving which we know were made. There are reminiscences in them of the dynastic works of Iranian Achaemenid Persepolis, and they thus reflect the dynastic pretensions of the conquering Mauryan emperors, chief of whom was Ashoka (*c.* 272–232 BC). Among them are tall footless pillars of polished sandstone, whose capitals are carved with symbolic animal figures. Some bear inscriptions by Ashoka, enjoining on his subjects a morality with a Buddhist flavour. Buddhist stupas, which may have been constructed a century or so earlier in the kingdoms of northern India to contain and honour the bodily relics of the Buddha, were enlarged and refurbished—a process often repeated later. A dynastic guild of sculptors seems to have grown up, able to carve colossal polished stone dedicatory figures, of which several survive, sometimes miscalled '*yakshas* and *yakshis*'. The two best know are the male from Parkham and the female from Didarganj, the latter dating from *c.* AD 50.

It was, in fact, in the decoration of major religious monuments that the next developments in Indian art showed themselves. At a number of sites, notably Bharhut, Sanchi, Mathura, and Bodh Gaya in the north, and Amaravati in the Kistna delta, decorative and figural relief carving was evolved to ornament Buddhist stupas and their railings. At first the style was in low and flat relief, the figures being carefully outlined and isolated against their backgrounds; often they were angular and primitive, a fresh start seeming to owe nothing to the Mauryan dynastic style. But this low-relief style was capable of its own kind of sophistication, as at Bharhut, where the pillars of the railing carried half-life-size figures of country godlings, pressed into service at the Buddhist shrine; its coping carries a continuous creeper design, framing small reliefs, which suggests that the whole structure was interpreted as an image of the mythical 'wish-granting tree'. Then, by the early years of the Christian era, at Sanchi, on the gateways of Stupa I the sculptural style evolved a characteristic softly rounded deep relief, which could also be developed to present virtually three-dimensional figures, as on the brackets and capitals. These works succeed in converting into stone what must have been a strongly developing style of two-dimensional narrative expression. The scrolled ends to the Sanchi lintels suggest that the Buddhist stories the lintels bear are transcriptions into a more permanent medium of the illustrations to the pictorial story-scrolls so popular in India throughout the ages.

The art first evolved in these early stupa decorations lies at the root of all the later Buddhist styles of South East Asia and the Far East. In India itself, during the later first, the second, and the third centuries AD the Buddhist (and Jaina) stupa became the focus of artistic attention, its decoration being much expanded and elaborated. Each stupa came to be metaphysically identified as 'the axis of the world', and ornamented with elaborate carvings which, for all their cosmic and sometimes dynastic symbolism, retained a fundamental humanity of scale. The skill of the sculptors in representing figures with a powerful plastic 'presence', and in composing complex narrative scenes full of overlaps, advanced rapidly. Especially in south-east India, at the Buddhist sites around Amaravati (for example Jaggayapeta, Nagarjunakonda), the stupas, with their railing and gateways, came to be almost totally clad in panels of white limestone carved with rich ornamental designs or sensuous figural relief. The style of these works is closely related to contemporary fragments of painting in the caves at Ajanta on the other side of the peninsula. At the vanished stupas of the most important site of all, Mathura in west-central India, what was to become the first classic style of Indian sculpture gradually evolved.

From at least the third century BC all the great stupa-sites have one constant feature: a large hall, aligned with the stupa, with an internal colonnade separating a nave from two aisles, linking them across the closed end by an ambulatory. The early halls were certainly built of wood. We know more or less what they look like from representations carved in the decorative reliefs. But in the western Deccan, among the volcanic ridges and gorges of the Western Ghats, a large number of man-made caves were excavated from about 200 BC onwards, which were virtually sculptures is stone of these wooden preaching halls.

It is clear that, in the course of time, the monks who preached the doctrine at these cave halls were gradually settling down actually to live on the sites. This process is clearly illustrated at Ajanta. Here, over about eight centuries from the third century BC, twenty-six caves were cut, four being preaching halls, the others all being progressively larger living caves, so that in the end there was accommodation for 600 or 700 monks. All save one were painted throughout on plaster, not once, but several times over, with scenes of Buddhist legend, most of the work being in a style so sensual that it can only have been executed by artists whose normal vein was the characteristic Indian secular eroticism. Only in some of the latest paintings before AD 600 do more schematic and austere doctrinal representations appear.

There is one regional style of Buddhist decoration which has attracted a great deal of attention in the West, that of Gandhara, comprising the Afghan Kabul valley with adjacent areas, in the north-west of the subcontinent. One group of invaders, the Central Asian Kushanas, took command of this region from about the end of the first century BC until well into the fifth century AD. Under their auspices,

during the second century AD, a land trade route was opened to the
eastern Mediterranean. Along this route, eastwards, came direct influence
from Romano-Hellenistic art. The features assimilated into the Buddhist
schist and stucco sculptures which encrusted the wealthy Gandharan
monasteries are semi-classical. The Buddha wears something resembling
a draped toga; deities develop classical muscular torsos; there are swags
and *putti*, and even illustrations of Greek legend.

The great importance of this regional styles lies in the effect it
had on the Buddhist art of Central Asia, China, Korea, and Japan, an
effect only modified, not replaced, by later waves of influence. Also
under the Kushanas the city of Mathura took on a special importance.
It lies at a focal point of several trade routes; and by the first century
AD it had become a centre for the manufacture of works of art.
Towards the end of that century the first representation on the
Buddha himself may have been made there; for all earlier Buddhist
illustration had avoided representing the person of the being whose
essential quality was that he had passed into Nirvana, and suggested
his presence in a narrative through symbols only. At Mathura it seems
that vestiges of the skill of the old Mauryan dynastic school of sculptors
may also have survived, and have been applied to the development of
massive three-dimensional sculpture, first for Buddhist subjects, and
then in the second century AD to represent the Hindu gods Shiva and
Vishnu who were adopted as patron dynastic deities by Kushana
kings. This skill also influenced the development of decorative relief
styles. The local pinkish sandstone is unmistakable; and images made
at Mathura have been found at other sites in northern India, for
example at Sanchi.

By the fifth century a smoothly finished, cool, and subdued type of
Buddhist sculpture had evolved there, which provided one of the
principal elements in the Gupta style of art (fourth to seventh centuries).
The fine echoing series of raised string-like folds of garments and their
curling lower hems, both influenced by Gandharan ideas, remained,
until the decline of Buddhism in India, features of many images, being
either suggested by incised lines or painted on to the surface.

Between the fifth and seventh centuries we find a unified Gupta style of Buddhist art established in northern India, which we know especially from the image excavated at Sarnath, again a dynastic site. But the accounts left by Chinese pilgrims describe numerous monastery-shrines throughout Bihar, Bengal, and Orissa, many of which have long disappeared, though a few have been located and excavated. There were 100-foot-high stupas and multi-storeyed monasteries built of wood, brick, and stone; and each site was filled with images, large and small, cut in stone, modelled in terracotta or stucco, and cast in bronze. Many of them were, no doubt, intended as costly testimonials to personal piety, since 'multiplying images of the Buddha' was considered an act meritorious in itself. Among the excavated sites is the earliest of the great Buddhist universities, Nalanda in Bihar, which expanded later in a rather haphazard way. It consists of clustered courtyards and buildings of different patterns, including, of course, stupas, many of which were decorated with particularly fine stucco sculptures of Buddhas and Bodhisattvas.

Although the Chinese visitors recorded many flourishing Buddhist centres, they also recorded their dismay at the decline of Buddhism relative to Hinduism. But in one region of India, the north-east, including parts of Orissa, Buddhism flourished greatly under the patronage of the Pala Dynasty (c. 750–1150) and took on a new and fascinating lease of artistic life, partly in direct response to the Hindu challenge. Other Buddhist universities were founded, notably at Vikramashila, and enormous effort was devoted to the elaboration of schools of philosophy, logic, ritual, medicine, and magic—to which, incidentally, Hindus were also admitted. The scholars gathered together all the available branches of learning into a monumental synthesis based upon certain medical and yogic symbolisms usually called Tantric. The art was a direct reflection of this syncretic activity.

In India most of this art has disappeared, leaving only strong traces of its presence in later Bengali folk-styles. We know its character best from the still-surviving traditions based upon it which were

External facade of an
Ajanta cave

transplanted directly into Nepal and Tibet (seventh century) and sustained by direct contact with the Pala universities. This joint imagery of man and world was transported during the eighth century into the Indianized kingdom of central Java, where its chief monument is Borobudur (*c.* 800). It is also virtually certain that continuously through this Pala period beautifully illuminated long palm-leaf manuscripts of Buddhist texts were made, the pages being bound between painted boards, both covers and pages being illuminated with figures from the Buddhist pantheon.

Hindu art developed later than Buddhist art in India as a whole. Hinduism, however, seems to have made during the second century AD a successful alliance with the Indian theory of kingship, whereby the metaphysical principal to which kings might appeal for supernatural patronage was awarded name and form as a deity. Only one of the major ancient Vedic gods, Surya, retained a central place for himself in later Hindu art as a dynastic deity. The overwhelmingly important gods of later art, to whom nearly all the major temples are dedicated, are Shiva, Vishnu, and the Mother Goddess under her various names (for example Durga), of all of whom there are only traces in Vedic literature. The numerous, much later, medieval representations of Vedic deities appear as the consequence of self-conscious attempts to brahmanize the iconography of religious art. It is thus natural that the evolution of Hindu stone architecture and temple carving—which is all that remains to us from the centuries earlier than *c.* AD 1200—took place at scattered single sites which were each for a time the capital cities of royal dynasties, large and small, and which had probably long been sacred localities.

The fundamental pattern behind the beautiful complexities of the Hindu temple is very simple, evolving naturally from the primitive hallows or sacred place. The sacred numinous object stands within an enclosure and a cell. The object is often a Shiva lingam (phallic emblem); it can also be a sculptural image, either replacing an older more primitive hallows, or ceremonially carved or cast, and dedicated as a new dwelling for the sacred. The cell is raised on a plinth and to it may be appended extra features, the commonest being a porch or portico, and a decorated door-frame. Then came an ambulatory, a crowning tower, one or more aligned approach-halls, one of which may be especially for dancing, and perhaps an encircling layout of lesser cells or even miniature temples. This last feature, in south India, might become a fantastically elaborate sequence of concentric enclosures with towering gateways. Each temple is conceived, as the Buddhist stupa was, as 'the axis of the world', symbolically transformed into the mythical Mount Meru, around which are slung like garlands the heavens and the earth. The heavens are represented on the exterior of developed temples by bands of sculpture containing icons of gods and other lesser superhuman creatures which popular legend ascribes to its heaven. Among these are the famous erotic carvings, which are images of the post-mortem delights awarded by celestial girls called *apsara*s to the spirits of heroes and sages.

The earliest certain examples of the basic form of the temple are of the early fifth century AD, on top of Sanchi hill. No doubt there were yet earlier examples which have perished, especially those at Mathura which housed the icons of Vishnu and Shiva produced there during the second and third centuries AD. Caves, which were also developed as Hindu shrines, were being used by the fifth century; a dynastic rock-cut sanctuary at Udayagiri bears the date of 401, and among its main features is a colossal sculpture of the boar 'incarnation' of Vishnu, the patron deity of the site.

Although there are regional styles in which the temple is conceived more as a constructed shelter (for example Kerala and Kashmir), the process of stone sculpture was one of the principal factors in the evolution of the fully stone-built Hindu temple.

The principal regional centres where Hindu architecture evolved are very numerous. Many remain to be properly investigated. But after about AD 650 it is possible to distinguish two broad types, the northern and the southern, both of which evolved as distinctive patterns out of a previous mixed experimental phase. At Aivalli, in particular, it is possible to discern among the seventy-odd ruined shrines successive phases of invention, when different layouts and decorative schemes were apparently being tried.

The fully characteristic northern temple stands on a plinth adorned with elaborately profiled and rhythmical horizontal mouldings. It is distinguished by its tall square-planned tower over the main cubical cell; this has a convex curve to its contour and may have, around its root, complex re-entrant angles, imitative pilasters, small duplicates of its own profiles, or ogival hood-mouldings based on the end windows of old wooden palaces. This tower is divided into horizontal bands which probably refer back to the actual reduplicated stories of earlier examples. Exactly such reduplicated stories do appear in early western Indian temples, and in the buildings of those regions in South East Asia where early Hindu patterns of temple were adopted, notably Cambodia and Vietnam.

The variations of the basic northern Hindu temple type are many. At numerous sites in the different regions local architectural schools flourished. In Rajasthan temples were built with tiers of open pillared balconies (for example Kiradu, c. 1100). In western India the temples tended to have squat towers buttressed with regular tiers of miniature repetitions of their own design, and some had superb, elaborately carved dance-pavilions aligned with the main shrine but standing free of it (for example Modhera, 1126). Perhaps the most famous sequences are at Khajuraho in central India and in the cities of Orissa, a Hindu state which never wholly succumbed to Islam. Both groups are distinguished by their superb figure sculpture.

At Khajuraho twenty-five temples still stand out of an original eighty-odd, all built between c. 950 and 1050 around a lake. One is constructed round a court on a ground-plan based upon a cosmic meditative diagram. The majority, however, follow the 'temple-mountain' design. The most beautiful individual buildings are also those which are carved with the most beautiful figure sculpture, notably the Vishvanatha and the Kandarya Mahadeva. The celestial figures carved around their heaven-bands, many of them in overtly erotic postures and groupings, all flavoured with a profound sensuality, are widely regarded as some of the greatest and most inimitable achievements of Indian art, an essential part of man's most precious heritage. The figures are all cut in what is, in fact, extremely deep relief. The depth of the cutting gives them a strong plastic presence even when they are seen from far off. The forms of the bodies are sinuous and totally convex; they seem to be bursting out of the fabric of the building itself—an intentional effect with a direct symbolic value in relation to the meaning of the temple as creative source and centre.

A number of fragments of wall-painting suggest that most of these temples, including their sculpture, were plastered and painted, as Hindu temples still are. It also seems likely that they were decorated with painted and dyed cotton hangings. We can, however, be sure that any temple of significance was elaborately decorated with precious metals and gems, just as shrines are in modern Catholic countries. The spoils gathered from Hindu temples by the early Muslim invaders are reported by the historians of Islam to have been immense. All that has now vanished, virtually without trace. However, painting and sculpture show how highly developed the arts of the Indian jeweller and worker in precious metal were; for nearly every figure represented is wearing a load of superlative necklaces, hip girdles, head ornaments, bangles, and anklets.

The second major group, in Orissa, now contains more than 200 temples, and once contained many more. At the cities of Bhubaneswar and Puri a continuous history of Hindu temple building can be traced through from the mid-eighth century almost to modern times. The sequence develops through modest stages and culminates in a handful of very large structures. The earliest typical shrine is the Mukteshvara, at Bhubaneswar. It has a tower with a curved outline and a substantial porch, both beautifully carved. Also at Bhubaneswar are the great Lingaraja, with its three aligned halls, and the Rajarani (*c.* AD 100). At Puri is the complex of temples surrounding the huge Jagannatha shrine, much restored. But perhaps the most famous Orissan building is the Black Pagoda at Konarak (*c.* 1230), an unfinished or ruined temple of the sun, conceived as a colossal stone celestial chariot. The entire

An Ajanta painting

sculptural scheme is dominated by erotic groups, superbly cut, once painted, and now world famous.

In Orissa today a tradition of illumination on narrow strips of palm-leaf still survives. The oldest known examples are probably fifteenth century, but there can be no doubt that this particular tradition preserves perhaps the most faithful record of what was in earlier times a widespread genre of Hindu art. Classical Hindu texts are impressed with the stylus on to the leaf-strip and colour is rubbed into the impressions; drawings to illustrate them are executed in the same way, and are painted in bright, clear colours. The figure types and conventions of design in the recent illustrations parallel very closely those which appear in the eleventh-century sculpture.

In south India, as in Orissa, artistic traditions as a whole did not suffer total eclipse at the hands of Muslim invaders, though some regions of the northern Deccan were occupied in the thirteenth century. In many parts of the far south, therefore, there are temples which have remained in worship down to the present day. Some of the oldest sites have virtually been abandoned without being systematically destroyed. The most important built temples are perhaps at Pattadakal, at Kanchipuram, and at Mamallapuram on the east coast of the Deccan. The early temples, founded at these places (late seventh to early eighth centuries) by the Shiva-worshipping Pallava Dynasty, standardize one of the experimental types evolved earlier by the Chalukyas at Badami. Thereafter it becomes the pattern upon which were based both later south Indian styles and styles of temples built in various parts of South East Asia, notably at Angkor and in Indonesia, during the period of Tamil overseas expansion.

Its essential characteristics are these: a pyramidal tower surmounting the cell, composed of a restricted number of storeys decorated with miniature pavilions and crowned by a kind of small faceted dome; an exterior wall uniting cell and main portico, which is vertically banded with pilasters between foot and lintel, in the panels of which there may be a few relief sculptures; a surrounding wall, often lined with cells, so close to the structure that it creates the feeling of a roofless corridor; pillars supported by lion caryatids, with broad-spread capitals; and curvilinear brackets under lintels and eaves.

Pallava sculpture, descended, no doubt, from that at Buddhist Amaravati, is notable for its restrained elegance. Its carvers were responsible for one of the most famous monuments in India. They produced a number of mythological relief carvings in caves and on rock faces; but the group of such carvings at Mamallapuram is one of the chief beauties of Indian art. The largest and most complete example (*c.* 670) is cut into a granite cliff facing the sea; it contains many figures of gods, sages, and animals illustrating the story of the descent of the celestial Ganga from heaven to earth.

In external architectural style—though not in sculptural—the colossal monolithic temple called the Kailashanatha at Ellora, on the other side of the Deccan (founded *c.* 775) is related to Pallava art. It belongs to a complex of caves, some Buddhist, some Jain, but is itself sacred to Shiva. This, too, is one of the splendours of Indian architecture. It was cut in two chief stages from a volcanic hillside, carved both inside and out, so that it stands free within an enormous quarry, the walls of which are pierced with flanking cave temples. The fundamental plan of cell with broad colonnaded hall is derived from a late type of Buddhist living cave at the monastery of Ajanta. The sculpture, however, is unique. Enormous figures in deep relief bound, leap, and twist, their energy bursting beyond their architectural frames. They were once plastered and painted; and here and there on the fabric a few fragments of pure wall painting survive.

Of slightly later date is the equally famous Shiva cave temple on Elephanta island near Bombay, far more modest in scale, and architecturally not very significant. But its vast sculptures, one being the well-known triple head (Trimurti) of Shiva, radiate an atmosphere of powerful tranquillity.

Under the immensely powerful Chola Dynasty, the eastern coast of the peninsula became the site of yet another flowering of art. About AD 1000 at Thanjavur (Tanjore) the greatest of the early Chola temples was built, a stupendous pyramidal shrine, sacred to Shiva, its tower nearly 200 feet high and crowned by an eighty-ton ornate dome capstone. On the inner walls of the ambulatory which runs around the cell under the main tower are the remains of an original series of wall paintings illustrating Shiva mythology and celestial female dancers—another hint at how lavish the use of colour originally was on Indian architecture. But the Cholas are perhaps more artistically remarkable for the extraordinary school of bronze sculpture which they patronized, and which has continued and evolved down to the present day. It produced icons, ranging from almost life size to a few inches high, of Hindu deities. The largest and most important of them were sometimes dedicated as 'portraits' of members of the royal family in the guise of gods. Many were meant to be carried in procession, and so they are modelled completely in three dimensions, with slender, elegantly rounded limbs in fluid postures. There were many images of Hindu saints in adoration; but perhaps the best-known type is that which represents the god Shiva as the beautiful 'Lord of the Dance', posing with one knee cocked, in an aureole of flame. This whole bronze art deeply influenced the arts of areas of South East Asia where south

Indian culture made its impact, especially Ceylon, Thailand, and the kingdom of eastern Java.

In the western Deccan the Western Chalukya Dynasty built its own temples in an extreme, mannered style, which is related to the general northern style (for example Ambarnath, Bombay, eleventh century; Gadag, Palampet, twelfth century). The exteriors were elaborate and often squat; but the interiors show a proliferation of columns with deeply cut horizontal mouldings, each with a variety of sections, and with facets for sculpture. The brackets become agglomerations of fantastic animals. The figures which adorn these brackets and the pillars develop extremely sinuous postures, their limbs becoming slender, almost insect-like. In the major icons hard, clearly defined forms often betray an insensitivity of touch which suggests a hardening impersonality in social and aesthetic attitudes.

The question of the value of this vast inheritance of early and medieval Indian art to the modern world is a most interesting one. For two centuries and more the West had been unable to come properly to terms with it. Indian society has long been, and still remains, so rigidly structured that foreigners have found it exceptionally difficult to enter sympathetically into Indian attitudes, aesthetic as well as social.

The fundamental point is that this Indian art incorporates, in its own terms, a set of ideal canons of form. The different categories of architecture were made according to strict principles of proportion, following prototypes whose patterns were considered sacred and were handed down from generation to generation of craftsmen, probably in manuals of written and diagrammatic formulae (some latish examples survive). Sculptures—and perhaps paintings too—were made according to clearly laid-down prescriptions for each type, both in iconography and in detailed proportions. These canons naturally seemed to be in violent conflict with the semi-classical idealist-realist canons of art which persisted in Europe virtually into this century. It was no accident that the first Indian art to attract widespread and serious attention in the West was the somewhat Helleno-Romanized art of Buddhist Gandhara of c. AD 120–500. Furthermore, even when the twentieth-century

Modernist and Cubist Revolution was under way, partly inspired by primitive arts, Indian art remained at something of an aesthetic disadvantage precisely because it incorporated a cannon; and canons were supposedly being rejected. But in the earlier twentieth century there were discerning collectors who recognized the immense virtues of Indian sculpture; two of the most important were themselves distinguished sculptors—Rodin and Epstein. British administrators who served in the old Indian Civil Service and the Archaeological Survey of India before India became independent also admired and collected works of early Indian art. But primary obstacles to earlier Western appreciation of all this art were those of its essential qualities which were deeply at variance with puritanical Western notions—its formal exuberance, its extreme sensuality, its vivid tactile presence, and its frequent unabashed concern with sexual love. Indeed, it would be true to say that the whole of the art so far discussed is meant in one way or another to stimulate the senses. For the heavens of the Indian imagination were characterized by joys of the most direct and uninhibited kind.

Music

N. A. Jairazbhoy

Music in the Indian subcontinent is a reflection of the diverse elements—racial, linguistic, and cultural—that make up the heterogeneous population of the area. The extraordinary variety of musical types is probably unparalleled in any other equivalent part of the world. Music plays a vital role in the religious, social, and artistic lives of the people. A great deal of it could be termed functional, as it is an indispensable part of the activities of everyday life, ranging from work and agricultural songs to the music which accompanies life-cycle events, such as birth,

initiation, marriage, and death. In spite of the great diversity of
music in the area, it is possible to make a few general
statements which would be valid for most of the music in
India. For instance, apart from modern developments,
Indian music is based mainly on melody and
rhythm; harmony and polyphony, as known
in the West, have no part in the music.
Much of the music is modal in
character and is often accompanied by a drone which estab-
lishes a fixed frame of reference and precludes key
changes which are so characteristic
of Western music. There is, however, such a great variety of melodic
and rhythmic forms in India that it would be injudicious to general-
ize any further.

In dealing with the origins of this exceedingly complex musical
culture, we are fortunate that music has been part of India's literary
tradition for nearly 2000 years, and references to music go back even
further; and that there are still areas in India which have remained more
or less isolated from the main cultural stream and appear to have
preserved their ancient musical forms relatively unchanged. Through
the literary sources, we can trace something of the history of Indian
classical music, which is predominantly an art form found in the cities.

A fundamental element of Indian classical music is the use of a
drone, usually provided by a wind instrument or a plucked stringed
instrument, which is tuned to a pitch convenient to the singer or
instrumentalist—there being no concept of fixed pitch. Classical music
is performed by small ensembles usually consisting of one main melody
instrument or singer, one or more secondary melody instruments which
echo, but may at times carry, the main melody line, and one or more
percussion instruments which mark the time measure and provide
rhythmic counterpoint. The melody line is largely improvised on
melodic entities called ragas, each of which prescribe a set of melodic

possibilities. These have been handed down as part of an oral tradition, from teacher to pupil over many generations. The bases of the rhythmic improvisations are called *talas*, each of which prescribes the length of a time cycle in terms of time units as well as the distribution of stresses within this cycle. Raga and tala are the two main elements of Indian classical music. In embryonic form these two elements are also to be seen in much of the folk music of the country.

Ancient Indian Music

The Vedas and their ritual are applicable to the *dvi-ja*, the 'twice born', the three upper castes of Hinduism. The fourth caste, the sudras, were introduced to Hindu mythology and religious philosophy through the originally secular epic poems, the Ramayana and the Mahabharata, and through the Puranas—popular stories depicting the lives of the various incarnations of the Hindu deities and other religious legends. These were probably sung and recited, perhaps even before the Christian era, by bards, in much the same way as they still are. These legends were also enacted on stage, and probably the first detailed description of music is to be found in this connection in the *Natyashastra* which has been variously dated from the second century BC to the fifth century AD. This work is, in many respects, a manual for the producer of stage plays and deals with all the aspects of drama, including dance and music. Much of the present-day musical terminology stems from this source, and the *Natyashastra* has inspired many treatises over the centuries.

Scholars are not all agreed on the nature of this early musical system which was associated with theatrical performance. It evidently included background music, performed by an orchestra, with singers, located just off stage, in what was very much like an orchestra pit. Melodies were apparently derived from modes (*jatis*) which were taken from the heptatonic serial progressions (*murchhanas*) of two closely related parent scales or tone systems, *shadjagrama* and *madhyamagrama*.

It is not clear just when the system of jatis fell into disuse, since many later texts refer to them merely out of reverence for Bharata, the author of the *Natyashastra*. There is, however, mention in the *Natyashastra* of certain musical entities, later called grama-ragas, which are said to be performed in the formal stages of Sanskrit classical drama. The connection between these and the elaborately described system of jatis is not established in the *Natyashastra*. The grama-ragas, seven in number, are mentioned in the seventh-century Pallava Kutumiyamalai music inscription in Tamilnadu, in the *Brihaddeshi*, written by Matanga about the tenth century, and in the *Sangitaratnakara* by *Sharngadeva*, written in the thirteenth century AD. In the *Brihaddeshi* the grama-ragas are said to have been derived from the jatis, but the evidence seems to suggest that they were more like the parent scales or tuning systems on which the jatis were based, namely the shadjagrama and the madhyamagrama.

In the thirteenth-century *Sangitaratnakara*, the total number of ragas had increased to 264, of which just over 10 per cent were said to be no longer popular. Modern scholars have not yet been able to reconstruct these ragas satisfactorily, in spite of the fact that a rudimentary form of notation, based on the Indian equivalent of the Western tonic sol-fa, was given by both Sharngadeva and Matanga.

It may have been, at least in part, because of the proliferation of ragas, and the number of overlapping categories to which they were ascribed, that new methods of classifying ragas seemed to become popular during the Muslim period. These were apparently not based on musical characteristics, but rather on associations involving the ethos of the ragas. From early times both jatis and ragas, in their connection with dramatic performance, were described as having particular moods (rasa) and being suitable for accompanying specific dramatic events. The term raga itself is derived from the Sanskrit root ranj 'to colour or tinge with emotion', and it was this aspect of raga which seemed to gain precedence.

The most popular method of classification was in terms of ragas (masculine), and their wives, called *ragini*, which was sometimes expanded to include *putras* (their sons) and *bharyas* (wives of sons). The number of masculine ragas is usually given as either five or six, each having six wives. These ragas and raginis are usually personified and are associated with particular scenes, some of which are taken from Hindu mythology, while others represent the states of feeling beginning to be expressed in the romantic-devotional literature of the period. The climax of this personification is found in the ragamala paintings, usually in series of thirty-six, which depict the ragas and raginis in their emotive settings.

The classification in terms of ragas and raginis is now no longer used, and although one still occasionally hears an older musician use the word ragini, only the term raga (in north India usually pronounced rag) is now in general use. This often leads to incongruities of gender, where the masculine word raga is followed by a word with a feminine ending, for instance raga *Bhairavi*, the wife of *Bhairava*, an aspect of the Hindu deity, Shiva.

Modern North and South Indian Classical Music

The thirteenth-century *Sangitaratnikara* was written in the Deccan, just before the Muslim conquest of this region by 'Ala'u'd-Din Khalji. It is shortly after this that one notices a gradual differentiation between north and south Indian music. Although orthodox Islam frowned upon music, the acceptance of the Sufi doctrines (in which music was often an integral part) by Islam made it possible for many Muslim rulers and noblemen to extend their patronage to this art. The attitude expressed by Amir Khusrau, a poet and musician at the Court of 'Ala'u'd-Din Khalji, who comments that the music of India was the finest in the world, was fairly representative of the Muslim attitude to Indian music. Although we know that musicians from Iran, Afghanistan, and Kashmir, were at the courts of the Mughal Emperors Akbar, Jahangir, and Shah Jahan in the sixteenth and seventeenth centuries, it is quite evident that it was Indian music which captured the imagination of the Muslim rulers. Famous Indian musicians such as Svami Haridas, Tansen, and Baiju Bavra have left their impress on the history of north Indian music as performers and innovators. Muslim musicians took to the performance of Indian music and added to the repertoire by inventing new ragas, talas, and musical forms, as well as musical instruments. This

Muslim influence was largely effective in the north of India and undoubtedly helped to further the differentiation between north and south Indian music, the two classical systems which are now generally referred to as Hindustani and Karnatak (Carnatic) music respectively.

The Muslim patronage of music has had two main effects on the music of north India. The first was to de-emphasize the importance of the words of classical songs, which were originally composed in Sanskrit and were, in any case, incomprehensible to anyone less than a traditional Hindu scholar. Sanskrit songs were gradually replaced by compositions in various dialects such as Bhojpuri and Dakhani. There were also compositions in Urdu and Persian, some of which can still be heard. The textual themes of the songs were often based on Hindu mythology and were of little meaning to the Muslims, yet Muslim musicians sang these songs, with Hindu religious themes, as they do to this day. The reverse is also true, that Hindu musicians sometimes sing songs dedicated to Muslim saints. Perhaps the best example of this broadminded attitude is to be seen in the poetry of the Muslim ruler Ibrahim 'Adil Shah II of the Deccan, who in his *Kitab-i-Nauras*, composed at the beginning of the seventeenth century, wrote poems in praise of both Hindu deities and Muslim saints. These poems were sung in specified ragas by both Hindu and Muslim musicians.

The second effect of court patronage on Indian music was to produce an atmosphere of competition between musicians, which placed no little emphasis on display of virtuosity and technique. A great deal of importance was also placed on the creative imagination of the performing musician and gradually the emphasis shifted from what he was performing to how he was performing it. Traditional themes remain the basis of Indian music, but, in north India particularly, it is the performer's interpretation, imagination, and skill in rendering these that provide the main substance of modern Indian music.

Mridangam

Beginning about the sixteenth century, we can see a direct connection between the textual literature and modern performance practice. An important feature of most of these texts is that a new system of classifying ragas in terms of scales was introduced. These scales are called *mela* in south India and *that* in north India. While north Indian music was evolving through its contact with the Muslims, south Indian musical theory was being thoroughly revamped by its theoreticians. Here a basic difference of approach becomes evident. North Indian musicians were little influenced by the musical literature written in Sanskrit because many of them were Muslim and had no background in the language. In addition, most Hindu musicians were unable to understand Sanskrit, which had become a scholarly language in north India. South India had, however, become the centre of Hindu learning, and Sanskrit literature continued to play an important part in the development of its music. Thus north Indian music seems to have developed, for the most part, quite intuitively during this period, and it was only in the twentieth century that musical theory has once again begun to come to grips with performance practice and to influence its development. In contrast, south Indian theoreticians had established most of the perimeters and the parameters of the system by the eighteenth century. This, unquestionably, retarded the rate of 'natural' evolution of south Indian music, but opened up a number of different avenues based on theoretical possibilities. As a result, there are now considerable differences of detail between the two systems to the point where they are, to a large extent, mutually incomprehensible.

Instruments

The ensemble used in south Indian music includes a main melody instrument or voice, a secondary melody instrument, one or more rhythmic percussion instruments, and drone instruments. Apart from the voice, the most commonly heard main melody instruments are: *vina*, a long-necked, fretted, plucked lute with seven strings; *venu*, the side-blown bamboo flute, usually with eight finger holes; *nagasvaram*, a long oboe-like double-reed instrument with finger holes; violin, originally imported from the West, played while seated on the floor, with the scroll resting on the player's foot; and *gottuvadyam*, a long-necked lute without frets, played like the Hawaiian guitar, with a sliding stop in the left hand.

The violin is by far the most commonly heard secondary melody instrument in south Indian music, and accompanies the voice and other melody instruments, except the nagasvaram. It plays in unison where the passage is composed, but imitates, with a slight time lag, the main melody instrument in the improvised passages. It is quite usual, during the course of a performance, for the main melody instrument to cease at certain points, when the violin temporarily takes its role.

Of the rhythmic percussion instruments, the double-conical two-faced drum, called *mridangam*, is the most commonly heard. The percussion group may also include the *kanjira*, a tambourine, the *ghatam*, an earthenware pot without skin covering, and the morsing, a metallic jews' harp. A special two-faced drum, called *tavil*—slightly barrel-shaped in appearance—usually accompanies the nagasvaram.

The most prominent drone instrument is the four-stringed *tambura*, a long-necked lute without frets. The nagasvaram is traditionally accompanied by the *ôttu*, a very long version of the nagasvaram, generally without finger holes. Sometimes, a hand-pumped harmonium drone, called *sruti* (or sruti box) replaces the ôttu or the tambura.

The north Indian ensemble varies in its constitution from vocal to instrumental music. It is now becoming increasingly common to hear two main melody instruments or two singers, who generally improvise alternatively. The most frequently heard main melody instruments are: sitar, a long-necked fretted lute; *surbahar*, a larger version of the sitar; *sarod*, a lucked lute, without frets and with a shorter neck than that of the sitar; *sarangi*, a short-necked, bowed lute; *bamsri*, a side-blown bamboo flute with finger holes; *shahnai*, a double-reed wind instrument, similar to the oboe, but without keys; and the violin, played in the same manner as its south Indian counterpart. The secondary melody line is very important in vocal music, but is not generally used in instrumental music. The most common secondary instruments are the sarangi and the hand-pumped harmonium, a keyboard instrument which was imported from the West at the end of the nineteenth century. Another secondary melody instrument often used, especially by Muslim singers, is the *surmandal*, a plucked board zither. On occasions, all three secondary instruments may be used at the same time. The most commonly heard drone instrument is the tambura, or *tanpura*, which has either four or five strings. It is a plucked long-necked lute, similar to the south Indian tambura but differing slightly in appearance. The drone may also be produced on the *sur-peti*, an instrument similar to the harmonium but without a keyboard, or on drone shahnais, called *sur*, when the shahnai is the main melody instrument.

The tabla, a pair of kettle-drums played with the fingers, is the most commonly heard percussion instrument in north Indian classical music, but the archaic *dhrupad* form is usually accompanied by the *pakhavaj*, a two-headed double conical drum, similar to the mridangam of south India, while the shahnai is generally accompanied by a small pair of kettle-drums, called *dukar-tikar*.

Some instruments, such as the sitar, are not only melody instruments, but have drone strings (*chikari*) which are often used rhythmically, and also have sympathetic strings (*tarab*) which provide an echo effect, something like the effect produced by a secondary melody instrument.

Tribal, Folk, and Devotional Music

Songs in a tribal society are mostly functional and often have the sanctity of a ceremonial rite. Such are, for instance, the songs which accompany the events of the life-cycle—birth, initiation, marriage, and death. Similarly, the agricultural songs which accompany the burning and preparation of the fields, planting, transplanting, harvesting, etc., have an element of ritual associated with them, and there is often a real fear that the harvest may not prove fruitful unless great care is taken over the formalities. Although many of the tribes practise this 'slash and burn'

method of cultivation, there are still tribes which are in the hunting and
food-gathering stage. Some of these have songs to propitiate their deities,
in the belief that this will ensure the success of their ventures, and songs
to give thanks at the successful conclusion of the hunt. When things go
wrong, in times of disease, drought, or shortage of food, the tribal shaman
is often invoked, and he generally has his own repertoire of songs.

Most tribes do, however, have more or less secular songs, such as
greeting songs, lullabies, love and courtship songs, ballads, and
humorous songs. On the occasion of certain festivals and celebrations,
members of the tribes may dance and sing for the pure joy of it. On
such occasions, one may also hear songs describing their ancestry and
the origin of the tribe.

The distinction between tribal music and folk music is not always
clearly defined. Nettle proposes that folk music is an oral tradition
found in those areas which are dominated by high cultures, having a
body of cultivated music with which it exchanges material and by
which it is profoundly influenced. This exchange is very much in
evidence in the folk music of India. Hindu mythology and religious
philosophy are an integral part of much of Indian folk music. Songs
sung at childbirth, for example the *sohar* songs of Uttar Pradesh, often
describe the birth of Krishna or Rama, and wedding songs might well
describe the wedding of Shiva and Parvati. A fisherman's song could
begin with an invocation to a protective deity (such as Jhule Lal in
Sind) and festival songs often have a predominantly devotional
character.

The *Bhagavata Purana*, which deals with the life
and adventures of Krishna, an incarnation of
Vishnu, is probably the most popular of the
Puranas and the story of Krishna
has had great influence on
both north Indian folk and
classical music. The ecstatic
devotion of the *gopis*
(milkmaids), especially Radha,

Sitar

to Krishna, and their yearning for him, occur over and over again, in both types.

This literature, composed in Sanskrit, has been received in oral form, generally through translations, by all except the erudite. The legends have been disseminated in a number of different ways, but most often in the form of sermons or readings with commentaries (such as *Hari katha*) at religious festivals, where they have attracted large audiences. These presentations generally include songs and music, and on occasions they may include secular, and even humorous material. A second very important source of dissemination is through religions mendicants, bards, magicians, and snake charmers, who travel from one village to another recounting the stories, often in song, and receive in exchange just enough remuneration to keep them going. A third source is through musical drama, which is found in one form or another in most parts of India, sometimes associated with the temples, as in the kathakali form in Kerala, sometimes produced by wandering bands of players, who travel from one village to another carrying their sets (if any), costumes, and musical instruments by bullock cart, during the festival seasons.

The role of the religious mendicant in the growth and spread of medieval Hinduism cannot be overstressed. Many of them have since then become sanctified and are now referred to as 'saint singers' or 'poet-saints'. The popular devotional movements began in Tamilnadu and gradually spread north through Maharasthra into north India. The songs of the poet-saints were generally composed in the vernacular languages and received immediate recognition in both the cities and the rural areas.

These songs have had a profound effect on Indian music. Modern Carnatic or south Indian classical music is said to have had its beginnings in the songs of one of the Karnataka saints, Purandaradasa (1480–1564), and to have reached its golden period about the beginning of the nineteenth century with the devotional and philosophical songs of the 'trinity', Tyagaraja, Dikshitar, and Shyamashastri. To this day, south Indian classical music maintains, for the most part, a highly devotional character. The influence of the bhakti saints on north Indian classical music is not quite so obvious. One of the most revered north Indian poet-saints, Jayadeva of Bengal (twelfth century), composed the *Gita Govinda*, a series of songs in Sanskrit, describing the love of Radha and the milkmaids for Krishna. Each of these songs was composed in a particular raga and tala. Unfortunately, although the songs are still sung in Bengal at Vaishnative festivals, the original music no longer exists; however, the themes of the songs have been carried over into north Indian classical music, particularly into the vocal form called *thumri*. Poet-saints such as Mirabai and Surdas have also undoubtedly had some effect on north Indian music, and specific ragas have been named after them (for example, Mirabai ki Malhar and Surdasi Malhar).

The greatest impact of these saint-singers on Indian music was in the upsurge of a new type of song, variously called *bhajan, kirtan*, or *abhang*. These devotional songs represent something of an intermediate stage between classical and folk music, less abstract than the classical, but more sophisticated than most folk music. While classical music placed emphasis on technique and beauty of performance, and thus became the preserve of specialists, the emphasis in the devotional songs lay in mystical and emotional experience. The sound produced was incidental to the act of singing and one did not need to be a good musician to derive spiritual benefit from the songs. The songs, however, often have 'catchy' tunes, many of which are derived from the ragas of classical music. The wide appeal of these songs can also be attributed to the lively rhythms with which they are accompanied. They have provided a repertoire for congregational purposes in temple services as well as in the many informal gatherings of devotees (bhajan *mandals*) which take place during the festival seasons.

While the devotional movements were spreading through Hindu India, a parallel phenomenon was taking place among the Muslims in India. Orthodox Islam, with its strict code of ethics in which music was generally thought to be illegal, was being tempered by the mystic Sufi movement, which emphasized a personal realization of God as its goal. One of the legitimate means of achieving this goal, according to some of the Sufi orders, was through singing the praises of God. Accordingly the Sufis had their own religious mendicants, usually attached to the shrine where they had been initiated, who wandered about the countryside visiting other shrines and singing their devotional songs, much like their Hindu counterparts. There is no doubt that both Hindu and Muslim mendicants exchanged ideas, and that they looked upon each other with respect. The famous poet-saint Kabir (1440–1518), originally a low-caste weaver in Varanasi (Banaras), reflects the extent of this communication, as he uses religious themes drawn from both Hindu and Muslim sources, as well as both Sanskrit and Persian vocabulary. The Indo-Muslim repertoire of religious songs, called *qawwali*, is said to have begun with Amir Khusrau, the famous poet-musician (c. 1300). This repertoire includes songs in praise of Allah, and of the prophet Muhammad and his descendants. It also includes songs in praise of the patron saint of the singer.

Like bhajans, qawwalis may be sung by individuals, such as the mendicants (called *darwesh* among the Muslims), or in groups, for instance at the annual festivals at shrines. Qawwalis may also be sung by professional singers at the homes of patrons, and nowadays in concerts as well. The technique and sensitivity of the professional *qawwals*, with their vast repertoire of poetry and command over music—much of which is similar to north Indian classical music—has resulted in a new form of musical expression which now seems to be spreading beyond its original Muslim religious environment. Not only may one hear bhajans rendered in the qawwali style, but also there have been occasions when qawwals have been invited to sing at Hindu religious functions. On such occasions the qawwal may sing songs composed by Kabir and others, where the basic theme is generally that there is only one God, whether he is called Ram or Rahim ('The Merciful', an epithet of Allah), and that all mystic paths lead to the realization of the One.

Ghazals are another form of song sung by qawwals. These are derived from an Urdu poetic form of the same name, composed of independent couplets. This is essentially love or erotic poetry; underlying it, however, are the themes of the Sufi mystics, for whom

God is the beloved. The verses of the ghazal are open to a number of different interpretations; secular, mystical, and philosophical. Modern poets have sometimes used this form for social and political comment as well. Thus a traditional theme, such as a moth sacrificing itself in the flame of a candle, could be interpreted as depicting the intensity of human love, divine love, or even the spirit of patriotism. The ghazal form has achieved a great deal of popularity in the northern part of the subcontinent, and special meetings, called *musha'ara*, are held expressly to enable poets to sing or recite their poems.

Modern Developments

Modern developments in Indian music could be said to have begun with the songs of the world famous Indian poet, author, and painter, Rabindranath Tagore. During his lifetime he wrote more than 2,000 songs, drawing his inspiration mainly from classical, folk, and devotional music. The result was a unique individual expression in which words and melody blend together in an extraordinary way. For Tagore, words without melody were like butterflies without wings, an attitude which captures one of the essences of Indian society. Purists

A Qawwali performance

in classical music have sometimes found objection to Tagore's songs on the grounds that they are not composed in pure ragas. This is indeed true, but the popularity of these songs in Bengal, especially among the intellectuals, shows that they are not without sophistication, and succeed in their intent.

The most significant factor in modern developments has been the influence of the mass media, particularly cinema and radio. Their influence is not limited to the cities; the travelling cinema and the temporary cinema in an open, thatched-roof structure, which has to be rebuilt each year after the monsoons, have made films available to the rural population at extremely low cost. In these cinemas the majority of the audience sits on the floor, only two or three rows of chairs being provided for the wealthier members. The influence of the radio, too, is steadily growing as relatively inexpensive transistor radios become available. In villages and small towns one may hear these radios blaring forth into the streets from the local shops.

Very early, with the introduction of sound films in the 1930s, the cinema industry in India discovered that if films were to be successful they had to include songs, and to this day nearly all successful productions are similar to the 'musicals' of the West. The songs were initially taken from traditional Indian sources, folk, devotional, and classical, as well as ghazals and qawwalis, and were presented in a more or less traditional manner. New songs were, however, needed to suit the plot and action in the films and gradually new instrumentation and techniques were introduced. The influence of Western music was delayed, partly by the fact that India had no indigenous tradition of orchestral music, which involves lengthy compositions and accurate performance from notation—neither of which were part of the training of the traditional Indian musician. There was also the lack of experience with harmony, counterpart, and orchestration, techniques which the West had gradually developed over a period of several hundred years.

Indian musicologists are generally unable to come to grips with these new trends and are apt to condemn them out of hand. This attitude is reflected in the policy of All India Radio, a government-controlled organization, which has sought to emphasize classical music. For a number of years, film music was not broadcast on All India Radio. This policy was modified when it was discovered that AIR was losing many listeners to the commercially controlled Radio Ceylon, which was presenting film music virtually all day. It is true that much film music is trite, and that some of the experiments are overindulgent, but these are necessary stages in the development of a new tradition. In the meanwhile, the popularity of film music is on the increase—sometimes to the detriment of age-old music traditions—and there is a growing audience for Indian film music in many parts of South East Asia, the Middle East, and Africa.

PART TWO

The Age of
Muslim Dominance

Muslim Architecture in India

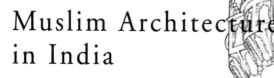

MARTIN S. BRIGGS

IT WAS IN 712 THAT the Muslim hosts first entered India and established themselves in Sind, but the colony there soon became detached from the Caliphate, eventually expired, and left no architectural remains of importance. In the tenth century, about 962, a former Turkish slave named Alptigin entered Afghanistan from Turkistan and established a small independent principality at Ghazni. His successor Sabuktigin, another ex-slave, became Amir of Ghazni in 977, raided the Panjab ten years later, and founded a dynasty. His son Mahmud, who succeeded him in 997, assumed the title of Sultan and soon began to make his power felt beyond the Indus, capturing Kanauj, the capital city of northern India, in 1019. But is was only in Ghanzi itself that he became famous as a builder, and the sack of that city by a rival chieftian in *c*. 1150 destroyed all the buildings except Mahmud's tomb and two others.

Ghanzi lies in the modern Afghanistan, and therefore does not strictly belong to our subject. But it must be recorded here that, in the days of its glory, it became a city of some importance. A contemporary chronicler, Firishta, wrote that 'the capital was in a short time ornamented with mosques, porches, fountains, aqueducts, reservoirs, and cisterns, beyond any city in the East.'[1] Important from the point of view of the later history of Muslim architecture are the two remarkable towers that Fergusson calls pillars of victory.

After Mahmud's death in 1030 the power of Ghazni began to decline, and it was occupied in 1173 by the rival prince of Ghur. Twenty years later, Muhammad, the Ghuri ruler of Ghazni, with his generals Qutbu'd-Din Aibak and Muhammad Bakhtiyar, conquered Hindustan and established the new Muslim capital at Delhi. This date, 1193, marks the real beginning of Muslim architecture in India itself.

Before describing the early architecture of Delhi and Ajmer it is necessary to indicate briefly the point of development to this Muslim building had attained in 1193 in Persia and the neighbouring counties whence its influence must have reached India, and then to study the nature of the existing indigenous architecture with which it became fused and on which, in spite of all statements to the contrary, it eventually impressed the unmistakable features of Islamic tradition.

The congregational mosque or 'Friday Mosque' (Jami' Masjid) had long attained its normal and almost standardized form consisting of a large open rectangular court (*sahn* in Arabic) surrounded by arcades or colonnades *liwanat* in Arabic) on all four sides. The *liwan* nearest to Mecca was usually made much deeper than the others and formed the sanctuary. In the centre of the back wall of the sanctuary, and on its inner side, stood the *mihrab*, a niche with a pointed head, indicating the proper direction (*qiblah*) for prayer, that is the direction of Mecca. The call to worship (*adhan*) was chanted by a muezzin (*mu'adhdhin*) from a gallery near the top of a minaret (*ma'dhana*), a tall slender tower. Within the mosque the chief ritual furniture consisted of a pulpit (*mimbar*) and facilities for ceremonial ablution. A large mosque might have several minarets, their form being usually cylindrical or polygonal in Persia, though the first known example, at Qayrawan near Tunis (eighth century), is a massive square tower, slightly tapered. Arches were freely

[1] Quoted in Fergusson's *History of Indian and Eastern Architecture*, revised edn, London, 1910, Vol. 2, p. 192.

Qutb Minar

used in all parts of the mosque, their form being generally 'Persian' (that is somewhat depressed and struck from four centres like the 'Tudor' arch), or less frequently of ogee type. Cusping was occasionally used. Windows were often filled with plaster or stone lattices or *claire-voies* to break the force of the sun, but glazing does not appear to have been introduced before the thirteenth century. Enamelled tiles were certainly employed, also banks of decorative lettering and geometrical surface patterns ('arabeseques') in profusion, while the famous 'stalactite' ornament, the hallmark of Muslim architecture in all countries, had made its appearance in the mosque of Al Aqmar at Cairo in 1125. Lastly, the masonry or brick dome had come into general use for tombs and tomb-mosques, though in ordinary congregational mosques it was normally of small size and placed over the space in front of the mihrab.[2]

The buildings which the Muslim conquerors found in India in 1193 were numerous and decidedly florid in character. The story of architecture in India prior to the Muslim invasion in 1193 has already extended backwards by 3000 years or more since the discoveries made at Harappa and Mohenjo-daro. In the prosperous reign of Ashoka (*c.* 272–232 BC) stone came into use, but the forms of timber members were often reproduced in stone. Ashoka, whose dominions included the whole of modern India except its southern extremity and part of Assam, became a devotee of Buddhism. Hence the monuments surviving from his day consist chiefly of great stone pillars inscribed with his religious edicts, and stupas, that is structures or shrines enclosing relics of Buddhist saints, or marking places where the Buddha lived or worked; a few artificial caves with highly polished interiors, used as hermitages for Ajivika monks, also go back to his day. In these buildings, which were scattered all over Ashoka's vast empire, there are many indications of foreign influence, even at this early data.

Thus the Ashokan pillars have capitals somewhat resembling the type used at Persepolis 700 years before, decorated with Persian mouldings,

[2] For a concise summary of the characteristics of Muslim architecture in general, see my chapter in *The Legacy of Islam*, Oxford, 1931, pp. 155–79.

and crowned with lions or other beasts. Where these lions were disposed
in pairs or in fours (as on the fine capital from the Sarnath pillar, which
was 50 feet high from the ground), we find the prototype of the famous
'bracket capital' which later played so important a structural part in
Hindu architecture and came to be freely used in Muslim mosques. The
stupas are extremely interestingly monuments, but do not appear to
have influenced mosque building to any marked extent.

The direct debt of Indian Muslim architecture to ancient Indian art
appears to be limited to the use of bracket capitals (a Persian heritage)
and certain arch forms, the latter being disputable. Other details
borrowed from Persia, Greece, and perhaps Rome (for example the
quasi-Doric capitals at Elephanta and the fluted pillars of the temple of
Martand in Kashmir and elsewhere) passed out of use long before the
Muslim invasion and so had no effect on Muhammadan architecture.

During the period between 650 and 1200 India was a mass of rival
states. Brahmanical Hinduism replaced Buddhism as the religion of the
majority of the inhabitants, but Jainism—which was as old as Buddhism
in its origin—continued to flourish abreast of it, and was responsible
for the erection of many important temples. The typical Hindu temple
of this period consists of two elements: a shrine cell crowned by a
curvilinear tower or steeple (*sikhara*) and an entrance porch or veranda.

In south India, instead of the curved sikhara, we find a more
primitive structure, a *vimana* or pyramidal tower with stepped sides,
not unlike the Babylonian *ziggurat*. Otherwise, variations from the
standard plan take the form of the addition of pillared halls
(*mandapam*) and enclosures (*prakara*) round the original shrine as a
nucleus, with lofty gateways (*gopurams*) at the various entrances. It is
only in the pillared halls that any noteworthy structural experiments
are to be seen, and there one sometimes sees primitive stone domes
on an octagonal arrangement of pillars, a system which found its way
into Muslim architecture.

If one can so far forget the overgrowth of ornament and the
complexity of subdivision as to penetrate to the underlying structural
forms and elements, it appears that the Hindu temples prior to 1193

were mainly of trabeated stone construction, based in large part on timber prototypes. Great stone lintels, beams, and purlins are freely used, and arches are almost if not entirely unknown, the tops of window openings and doorways being flat. Bracket capitals are employed to reduce the span of openings. Pyramidal roofs are formed by successive projections of masonry courses, and domes of primitive type are constructed in the same way on an octagonal base of stone lintels, themselves supported on stone columns in late examples (after the tenth century). The top or cap of such structures, the *amalaka*, sometimes appears to be carried on the slightly curvilinear piers or ribs forming the skeleton of the sikhara, where the walls of the sikhara are not entirely solid. There is no doubt that the Muslims borrowed many of these structural features, notably lintels and bracket capitals, from Hindu tradition; and it is equally certain that the domes they built in India showed similar influence.

When the Muslims under Muhammad of Ghur invaded India in 1191, they at first encountered defeat from the Hindu raja who ruled over Delhi and Ajmer. In the following year, however, they were successful, and in 1193 Delhi, Kanauj, and Varanasi (Banaras) were captured. The surrender of Gwalior occurred three years later, the conquest of Upper India being completed in 1203. Most of the Muslim rulers were of Turkish or Arab blood, and several of the early sultans of Delhi were Turkish slaves who, like the Mamelukes of Egypt including the famous Saladin himself, rose to the highest positions in the state from this lowly origin. The general in command of the army which conquered Delhi in 1193 was one such slave, by name Qutbu'd-Din Aibak, a native of Turkistan, and it was he who, even before he became the first sultan or king of Delhi on Muhammad's death in 1206, put in hand the building of two large 'congregational' or metropolitan mosques in Delhi and Ajmer. Undoubtedly this step was intended as a symbol of conquest, as an evidence of the Muslims' belief in the faith of their fathers, and possibly also as a memorial of their triumph over idolatry.

It may be assumed that the workmen were mainly if not entirely Hindus: that fact is proved by the clumsy way in which they dealt with the few non-Hindu items of construction required by the conquerors. Moreover, this was the practice in all the countries subdued by the Arabs in the early days of Islam. The plan of the mosque, utilitarian as well as symbolical in its nature, was prescribed by tradition and was insisted upon by the Muslim governor or ruler; the materials employed, and the constructional methods used to achieve the desired effects, were largely left to be determined by the local circumstances and the particular skill of the native craftsmen.

The first mosque at Delhi, dedicated to the Quwwat-ul-Islam ('Might of Islam'), is admirably situated on a slight eminence and was completed in 1198. It originally measured externally about 210 feet from east to west (that is from front to back) and 150 feet from north to south, the measurements inside the colonnade being 142 by 108 feet. (In India, the mihrab is always at the west end.) It was erected on the site of a Hindu temple, but an Arabic inscription on the east wall states that the materials of twenty-seven 'idolatrous' temples were used in its construction. The sanctuary at the west (Mecca) end is now in ruins, only twenty-two of its numerous columns remaining, but the fine stone arcade or screen forming its frontage to the courtyard survives to show the magnificence of the original design, with a central arch of slightly ogee shape, 22 feet wide and 53 feet high. The low colonnaded sanctuary behind it, like the other colonnades surrounding the courtyard, appears to have survived from the earlier temple, so that Qutbu'd-Din's work was mainly confined to the erection of this huge arcaded sanctuary façade. The Hindu craftsmen employed were unaccustomed to the construction of arches; hence, instead of proper voussoirs, they used projecting courses of masonry such as were familiar to them in building sikharas.

After Qutbu'd-Din's death, his son-in-law and successor Iltutmish proceeded in *c.* 1225 to extend this arcaded screen to treble its original width north and south, and also to erect a new east colonnade to the mosque, so that it now measured some 370 by 280 feet. Within the extended courtyard he built the great Qutb Minar, a detached tower or minaret 238 feet high, which may possibly have been commenced by Qutbu'd-Din himself. There is some doubt as to the real purpose of this remarkable monument. An inscription, and a reference by the poet Amir Khusrau, support the theory that it was a normal minaret used by a muezzin; but many authorities hold that it was a tower of victory, perhaps inspired by the 'pillars of victory' which still stand on the plain of Ghazni.

The tomb of Iltutmish, who died in 1235, lies near the mosque, and is a beautiful example of nearly pure Persian art, though there are certain features of its decoration—such as the design of the shafts and the cusped arches—that suggest Hindu taste, and much of the ornament betrays an inexperienced hand. The mosque at Ajmer, already mentioned, was commenced c. 1200 and finished during the reign of Iltutmish. It originally measured 264 by 172 feet and was erected on the site of a Jain temple or college built in 1153. As at Delhi, the chief alteration to the temple consisted in erecting a great screen or arcade of Persian arches in stone, bordered with characteristic

Arabic decorative lettering, and as at Delhi the arches are quite
unconstructional, having horizontal joints formed by projecting
courses of masonry.

The Mongol wars which devastated Central Asia in the thirteenth
century, and the weak character of the rulers of Delhi after Iltutmish,
may account for the fact that no outstanding monument was erected
for nearly a hundred years by the Muslims of India. Then in 1300
'Ala'u'd-Din, who had succeeded to the throne of Delhi in 1296 and
had previously conquered part of south India, began to enlarge the
Quwwat-ul-Islam mosque and to build a *minar* which was intended to
be more than double the height of the lofty Qutb Minar. 'Ala'u'd-
Din was a megalomaniac, and his vast projects remained
unfinished, but in the so-called Darwaza, a noble south
gateway to the mosque enclosure (1310), he has left us a
very charming and delicate little building which may
be considered to mark to culmination of early Indo-
Muslim art.

For the next period, corresponding with the
duration of the Tughluq Dynasty in Delhi (1321–
1421), that city continued to be virtually the

Tuglukabad Fort

capital of Muslim India, though from time to time various principalities, such as Bengal, asserted their independence. Delhi was certainly a flourishing place when the Muslims captured it in 1193. Its favourable strategical situation is considered to explain its continuance as a capital through a thousand years. The site of the old 'cites' of Delhi, reckoned at least seven in number without the pre-Muslim town, is spread over a triangular area measuring some ten or eleven miles from north to south, with the apex of the triangle at the junction of the 'Ridge' with the River Yamuna. The site of New Delhi is about in the centre of this triangle, and that of Old Delhi, the first Muslim city, founded by Qutbu'd-Din, at its south-west corner. The second city, Siri, lies north-east of Old Delhi, and the third, Tughlugabad, founded in 1321, in the south-east corner of the triangle. The fourth and fifth cities, Jahanpannah (1327) and Firozabad (c. 1354), were also established during the rule of the Tughluq Dynasty, which provided a number of interesting buildings, very different in character from the earlier architecture just described.

Outside Delhi the chief Muslim buildings of the fourteenth century were erected in Gujarat, Bengal, and the Jaunpur area. Gujarat was a seat of Hindu craftsmanship, and such mosques as the Jami' Masjid at Cambay (1325) and the mosque of Hilal Khan Qazi at Kholka near Ahmadabad (1333) contain numerous Hindu fragments as well as Hindu ideas, the columnar or trabeated effect being frequently produced. At Gaur in Bengal the enormous Adina Masjid near Pandua (c. 1360) has a huge courtyard surrounded by five aisles of arches on the Mecca side and three aisles on the remaining sides. These arcades, constructed of brick, originally carried 378 domes of identical size and design, a most unimaginative and monotonous conception. Nothing could be less characteristic of Hindu art.

At Gulbarga in the Deccan is another large and very remarkable mosque, the only one of its kind in India, built about the middle of the century. There is a tradition or legend to the effect that it was designed by an architect from Cordova, and certainly it resembles the famous mosque in that city to the extent that the whole area is covered. There are the usual arcades on the north, south, and east, with domes at each angle and a large dome over the mihrab; but the roof over the remaining area (normally occupied by the open court) and over the sanctuary consists of sixty-three small domes resting on arcades. With its stilted domes, its foliated battlements, and its fine arcades of Persian arches this striking building is essentially 'Saracenic'.

Returning to north India we find two interesting mosques at Jaunpur, near Varanasi (Banaras): the mosque of Ibrahim Naib Barbak in the fort, completed in 1377, and the fine Atala Masjid (1408). The latter has a truly impressive propylon or central feature in the Persian style, with a great Persian arch over the entrance, but the walls of the square flanking towers, which look as though they ought to carry minarets, are battered and are frankly Hindu, as are the colonnades on either hand. Yet the interior arches and dome are distinctly Muhammadan in character.

The next century, from 1421 to 1526, was interrupted by frequent wars, and Delhi ceased to occupy its predominant position of control over the semi-independent kingdoms of Bengal, Jaunpur, Gujarat, Malwa, the Deccan, etc. Nevertheless many notable buildings were erected in the area, most of them being tombs. The group of three, known as Tin Burj ('Three Towers') are rough and massive square structures with blank arcading on their exteriors, the Persian arch being used. The domes are rather lower than the typical high Saracenic dome, and thus approximate nearer to the Hindu form. The tombs of Mubarak Shah Sayyid and Muhammad Shah Sayyid, in or near Khairpur, are plain octagonal structures with domes, 'kiosks' surrounding the domes, and external arcading. Rather later is the plain but impressive tomb of Sikandar Lodi (1517) at Khairpur, surrounded by a fortified enclosure. The chief Delhi mosques of the period are the beautiful Moti-ki-Masjid, a remarkable composition with high blank walls flanked by arcaded pavilions and with effective domes, and the splendid domed mosque of Khairpur.

The two chief mosques of this century at Jaunpur are the fine Jami'Masjid (begun in 1438) and the small Lal Darwaza mosque. Both have been frequently illustrated, and both have the characteristics already mentioned in connection with Jaunpur mosques of the preceding period.

Gaur, the capital of Bengal at this time, similarly followed and developed its fourteenth-century tradition of brick arcuated construction, a curious medley of Muslim and Hindu methods. Among its buildings may be mentioned the so-called Firuz Shah Minar (dated 1490), a curious structure resembling an Irish 'round tower' rather than a minaret; the Eklakhi mosque and tomb, a fine domed building 80 feet square of uncertain data; and the Sona Masjid or 'Golden Mosque', so styled because of its gilded domes, erected in 1526, and now the finest ruin in Gaur.

Another great centre of building activity at this period was Mandu, the capital of the old kingdom of Malwa, in the former principality of Dhar. The Jami' Masjid, finished in 1454, is a magnificent congregational mosque, of which Fergusson says that 'for simple grandeur and expression of power it may, perhaps, be taken as one of the very best specimens now to be found in India'.[3] The great courtyard is surrounded by five arcades of pointed arches on the Mecca side, two on the east, and three on the north and south. There are large domes over the mihrab and the north-west and south-west corners, the remainder of the arcades being covered by an enormous number of small domes. This is an essentially Muslim building, free from Hindu trabeated construction, and is carried out in red sandstone with marble enrichments. In south India and most notable Muhammadan architecture of the period 1421–1526 is to be found in the city of Bidar, which supplanted Gulbarga in 1428. Here there are many interesting royal tombs, and a fine *madrasa* (college) and mosque.

But the most important architectural centre of the time was Ahmadabad, the capital of the kingdom of Gujarat. Here the mosque and other buildings erected by the Muslims are predominantly Hindu in

---

[3] Fergusson, *History of Indian and Eastern Architecture*, Vol. 2, p. 249.

character, in spite of the occasional use of arches for symbolical purposes. The Jami' Masjid (begun *c*. 1411) is a huge mosque of this type, all interest being concentrated on the Mecca liwan, which has 260 slender pillars supporting fifteen symmetrically arranged stone domes, built up of horizontally projecting courses in the Hindu fashion. The method of lighting the liwan is ingenious and admirably suited to climatic needs. At Sarkhej, about five miles from the city, is another large mosque completed in 1451, which is skilfully designed and is devoid of arches. The Jami' Masjid at Champanir (finished in 1508) is a large mosque resembling the Ahmadabad example in general arrangement but with two graceful minarets flanking the central doorway of the liwan, which has eleven domes in its roof as against fifteen at Ahmadabad. This is one of the largest and finest of Indian mosques; certainly one of the most Indian. The most notable of many fine tombs in Ahmadabad are those of Sayyid Usman (1460), Sayyid Mubarak (1484), and Rani Sipari (1514); and the tomb of Ahmad Ganj Baksh at Sarhej, begun in 1446. The second of these has arches, but for the most part the tombs of Gujarat have domes carried on an arrangement of columns in the Hindu manner.

With the year 1526, when Babur the Mughal king of Kabul, with the aid of 700 field-guns, defeated the vast army of the Sultan of Delhi on the plain of Panipat, we enter on the Mughal period of architecture, which lasted nominally until 1761, but which may more conveniently end for our purpose at the death of Aurangzeb in 1707. The Muslim buildings of these two centuries form a more distinctive and homogeneous group than the architecture described hitherto, which varied greatly from province to province, and they are more familiar to foreigners, all of whom have at least heard of the Taj Mahal. The term 'Mughal' as applied to architecture has its drawbacks, but the fact remains that the buildings ereted under the Mughal emperors were more definitely Muhammadan in character than those which preceded them and need to be classified as a separate school. The chief monuments were erected by Akbar (1556–1605) and Shah Jahan (1628–58); during the reign of Aurangzeb (1658–1707) architecture progressively declined.

Most of the buildings of this important period are to be found in the north-western part of India, especially in Delhi, Agra, Lahore, Fatehpur-Sikri, and Allahabad, with an isolated group at Bijapur. Babur established his capital at Agra, but his stormy reign only lasted four years, and only two of his numerous buildings remain: the mosques at Panipat and at Sambal in Rohilkhand. His son Humayun ruled from 1530 to 1540 and again from 1555 till his death in 1556, the intervening period being occupied by the reign of an Afghan usurper, Sher Shah. Of buildings erected between 1526 and 1556, the best known are in Delhi. They include the Jamali Masjid (1528–36); the mosque of 'Isa Khan (1547); and his richly decorated tomb adjoining, with 'kiosks' grouped round the central dome, altogether a bold combination of Hindu and Islamic elements. Then there is the walled 'sixth city' of Delhi known as the Purana Qila, in which stands the splendid mosque of Sher Shah, a clever blending of richness and refinement. At Fathabad, in the Hissar district of the Panjab, is a mosque (c. 1540) of massive proportions, well designed and decorated with tiles in Persian fashion. Sher Shah's tomb stands on a high platform or podium of masonry in the middle of a lake at Sasaram in the Shahabad district. At the corners of this podium are little domed kiosks, while two tiers of still smaller kiosks are grouped round the great octagon beneath the dome. This is a picturesque and delightful group, thoroughly Indo-Muslim.

One of the first monuments erected during Akbar's reign was the tomb of his father Humayun at Delhi, built in 1565–9 by Humayun's widow, who was afterwards buried there. It is surrounded by a formal garden which still retains its original layout, though many of the trees have vanished. The base of the tomb consists of a huge podium of red sandstone 22 feet high, with arches ornamented with white marble. From this noble foundation rises the tomb itself, 156 feet square and 125 feet high to the top of the dome. But though the building forms a square on plan, in fact it consists of a central domed octagon buttressed by four octagonal towers. The facing material is red sandstone, picked out with white marble, and the dome is faced with white marble. In shape the dome is slightly bulbous, thus introducing into India for the first time a feature characteristic of late work in Persia and Turkistan, and in construction it is double, another innovation. Its summit is crowed with the Arab finial, not the Hindu water-pot finial (kalasa), and indeed it is a decidedly 'Saracenic' design. The exterior of the buildings has Persian arches and severely flat surfaces, relieved only by the brilliant marble inlay; and the kiosks on the angle towers are the sole legacy from Hindu tradition. Everything here suggests the experienced hand of a Muslim architect from Persia, or more probably from Samarqand, where the rulers had developed tomb building to a fine art. It is generally considered that this splendid monument was the prototype of the Taj Mahal.

Akbar resided in several cities, among them Allahabad, Lahore, where he held his court from 1585 to 1598, and Agra, where he remained from that date until he died in 1605. At Agra he began building the famous fort in 1566, and within it he laid out the first part of the palace, which was continued by his successors and has since been so much altered that the various stages of extension are difficult to trace. The courtyard of the Jahangiri Mahal, probably Akbar's work in spite of its name, is an Indian design with square pillars and bracket capitals, richly carved, and rows of small arches constructed in Hindu fashion without voussoirs. Other parts of Akbar's palace are slightly more Persian in style. The hall of the palace of

Lodhi Tomb

Allahabad (1583), with its boldly projecting veranda roof supported on rows of Hindu pillars, is a definitely Indian design, with hardly a single 'Saracenic' feature in it.

But the chief centre of Akbar's building activity is the city of Fatehpur-Sikri, twenty-three miles from Agra, which he founded in 1596 and was the seat of his court until 1584 or 1585. It was systematically laid out by him, has hardly been altered since, and is now deserted. It originally had a circumference of nearly seven miles, with walls on three sides pierced by nine gateways and a very large artificial lake on the fourth side. The Jami' Masjid of the city has a quadrangle 433 feet by 366 feet, surrounded by cloisters, with a vast number of small domed cells, one behind each bay of the cloister, which accommodated the Muslim teachers and their pupils, for this mosque served as the university of Fatehpur. The Mecca liwan with its three domes, its rows of pillars supporting the roof, and its lofty central propylon, follows an Indo-Muslim type we have met before. Two tombs stand in the quadrangle on the north side; there is a central gateway in the east colonnade; and in the middle of the south side is the magnificent Buland Darwaza ('high gateway'), 130 feet wide, 88 feet deep, and 134 feet high. Built to commemorate Akbar's conquests, it is universally recognized as one of his greatest buildings. Though its huge recessed and vaulted portal, with a wide rectangular frame of flat ornament, is essentially Persian in character, the kiosks on its roof give it an Indian flavour. The palace of Fatehput-Sikri contains a number of remarkable buildings, including Akbar's office or *Diwan-i-'Am*, a Hindu design with a projecting veranda roof over a colonnade; and the wonderful Hall of Private Audience (*Diwan-i-Khas*), a masterpiece of planning, construction, and ornament, all of a distinctly Indian character. The city also contains two large houses of notable and unusual form, the palaces of Raja Birbal and of Jodha Bai.

Akbar's mausoleum (c. 1593–1613) is at Sikandara near Agra. It is a colossal structure standing on an enormous arcaded podium 30 feet high and 320 feet square. The mausoleum proper is rather more than

150 feet square and several stories high, with stepped walls of marble pierced with delicate trellis work. The roof of this structure is flat, with a small kiosk at each corner, and it seems probable, if not certain, that a central dome was originally intended to complete the group.

Akbar was followed by Jahangir (1605–28), who lived mainly at Lahore, where he carried out the charming Moti Masjid ('Pearl Mosque') and a considerable amount of extension to the palace in the fort. Jahangir, even more than Akbar, was a lover of gardens, some of them laid out in patterns like a Persian carpet. He built 'paradises' at Udaipur, Srinagar, and Fatehpur-Sikri; but the chief examples were the Shah-Dara or 'Garden of Delight' near Lahore, surrounding his own mausoleum, and the garden of the tomb of I'timadu'd-daula at Agra. This last monument (1621–8) is noteworthy less for its general design than for its decoration, the exterior being covered with an inlay of *pietra dura*, a fashion which may have been imported and thereafter became popular.

The reign of Shah Jahan (1628–58) was the golden age of Mughal architecture in India and produced a series of noble buildings. By far the most magnificent of all these was the celebrated Taj Mahal at Agra (1631–53), erected in memory of his favourite queen, Mumtaz-i-Mahal ('the Elect of the Palace'), after whom it is named. The design is more Persian and less Indian than any building we have encountered hitherto, yet nothing quite like it is to be found in Persia. The mausoleum itself closely resembles the tomb of Humayun, being a square (of 186 feet) with canted angles rather than an octagon. The square is composed of a high central block, octagonal within, buttressed at each angle by projections, with a great Persian portal between each pair. The slightly bulbous dome rises from a circular drum. All the arches are of Persian type. On each angle of the sub-structure stands a small domed kiosk. The beautiful central chamber is restfully lit through marble trellis work in the window openings, to break the glare of the sun. The mausoleum stands on a terrace 22 feet high and 313 feet square with a cylindrical minaret, divided into stages by galleries, at each angle. The whole of these buildings are a dazzling white marble and large parts of them are inlaid with coloured marbles and precious stones in delicate Persian patterns. The group is surrounded by a lovely formal garden, with avenues of cypresses and long lily ponds leading up to the mausoleum, and the river which bounds the garden on the north provides marvellous reflections. The Taj Mahal is one of the great buildings of the world, and has inspired every serious critic who has seen it to express his admiration.

Only second in importance to the Taj is Shah Jahan's work in the palace at Agra, carried out between 1638 and 1653, and including the Diwan-i-'Am, the Diwan-i-Khas, and the Moti Masjid. In these various

Purana Qila

buildings, though red sandstone is used to some extent, white marble
with coloured inlay is the prevailing material. Opulent elegance
pervades the whole scheme, and the effect is a satisfactory blending of
Indo-Muslim elements. Some writers indeed profess to rate the Moti
Masjid higher than the Taj. Shah Jahan also laid out charming gardens at
Delhi and Lahore, and in the latter city the mosque of Wazir Khan
(1634) was built in his reign. It is the chief mosque of the town, Persian
in general character, and freely decorated with coloured and glazed

tiles. At Ajmer are some beautiful marble pavilions on the embankment of the lake, also due to Shah Jahan.

His work at Delhi, too, was considerable. It included the walls of the 'seventh city' of Delhi called after him 'Shahjahanabad', and built between 1638 and 1658. Its fine walls and gates have been well preserved, as have his fort and the palace within it. Bounded on one side by the river, this vast complex of buildings, covering an area over 1000 yards by 600 yards, is admirably laid out in an ordered sequence of courts, but it suffered severely from British military occupation in the unimaginative period before Lord Curzon came on the scene. As in the other Mughal palaces described, the two chief buildings are the Diwan-i-'Am and the Diwan-i-Khas, and here they are of great beauty, richly decorated with marble inlay, and Indo-Muslim in character.

Shah Jahan also built in 1644–58 the huge Jami' Masjid near the fort at Delhi, with a quadrangle 325 feet square and two fine cylindrical minarets. Its outstanding feature is its commanding position, for it is placed on a high podium, a most unusual arrangement for a Muhammadan mosque. Whereas the domes, the minarets, and certain other parts of the building are Persian, the general effect is hybrid, and the angle pavilions are definitely Indian. Marble is used here too, but in combination with red sandstone.

At Bijapur, which was the capital of an independent kingdom from 1489 until it was taken by Aurangzeb in 1686, there was a flourishing school throughout the Mughal period, characterized by many distinctive features of design. These included the use of purely ornamental minarets—the call to prayer being chanted by the muezzin from a small platform elsewhere—rich cornices, and ingenious dome construction in which pendentives were employed. Fergusson wrote of the architecture of Bijapur in terms of the highest eulogy. Cousens, whose survey of the buildings of Bijapur provides a mine of information, says that 'there is abundant evidence to show that first-class architects were induced to come south from Northern India' to Bijapur, while there are traces of Hindu tradition in some of the buildings, proving

that the Hindu craftsmen retained some of their individuality. Bijapur at
the height of its prosperity, early in the seventeenth century, is said to
have contained nearly a million inhabitants and some 1600 mosques;
but during the Maratha supremacy in the eighteenth century it fell into
ruin and its buildings were freely plundered for stone and other material.
They were then smothered in jungle up to 1883, when Bijapur became
a British headquarters.

Lack of space forbids more than a mention of the chief examples.
The large but incomplete Jami' Masjid, commenced about 1576, is one
of the finest mosques in India, severly plain but relieved by delicate
claire-voies (pierced windows). In front of the mihrab is a large dome
of unusual construction, the external appearance of which would be
improved by the addition of a drum. The rest of the Mecca liwan is
covered with a number of small stone domes supported on piers and
arches but concealed externally by a flat terrace roof. The gorgeous gilt
and coloured mihrab is of later date (1636). The numerous halls,
pavilions, and mosques in the citadel include the graceful Mihtar Mahal
(c. 1620), a small mosque with a striking gate tower, said by Fergusson
to be 'equal if not superior to anything in Cairo'; the Sat Manzil, a
small palace of many stories; the Gegen Mahal (? 1561), an assembly
hall with a noble archway; and the Jalamandir, a dainty water pavilion.
Elsewhere in the city are two large isolated monuments: the tomb of
Ibrahim II and his family (1626–33), commonly called the 'Ibrahim
Rauza', and the mausoleum (Gol Gumbaz) of Muhammad, his successor,
which was finished in 1659. The former is chiefly notable for its rich
decoration, the latter for the remarkable and daring construction of its
enormous dome.

Shah Jahan, whose private life was less creditable than his
architecture, was deposed in 1658 by Aurangzeb, his third son. The
buildings of Aurangzeb's reign are inferior in all respects to those of
Shah Jahan. Among them may be mentioned the Moti Masjid at Delhi
(1659) with delicate marble decoration; and the Badshahi mosque at
Lahore (1674), which is almost a copy of the Jami' Masjid at Delhi,

though inferior to it in several respects. From that date onwards Muslim architecture in India declined but never died. The superb standard set by the Taj was imitated in buildings of all kinds—mosques and tombs, palaces and houses—till the British finally introduced Indo-Muslim railway stations and hotels. Thus the well-known buildings erected by Tipu Sultan at Srirangapatnam in the eighteenth century are Muslim architecture of a sort, though in its most Indian form, but they are decadent in their elegance.

Medieval Hindu Devotionalism

J. T. F. JORDENS

DURING MEDIEVAL TIMES (THIRTEENTH TO seventeenth centuries) Hinduism underwent a transformation so great that it has been compared to that wrought in Western Christianity by the Reformation. The focus of religious attention moved from the great gods and the liturgies connected with polytheism to the One God and his avatars, especially Krishna and Rama. A new attitude to God, emotional, passionate bhakti, replaced the old approaches of sacrificial rite and monistic mediation, just as a new mysticism, practical yet ecstatic, replaced the former philosophical type. Forms of religious expression changed: love songs to the Lord were sung, and group singing created a new popular cultural form, the kirtan. Pushing aside old gods, old attitudes, old cultural forms, the new movement also drove the sacred language, Sanskrit, back into the memories of the pandits and the deepest precincts of temples and monasteries. In the first centuries of their growth all modern Indian vernacular literatures were moulded by this religious movement, and thus were essentially

mass literatures. The socio-ritualistic order dominated by the
brahmans was not overthrown, but the brahmans lost much of their
spiritual authority, which passed to the saints and the gurus, whose
songs and biographies soon became a new scripture. The new
devotional religion, without destroying the Hindu social framework,
fostered ideas of brotherhood and equality before the loving Lord,
and its saints drawn from all levels of society proclaimed that in bhakti
caste had no meaning.

Origin and Spread

The divinization of Krishna and later of Rama emerged around the
beginning of the Christian era, and connected with it was the earlier
type of bhakti: a personal devotion, contemplative and sober, to a
personal loving Lord, as we find it supremely expressed in the Bhagavad
Gita. But the first clear manifestation of the new bhakti, emotional,
ardent, ecstatic, often using erotic imagery, appears in the Tamil country
in the early seventh century, in the poems of the Nayanars, devotees of
Shiva, and of the Alvars, devotees of Vishnu.

How did this new bhakti spread from the south into Maharashtra,
Bengal, and the northern plains? Obviously Tamil could not be the
vehicle, so it happened through the Sanskritization of the new spirit.
The Vaishnavite brahman scholars infused this new spirit into the
Bhagavata Purana (ninth century) which travelled the highroads of
Sanskrit tradition and soon became the principal text of Vaishanavism
all over India, marking a turning point in the history of the Vaishnavite
faith. Whereas the other books of this work are very much in the old
puranic tradition, the tenth book erupts in a magnificent exposé of the
new bhakti, centred on Krishna's childhood and youth.

This puranic development of the new bhakti was paralleled by
its growth in the work of the great theologians, both Saivite and
Vaishnavite. They formed religious orders, and their monks carried
their message all over India. The first and greatest among them was

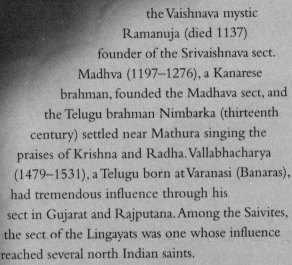

the Vaishnava mystic Ramanuja (died 1137) founder of the Srivaishnava sect. Madhva (1197–1276), a Kanarese brahman, founded the Madhava sect, and the Telugu brahman Nimbarka (thirteenth century) settled near Mathura singing the praises of Krishna and Radha. Vallabhacharya (1479–1531), a Telugu born at Varanasi (Banaras), had tremendous influence through his sect in Gujarat and Rajputana. Among the Saivites, the sect of the Lingayats was one whose influence reached several north Indian saints.

Another cluster of sects influenced bhakti in the later stages, especially in Bengal, the chief of which were the Buddhist Siddhas, the Sahajayana, and the Natha Yogis. It was mainly the Bengali Vaishnavas and also some Hindi saints like Kabir who came under this influence.

Maharashtra

Among the Indo-Aryan vernaculars devotional bhakti first appeared in Marathi. It started in the thirteenth century with Jnanesvara (1271–96, also known as Jnanadeva), who wrote a long Marathi commentary on the Bhagavad Gita, called *Bhavarthadipika*, more commonly known as the *Jnanesvari*, the fountainhead of Maharasthrian devotionalism. Namdev (1270–1350) was a contemporary of Jnanesvara, but outlived him by

over fifty years. A
tailor by caste, he was
surrounded by other low-
caste hymnodist-saints: Gora
the potter, Samvata the gardener,
Chokha the untouchable, Sena the
barber, and Janabai the maid. The
object of his devotion was Vithoba, the
form of the great god Vishnu residing in the
Pandharpur temple. This Vithoba was the god
of the Varkari-Panth, a sect that has an
important place in the history of
Maharashtrian devotionalism. It differs from
most other sects in several ways. Its members
are householders, and have a strong aversion
to asceticism. Their main cult is the twice-a-
year pilgrimage to Pandharpur, when
thousands of Varkaris walk from village to
village, from town to town, singing the praises
of Vithoba. The membership cuts across the
whole caste structure, and their most
important aid to religion is the society of
saints, by which term is meant their brothers
and sisters in the faith and the saints who have
died but left their immortal songs behind. The
spread of this intensely devotional movement
over the whole of Maharashtra was connected
with the names of Jnanesvara
and Namdev.

The coming of the Turks and of Islam
drove the movement underground as it were.

The temple at Pandharpur was razed, but the spirit did not die. It was Eknath (1533–99) who revived the inspiration and the tradition. He was a brahman born in a family of celebrated saints. As a scholar, he published the first reliable edition of the *Jnanesvari*. He was a family man, devoted, austere, whose life was regulated around his hearth and his manuscripts, and yet he was a mystic. He showed how, whatever obstacles the Muslims put in the way, the Hindu could aspire to the deepest experience of his religion within the ordinary framework of life. Every day he practised kirtan, and his songs are part of the Marathi heritage. They have a strong moral basis, are concerned with the simplest aspects of life, and yet often soar to great heights of personal mysticism.

Tukaram (1598–1650) was no doubt the greatest bhakti poet Maharashtra produced, and has high claims to be the greatest in the whole of India. He was born in a rural family of grain traders and great tragedy set him on the path of devotion. A famine took one of his two wives and his son, and left him heartbroken and ruined. His work consists of a collection of hymns, expressing the cry of his soul.

> They say that I fabricate poems
> Yet words are not mine, but Another's.

Humayun's Tomb

It is not my art that clothes them in beauty,
It is the Cosmic Lord who makes me speak.

I am only an ignorant peasant,
How would I know those subtle words?

I am only a simple secretary, says Tuka.
On my books I print the seal of His name.

Tukaram's hymns are the glory of devotional poetry, the favourites
of the Varkari pilgrims, and they are woven into the very texture of
the Pandharpur rites. More than any other of his fellow saints, Tukaram
was a mystic overpowered by love, by the presence or the absence of
his Lord.

Ramdas (1608–81) was the last of the great Maharashtrian
hymnodists and in several ways quite different again. His main work,
the *Dashabodha* is not written in the commentary form, but is rather a
compilation of his writings and sermons produced over many years.
The content too is new, for we have not only a theologian discussing
ideas, but also a reformer concerned with the contemporary state of
society, with the bad condition of the brahmans, with the threat of
Islam. There is evidence of what today we would call 'political'
concern in the relationship he had with his pupil Shivaji, the founder
of the new Maratha Hindu kingdom. In him devotionalism and
activism were closely wedded: whereas his predecessors were
householders, their concern for society was less than that of Ramdas,
the ascetic. And whereas the others centred their devotion on Krishna
and the Vishnu of Pandharpur, Ramdas, as his name proclaims, was a
devotee of Rama.

Bengal

Medieval devotionalism in Bengal has different roots from that of
Maharashtra, and developed in quite a different way. Two distinct streams
of religiosity determined its growth. On the one hand there is the
influence of the Vaishnava tradition, and on the other the non-Vaishnava

influences from Buddhist and Hindu sources. The Vaishnava impetus came first of all through the *Bhagavata Purana* with it glorification of the Krishna-*lila*. This came to Bengal under the Pala Kings and found its typically Bengali literary transformation in Jayadeva's passionately lyrical *Gita Govinda* towards the end of the twelfth century. The *Gita Govinda* brings into Bengali Vaishnavism a new aspect, derived from another source than the *Bhagavata*, namely the prominence given to Radha, the favourite of Krishna. The erotic-mystical theme of the love of Krishna and Radha occupies here the centre of the stage, and henceforth dominates Bengali devotionalism.

Non-Vaishnava influence came from two sources, distinct yet interrelated. Buddhism had been on the decline in India for some time, but in Bengal it survived under the Pala Dynasty, after which it became decadent. In its decadence it produced forms that affected the development of Vaishnavism, and both these Buddhist and Vaishnava forms then influenced Bengali devotionalism. Their emphasis was on the female principle of the universe and they exalted the religious value of sexual passion.

Chandidas (fourteenth century) is the first great name in Bengali bhakti literature. His poems, which include poems to the Mother Goddess and to Krishna and Radha, testify to his being influneced by both the *Gita Govinda* and the Sahajya doctrine.

Although Vidyapati (fourteenth to fifteenth century) did not write in Bengali, but in Maithili, an allied dialect, his songs on Radha and Krishna are part of Bengali Vaishnavism. The saint who gathered together the various strands of Bengali Vaishnavism, became a reformer, and founded a sect with enormous influence on Bengal religious life, was Vishvambhar Mishra, called Chaitanya (1485–1533). He was unique in medieval bhakti history in that he was the initiator of a very broad movement which covered Bengal and spilled out into the whole of east India. It was a movement which encompassed an organized sect, a strong theological school, and a broad-based popular cult. Chaitanya was probably at first a member of the Shankarite Dashnami sect, and he did not leave any theological writings, but only a few devotional songs. He himself was primarily a visionary ecstatic.

Chaitanya expressed himself in the *sankirtan*, a session of hymn singing by a group of devotees. These songs were often accompanied by ecstatic dancing to the sound of tambourines. Sessions took place in homes or temples, or erupted in the streets in the form of processions. Chaitanya, the ecstatic par excellence, was the centre of the cult, and a whole literature of hymns, biographies, legends, and dramas sprang up around him. In fact Chaitanya himself became the object of popular devotion, and was considered the living Krishna, or rather the incarnation of Radha-Krishna. The Chaitanyites were no social reformers militating against the caste structure, but within the sphere of devotional practice they completely rejected all distinction of caste and thus promoted a sense of equality that penetrated deep into Bengali life.

The Chaitanya movement had a great impact on Bengali life as a whole. It gave it a special identity which persisted even through periods of stagnancy, and provided time and again new inspiration to its religious reformers and poets: Keshub Chandra Sen, Bankim Chandra Chatterjee, and Rabindranath Tagore cannot be properly understood without reference to that tradition.

The Land of Hindi

In the Hindi-speaking areas the new movement started not around the figure of Krishna, but around Rama, and found its leader and organizer in Ramananda (1400–70). He looks upon Rama as the supreme God, who is to be adored with his shakti, Sita, and whose close companions like Hanuman should also be venerated. The literature of the sect is not important—only one hymn of Ramananda himself is extant—and its theology and ritual are largely modelled on those of Ramanuja.

Its main influence lies in a different direction. Ramananda
was strongly opposed to the restrictions and injustices of caste. He
threw his sect open to all, and his twelve personal disciples are
said to have included women, an outcaste, and even a Muslim. This
frank egalitarian basis and the exclusive use of the vernacular set the
sect apart from many others. Although egalitarian ideas
did exist in India before, one cannot discount here the possible
influence of the contemporary Muslim Sufis. The
Ramanandi sect has great historical
importance because its followers initiated a
number of other sects and movements
which covered north India.
The Ramanandis stand at
the source of important

later sects like the Sikhs and the Kabirpanthis, who inherited their social concern.

Kabir (1440–1518) started out as a disciple of Ramananda, but later developed his own characteristic eclecticism. Probably a Muslim by birth, or at least brought up in a Muslim home, he was and remained a low-caste weaver. His poetry, of which a good collection has come down the ages, is essentially a poetry of the people: it is unpolished and has a rustic, colloquial quality, yet it is pervaded with a profound symbolism and often reaches great lyrical power. It is a poetry of epigrams and short verses, easily remembered, that has penetrated the life of north India nearly as much as the poetry of Tulsidas.

For Kabir there is only one way to God: the way of personally experienced bhakti, which gives one the vision of the Lord, and which is a gift of God's grace. Man must purify his soul by righteousness and humility, by renunciation and love, and by praise of God in his kirtan and in his quiet meditation. Kabir's idea of God, like his whole theology, is eclectic, with strong influences from Vaishnavism, hatha yoga, Vedantic monism, and Sufism. He called God by many names, like Ram, Hari, Allah, Khuda, *Nirguna*, *Tat*, and even *Shunya* (the Void) and *Shabda* (Sound). No wonder the Muslims claimed him as a Sufi, the Hindus looked on him as a *Rama-Bhakta*, and the Sikhs incorporated his songs in their *Adi Granth*.

Kabir was at heart a reformer and an iconoclast. Continuously he attacks the externals of religion, scriptures, pilgrimages, rituals, superstitions, and idols.

Fatehpur Sikri

There is nothing but water at the holy bathing places;
    and I know that they are useless, for I have bathed in them.
The images are all lifeless, they cannot speak;
    I know, for I have cried aloud to them.
The Puranas and the Koran are mere words;
    lifting up the curtain, I have seen.[1]

To this religious iconoclasm he adds a social iconoclasm that incessantly attacks the injustices of caste, and denounces the pride of the brahmans. Humanity to him is a brotherhood, and all varieties of human nature are but refractions of the divine.

It is but folly to ask what the caste of a saint may be;
The barber has sought God, the washerwoman, and the carpenter—
Even Raidas was a seeker after God.
The Rishi Svapacha was a tanner by caste.
Hindus and Muslims alike have achieved that End, where
    remains no mark of distinction.[2]

Kabir founded a community, known as the Kabirpanth, which exists to this day, and a dozen other sects sprang from his direct teaching. The most important of these sects, which was to have quite a different history, was that of the Sikhs, founded by Guru Nanak, a disciple of Kabir.

Tulsidas (1532–1623) was the other most famous spiritual heir of Ramananda. His *Ram-charit-manas*, the *Lake of the Story of Rama*, has been rightly called the Bible of north India. This was a new Ramayana in the vernacular, a conception so daring that it aroused the ire of the brahmans and made the people consider Tulsidas a reincarnation of Valmiki. It is the favourite book of a hundred million people, for many of whom it is their main source of religious inspiration.

In his attitude to the traditional framework of Hinduism he also moves away from his predecessors. He is not a revolutionary as they

---

[1] *One Hundred Poems of Kabir*, trans. Rabindranath Tagore, London, 1962, poem No. XIII.

[2] Ibid., poem No. II.

were, but upholds firmly the broad basis of traditional Hindu society and of the scriptures, and repeatedly attacks those many sects that endangered these basic structures. For him reform had to be brought about within the compass of Hinduism itself through the loving power of bhakti. Caste should stand, but, for a devotee as devotee, caste was of no importance, and bhakti was open to all.

Tulsidas's bhakti is the love of the servant for his loving master. His work is totally free of even the slightest hint of sensuality, showing in fact a scrupulous concern for purity.

The Hindi world also produced its devotees of Krishna. Mira Bai (1503–73), a Rajput princess, was the first to achieve poetic fame. She was widowed at an early age, and left the Court of the Rana to devote herself to the worship of Krishna. She was no theologian, nor did she leave a great number of songs, but those that are extant have a quality all their own. There is a freshness and femininity about them, a deep pathos that expresses itself in lyrical simplicity, without the frills of conscious artistry. It is not so much the myth of Krishna that interests her as her own relationship with him, consisting of a spiritual marriage. In their nuptials the erotic element is totally absent; there is no voluptuous imagery. It is in her poems of separation that she reaches her greatest heights, projecting her sorrow and pining for Krishna on to nature around her.

> Thunderclouds came and went, but no message from Hari,
> Frog, peacock, partridge and cuckoo started to call.
> Lightning flashed in deep darkness, but I was alone,
> Trembling in the roar of fragrant wind and pelting rain.
> Loneliness burnt and stung like a jet black cobra,
> And Mira's heart overflowed with love for the Lord.

Surdas (1483–1563) was one of the eight main disciples of Vallabha, and the most brilliant. Born in a brahman family and blind, possibly from birth, he was musician attached to the temples at Agra and Mathura. He left a great number of songs, collected in the *Sursagar*, which he himself tells us was inspired by the *Bhagavata Purana*. His songs have as their theme the love of Krishna, whose life he sings, taking particular delight in the child Krishna, and the lover. His verse is renowned for its exquisite melody, and the conciseness of the little tableaux reminds one of the contemporary Rajasthan Krishna miniatures, which also vividly evoke the village life of the time.

> As the moth for love of the lotus loses itself in the flower
>   and yet is happy; so am I Thy devotee, my Lord!
> As the stag for delight of a tune stands unconcernedly near the
>   axe of the huntsman; so am I Thy devotee.
> As the pigeon for desire of the sky soars higher though only to be
>   dashed to the ground; so am I Thy devotee, Beloved!
> As the rain-bird in its utter loneliness calls its lover continuously,
>   so I wait for a vision of Thee, my Lord!
> For I feel forsaken and lonely and sad.[3]

South India

In Tamil, the hymns of the Alvars and the Nayanars continued to dominate the scene, and they soon gained the status of divine scripture and became part and parcel of temple worship as well as of popular devotional life. The first great poet to follow them is Kamban (twelfth century), author of the famous Tamil Ramayana, which is replete with descriptions of the country and times of the Cholas. The Mahabharata and the *Bhagavata Purana* also found their Tamil translators. Much of the Vaishnavite effort, however, went into Sanskrit compositions, and even much of its vernacular literature derived closely from the Sanskrit, and preferred the puranic approach and style.

The Shaivites produced a new devotional literature by the hymnodists called Sittars or Siddhas. Their innumerable songs gained great popularity, and, in their fierce monotheism and equally fierce condemnation of idolatry, they arrayed themselves against the powers of orthodoxy.

The earliest Kannada literature was predominantly Jain, but the

---

[3] A.J. Appasamy, *Temple Bells*, Calcutta, n.d., p. 27.

Hindu renaissance was inaugurated by Basava towards the end of the twelfth century. He founded the sect of the Virashaivas or the Lingayats, characterized by its numerous monasteries and by the large measure of its social equality, which had a tremendous influence on the Kannada country. They invented a new kind of vernacular literature, the *vachana*, little pieces of rhythmic prose sermons, meant for the people and inculcating bhakti to Shiva.

Oh pay you worship to God now—before the cheek turns wan, and the neck is wrinkled, and the body shrinks—before the teeth fall out and the back is bowed, and you are wholly dependent on others—before you need to lean on a staff, and to raise yourself by your hands on your thighs—before your beauty is destroyed by age and Death itself arrives. Oh *now* worship Kudala-sangama-deva.

Vaishnava literature in Kannada really started from the sixteenth century, during the Hindu kingdom of Vijayanagara, first with translations from the Sanskrit classics, the Mahabharata, the Ramayana, and the *Bhagavata Purana*. These were then followed by popular songs composed and sung by the dasas, or mendicant singers, inspired by *Madhvacharya* and stimulated by the visit of Chaitanya to the south in 1510. This tradition continued for a couple of centuries, producing songs in praise of Vishnu, some venerating him in the form of the Vithoba of Pandharpur, thus linking up with the Maharashtrian tradition.

The Telugu country saw a couple of figures who in many ways closely resemble some of the contemporary north Indian saints. Potana (1400–75) was a poor man without scholarship, who lived and died in the countryside. His voluminous translation of the *Bhagavata* gained immediate popularity, because it combined a simple language of great narrative power with a deep intensity of devotion. Among Vaishnava popular devotional literature it is one of the classics. Vemana (fifteenth century) was a low-caste Shaivite, and very much an individualist and a revolutionary. His *shataka* (century) of gnomic verse is known to all Telugus, and to most south Indians. His verses bristle with sarcastic attacks on the brahmans, on polytheism, idolatry, and pilgrimages.

Other modern languages too like Oriya, Assamese, Kashmiri, Gujarati, and Malayalam had their devotional hymnodists. In fact, devotional bhakti changed Hinduism profoundly over most of India, from the eleventh century onwards. Up to the seventeenth century it remained the most important single power in Hinduism, and it was only in the nineteenth century that the impact of the West was to challenge Hinduism again, and stimulate yet another renewal.

Islam in Medieval India

S.A.A. RIZVI

ISLAM MEANS 'SUBMISSION' OR 'RESIGNATION' to Allah (God). The Qur'an, the highest authority, calls it 'the only true religion', perfected for those whom Allah intends to guide. The Qur'an is revealed and not created, being the eternal word of God incarnate. It requires Muslims (the word Muhammadan is taboo among modern Muslims) to believe in God, His Angels, His Books, and His Messengers. All the prophets from Adam to Muhammad, and all the books revealed to them, are regarded as the religious heritage of Islam; but as Muhammad is the last of the prophets, Islam is the last word in the cycle of divine revelation.

Islam's condemnation of the idols of Mecca applies equally to all idol worship. The oneness of God and the mission of Muhammad are recognized in the profession of faith (*shahadah*): 'There is no God except Allah and Muhammad is Allah's messenger.' Five times a day, their faces turned towards Mecca, Muslims are enjoined to pray in a prescribed form. The noon prayer on Friday is the only public one; but these congregational prayers have obliged Muslims, both rulers and private men, to build mosques in which to hold them. Another obligation laid on the Muslim is to give a fixed proportion of certain categories of his property as alms. Then, during the month of Ramazan, the ninth of the Muslim calendar and that in which the Qur'an was first revealed, he must neither eat nor drink from dawn to sunset. Every Muslim who possesses the means must also make the pilgrimage to Mecca at least once in his life.

Islam has no priesthood or sacerdotal hierarchy. During the first century of its history, Islam split into two sects divided on political as well as religious grounds, Sunnis and Shi'is. The religious differences between the two arose over the interpretation of verses of the Qur'an and over the *Hadis*, or corpus of traditions about Muhammad's sayings and doings. The Sunnis, who have always predominated in India, believe that Muhammad appointed no successor, and left this matter to the discretion of the élite of the *Umma* or community of believers. The Shi'is assert that Muhammad's being the last of the prophets does not end men's need of intermediaries between themselves and God. They call such intermediaries Imams, and regard 'Ali, the cousin and son-in-law of Muhammad, as their first Imam. Their jurisprudence and religious practices are based on the teachings of their Imams.

All Shi'is are in agreement about the legitimacy of the first six Imams, but differ as to who succeeded the sixth Imam, Ja'far al-Sadiq, who died in 765. One group, the Isma'ilis, believe that the succession then continued through Isma'il (died 760/1), Ja'far's son. The other group, the Isna 'Asharis, to whom the Shi'is of Iran belong, believe that the line was continued by Musa al-Kazim, followed by five others. The Isma'ilis, who from the ninth to the thirteenth centuries propagated their beliefs effectively by giving inner or esoteric meaning to their religious teachings, which they explained allegorically, ruled Multan more or less continuously to 1160. Even after losing their political power there, they continued to preach their doctrines secretly in India, and one of their leaders, Nur Turk, made a final bid for power through a *coup d'état* in Raziya's reign.

The Isna, 'Ashari faith was recognized as the state religion of Iran by Shah Isma'il I (1501–24), the founder of the Safavid Dynasty. In India the acceptance of this faith by the sultans of Ahmadnagar, Bijapur, and Golconda, together with their patronage of Shi'i scholars and learning in their kingdoms, sharpened the Shi'i–Sunni controversy in northern India, where there was a considerable influx of Shi'i élite from both the Deccan and Iran.

The rulers of northern India were of the Sunni faith, as were most of their subjects. Among the Sunnis there are four principal schools of jurisprudence named after their founders: the Hanafi after Abu Hanifa of Kufah (*c.* 699–767); the Malikite after Malik ibn Anas (died 795), the leader of the Medina School; the Shafi'ite called after ash-Shafi'i who flourished in Baghdad and Cairo (767–820); and, a late-comer, the Hanbalite after Ahmad ibn Hanbal (780–855) of Baghdad. The greatest challenge to orthodox Sunnism came from rationalism in the form of the Mu'tazilas, who had much in common with the Shi'is. They professed a strict monotheism, denying any resemblance between Allah and His creatures.

The Mu'tazilas made a positive contribution to Sunni orthodoxy through Abu'l Hasan al-Ash'ari (875–935) a zealous Mu'tazilite who had learnt their techniques before deserting them, and evolved his own system of rational argument for the defence of orthodox doctrine, known as *kalam*. The Ash'ari system made great progress under the leadership of its most outstanding protagonist, Abu Hamid al-Ghazali (1058–1111). The influence of Ghazali was much greater because of the new Muslim religious leaders produced by the educational system devised by the Saljuqid vizier, Nizamu'l Mulk Tusi (*c.* 1018–92). This centred on seminaries of higher Sunnite learning known as madrasas, designed specifically to produce scholars of the Ash'ari School qualified to run the government in accordance with orthodox Sunni ideas. Known as 'ulama' (singular, 'alim,), these scholars were mostly government officials whose religious prestige was exploited by the sultans as a counterpoise against ambitious military adventurers.

Contrary to the 'ulama', who specialized in the formal structure of Islamic law and dealt with the practical requirements of political, social, and economic life, the sufis claimed to penetrate to the very root and spirit of Islam. Professor Arberry describes sufism as 'the attempt of individual Muslims to realize in their personal experience the living presence of Allah'.

In the formative period, sufis generally led a retired ascetic life; but gradually they evolved a corporate system of their own, ideas and practices being borrowed from Christian and Buddhist monasticism and philosophy from Neoplatonism and Upanishadic concepts. Their originality lay in incorporating these influences within the framework of Islam, thus making them an integral part of Muslim life.

The most authentic exposition of sufism is contained in the *Risala* (Epistle) of Abu'l Qasim al-Qushairi (d. 1074). By the twelfth century, sufis were divided into different *silsilas* (orders), each with its *pir* (preceptor), also known as *Shaikh* or *Khwaja*, as an infallible guide for the neophyte. Until the fourteenth century, a pir only initiated disciples into his own order, but later on distinguished preceptors were authorized to initiate disciples into other orders too.

The *Khanqah* (hospice) was the centre of the pir's activity, attracting from afar men seeking the spiritual life. The earliest sufi of eminence known to have settled in India, where the rich Hindu mystic traditions gave a new vitality to sufism, was Hujwiri, also known as Data Ganj Bakhsh (died after 1088), the author of the celebrated manual of sufism entitled *Kashfu'l Mahjub*.

The development of several new sufi orders in the twelfth century led to the establishment of a network of khanqahs, mainly in Iran, Central Asia, and India. In India the first leading khanqah was established at Multan by Shaikh Baha'u'd-Din Zakaraiya (1182–1262). He was also the founder in India of the Suhrawardi order originated by Shaikh

Shihabu'd-Din Suhrawardi (1145–1234), the author of an Arabic manual of sufism entitled '*Awarifu'l-Ma'arif*. Rulers, high government officials, and merchants lavished gifts upon these khanqahs, and the hagiological literature relates how, with its overflowing granaries and general affluence, the khanqah was often able to give financial assistance to the state. Shaikh Baha'u'd-Din Zakariyya openly took Iltutmish's side in his struggle against Qabacha, and received from him the title of *Shaikhu'l Islam*, ('Leader of Islam'). He avoided ordinary men and associated only with the religious and political élite. His grandson, Shaikh Ruknu'd-Din Abu'l Fath (died 1335), in his turn was highly respected by Sultan 'Ala'u'd-Din and the Tughluq sultans. Another Suhrawardi sufi, Shaikh Shihabu'd-Din's disciple Shaikh Jalalu'd-Din Tabrézi, failed in his efforts to establish supremacy in Delhi, and retired to Bengal, where he established a khanqah and a *langar* (centre for the distribution of free meals), first at Lakhnauti, and then at Devatalla near Pandua. He is said to have converted a large number of Bengalis to Islam. The Panjab, Sind, and Bengal thus became three important centres of Suhrawardi activity.

The second outstanding order to establish khanqahs in the towns conquered by the Ghurid invaders was the Chishtiyya, originating from a village near Herat called Chisht or Khwaja Chisht. It was brought to India by Khwaja Mu'inu'd-Din who was born in Sijistan in *c.* 1141. Having visited the important centres of Islamic culture in the Middle East, where he came in contact with Shaikhs of all the important sufi orders, he went to Lahore, finally settling in Ajmer about 1206. By the time he died in 1236, Chishti khanqahs were firmly established in many parts of the Delhi sultanate.

The Chishti centre in Delhi flourished because of the towering personality of Khwaja Qutu'd-Din Bakhtyar Kaki (died 1236), the successor there of Khwaja Mu'inu'd-Din Chishti. Although he took no interest in political activities, his immense spiritual prestige made his khanqah a rendezvous for Muslims from all walks of life. His successor, Baba Faridu'd-Din Ganj-I-Shakar (died 1265), continued living in his own khanqah in Ajodhan (Pak Pattan), so the Delhi centres became the charge of Khwaja Qutbu'd-Din's other disciples, in particular Badru'd-

Taj Mahal

Din Ghaznavi. Delhi became the real Chishti centre, mainly because of
Baba Farid's talented successor, Shaikh Nizamu'd-Din Auliya', who from
1287 until his death in 1325 was the focus for Muslims all over northern
India. Muhammad bin Tughluq has been blamed by scholars for
destroying the importance of Delhi as the centre of the Chishti order,
but in actual fact Nizamu'd-Din's successor, Shaikh Nasiru'd-Din Chiragh-
i-Dihli, died in 1356 without bequeathing the Chishti mantle to a
successor. And in any case centralization was no part of the sufi tradition.

In Bengal, the Chishti order was introduced by Siraju'd-Din Akhi
Siraj (died 1357), who lived in Gaur. His successors, the most popular
of whom was Nur Qutb-i-'Alam (died 1410), established their
khanqahs in Pandua. In close touch with this Bengal centre was the
Rudauli centre, about fifty miles east of Lucknow. Another Chishti,
Saiyid Muhammad Gesu Daraz (c. 1320–1422), made the first capital of
the Bahmani Dynasty, Gulbarga (in the north of the present Karnataka
State), the centre of his activities. A number of other Chishti 'saints',
compelled by Sultan Muhammad bin Tughluq to leave Delhi for
Daulatabad, also became instrumental in spreading Chishti sufism in the

Deccan. The disintegration of the central power, and the emergence of the provincial dynasties in the fifteenth century, provided more patrons, and led to the establishment of Chishti khanqahs all over India.

The Chishti sufis urged their disciples to lead a life of poverty and asceticism. Their simple life devoted to Allah, their dependence upon the charity of ordinary people, and their immediate distribution to the poor of any money they received, made a favourable impression upon all sections of the Muslim population, and even upon Hindus. Their most popular practice was *sama'* (the recital of holy songs), which was intended to arouse a state of ecstasy in their audience. In the thirteenth and fourteenth centuries the 'ulama' tried to have the government stop the practice, and several open debates were held to condemn sama', but they were foiled by sufi influence. In attempting to restore orthodoxy and forge an alliance with the 'ulama', Shaikh Nasiru'd-Din Chiragh and some of his disciples managed to persuade the 'ulama' in their turn to moderate their attitude towards sama', which gave it some respectability in strict circles.

By the thirteenth century, the sufi theory of the Unity of Being, or Oneness of Existence, known as *Wahdatu'l Wujud*, which had emerged through the works of the sufi scholar Ibn 'Arabi (1165–1240), had made an impact on the whole ethos of Islam. It differed both from the Ash'arite conception of 'the necessary (*wajib*) existence of the Creator, Who alone exists from all eternity and alone is self-subsisting', and from the Indian monist view 'Thou Art That'. Ibn 'Arabi emphasized that, as transcendence and immanence are two fundamental aspects of Reality, God is both Transcendent and Immanent. 'He is absolute Being, and is the sole source of all existence; in Him alone Being and Existence are one and inseparable.' 'There is no such thing as union with God in the sense of becoming one with God, but there is the realization of the already existing fact that the mystic is one with God'.

This philosophy was very compatible with the theistic philosophy of Gorakhnath and his followers, known in sufi literature as Nath Yogis, Nath Panthis, Kanphata (split-ear) Yogis, or simply as Yogis or Jogis, who dominated the popular level of Hindu religious and ethical life from the thirteenth to the fifteenth centuries. Various anecdotes indicate that sufis approved of some ethical values of the Yogis as well as of their corporate way of living.

At sama' gatherings in many khanqahs, Persian poetry began to be relegated to the background as Hindawi poetry, with all its Shaivite and Vaishnavite imagery, came to the fore. Since Hindawi poetry was already at a highly developed stage by the time Mulla Daud (a nephew of Shaikh Nasiru'd-Din Chiragh) wrote the *Chanda'in* in 1379–80, it would seem that there must have been a much earlier Hindawi poetry now lost. Fifteenth- and sixteenth-century sufi Hindi poetry developed equally well in both rural and urban environments. The emergence of fifteenth-century *sants* ('saints') such as Kabir and Nanak, and the devotional literature associated with them, which constituted a new phase in bhakti, were the result of two centuries of interaction between Hindu sants and sufis.

The development of madrasas changed the intellectual and ethical climate. In the main they followed the curriculum evolved by Nizamu'l Mulk, and trained 'ulama' (scholars) to man the civil service. This training for an administrative career included the study of works of Qur'anic exegesis, Hadis, and some sufi texts, but the main emphasis was on *fiqh*. The madrasas and their teachers were mostly supported by state grants and stipends, but the system was free enough for madrasas to be established by nobles and the pious rich. The 'ulama' tried to influence state policy, and prevailed upon the rulers to enforce orthodoxy. Balban, 'Ala'u'd-Din Khalji, and Muhammad bin Tughluq, however, ensured that the 'ulama' had as little influence as possible upon affairs of state.

Scholars have differed in their interpretation of the process of Islamization. Sir Thomas Arnold, nurtured in the liberal traditions of Europe, seeks in his *Preaching of Islam* (1895) to present the process as a purely peaceable movement led by the sufis. Modern Muslim scholars, particularly Indian Muslims, think that the rigidity of the caste system was responsible for the conversion of low-caste Hindus to Islam. A contemporary view, expressed by the eminent Chishti saint, Ja'far Makki, whose long life stretched from the close of Muhammad bin

Tughluq's reign to the early years of Sultan Bahlol Lodi's, was that
conversions were very complex phenomena. Fear of death or of the
enslavement of families, promises of rewards and pensions, prospects of
booty, and, lastly, the bigotry of the Hindus, were the main factors in
proselytization. He considered that Muslim preaching also contributed
to Islamization, but that there was no place for such preaching in
Chishti khanqahs. By withdrawing state support for proselytizing
actively and stopping forced conversion to Islam, Akbar compelled the
preachers and the orthodox to rely on their own resources, thereby
courting their hostility.

The fifteenth and sixteenth centuries saw the introduction of many
new elements into Islam in India. One was conflict between the
followers and opponents of *Wahdatu'l Wujud*, exacerbated by the arrival
of the disciples of Shaikh 'Ala'u'd-Daula Simnani (1261–1336), the
great Irani opponent of Ibn 'Arabi. He believed that Wahdatu'l-Wujud
was the initial stage in the development of sufism, the final stage being
his own theory of *Wahdatu'sh-Shuhud* (Unity of Perception). He urged
his followers to lead an active life of missionary work, and strongly
denounced the quiet and passive life of the khanqah. Simnani's *Shuhudi*
ideology received its main setback when the Shattari order was
established by Shaikh 'Abdu'llah Shattari, who reached India towards
the end of his life, after visiting many sufi centres in the Middle East. In
India he travelled as far as Bengal before returning to Malwa, where he
died in 1485. He loudly challenged everyone, sufi and yogi alike, either
to teach him Unity of Being if they knew more than he, or to learn
about it from him. While he himself propagated his mission in Malwa,
his disciples established strong Shattari centres in Bengal and Jaunpur,
where the writing of beautiful sufi poetry in local dialects blossomed.

The Emperor Humayun's devotion to the Shattaris made him
unpopular with all other sufi orders, particularly with the Naqshbandis,
who were the patron saints of the Turanis or Central Asian Muslims and
so also Babur's. In Humayun's reign the Naqshbandis suffered
temporary eclipse, but under Akbar many Naqshbandi saints occupied
high government posts.

In the fifteenth century the Qadiri order, started by Shaikh 'Abdu'l Qadir Jilani (1077–1166), established a firm hold in the Panjab and Sind. The celebrated sufi scholar, Shaikh 'Abdu'l Haq Muhaddis of Delhi (1551–1642), had Qadiri preceptors, but the order owed its popularity not to him but to the Sindhi, Miyan Mir (1550–1635), who advocated a broad and humane outlook on life, and urged both Jahangir and Shah Jahan to be considerate to all groups of their subjects. Distinctions between believers and *kafirs*, and heaven and hell, were frivolous; true prayer was devoted obedience to the will of God. His disciple Mulla Shah was both a mystic and a poet. He defined a believer as one who could reach God and behold him, and a kafir as one who failed to do so. Mulla Shah had been Dara Shukoh's preceptor, and after his execution Aurangzeb tried to harass him, but such was his popularity that the Emperor was unable to do anything more drastic than banish him from Delhi.

Babur and Humayun were accompanied to India by a large number of Irani scholars, poets, and philosophers, as well as by soldiers of fortune, and Akbar's patronage of the arts and sciences accelerated the immigration of the first three groups. Bada'uni, the orthodox Sunni historian at Akbar's Court, gives us to understand that all of them were Shi'is, but in fact many of them were Ishraqis or Tafziliyas. Both the latter schools believe that although 'Ali should have succeeded Muhammad as the first Caliph, the matter was not of sufficient importance to let it cause bitterness so long afterwards.

Akbar's tolerant administrative laws, which deprived Sunnism of its position of dominance, upset many of the orthodox. They made common cause with elements

Tomb of Itmadu'daula

dissatisfied for political reasons and in 1580 organized an abortive rebellion; as a result, not only the political leaders, but also their supporters from among the theologians, were punished. This made the orthodox change their tactics. Instead of opposing Akbar, they now sought to influence his policy by making a show of loyalty to him. At the same time, they misrepresented his policies and activities so as to arouse hatred against him, and also reviled the élite supporting the Emperor, blaming them for the downfall of orthodoxy. As a result of their efforts, Akbar has gone down in history as the founder of a new religion, which subsequently came to be called Din Ilahi, but which was never defined by his accusers, who merely presented a distorted view of his eclecticism and new policies. The orthodox Sunni point of view is voiced in *Najatu'r Rashid*, written by Mulla 'Abdu'l Qadir Bada'uni in 1591.

Tension between the various religious groups mounted during Jahangir's reign. Immediately after his accession he banished Shaikh Nizamu'd-Din Faruqi Thaneswari, an eminent Chishti saint, for blessing his rebellious son Khusrau. Jahangir then imprisoned Saiyid Ahmad Afghan, a devoted supporter of 'Ala'u'd-Daula Simnani's Wahdatu'sh-Shuhud, for he was known to have a great following among the Afghans and thus be a likely danger to the state. In 1610 Jahangir had a distinguished Irani Shi'i, Qazi Nuru'llah Shustari, flogged to death, although he was seventy years old.

Striving to benefit from the accession of Jahangir were Shaikh 'Abdu'l Haq Muhaddis Dehlawi and Shaikh Ahmad Sarhindi. They wrote letters to distinguished nobles and imperial officials urging them to persuade the Emperor to accord dominance to the Sunni Shari'a. Naqshbandi hagiological literature has exaggerated Sarhindi's achievements, and modern scholars regard him as having been the saviour of Sunnism, but in fact his efforts failed to induce Jahangir to make any noticeable change in Akbar's policy of universal concord. The Emperor continued to admire saints of peaceable disposition, such as Miyan Mir and Mulla Shah. In Shah Jahan's reign, the Chishtis again became prominent, although the Qadiri was the predominant sufi order.

In Akbar's reign a large number of Sanskrit works were translated into Persian under his patronage, and after his death such translations continued to be made by Muslim scholars working on their own initiative. Of paramount importance was Dara Shukoh's *Majma'u'l Bahrain*, proving that Hindu and Muslim mysticism were parallel streams which could be made to meet without much difficulty. His most valuable contribution to religious literature was a Persian translation of fifty-two Upanishads, which he completed within six months in 1656–7, with the collaboration of Hindu Sanskritists. His approach to Reality was Vedantist, and differed from that of other sufis whose system was more compatible with that of the Nath Yogis.

The reign of Shah Jahan saw the reconciliation of Avicennian philosophy with Sunni orthodoxy. The leader of the movement which brought this about was Mulla 'Abdu'l Hakim Sialkoti, who wrote several works on Peripatetic philosophy and the physical sciences.

By Shah Jahan's time two Naqshbandi schools had emerged, Khwaja Baqi Bi'llah's sons followed the general pattern of sufism in Delhi; they indulged in sama', believed in Wahdatu'l-Wujud and paid little attention to the admonitions of Mujaddid, the title by which Shaikh Ahmad Sarhindi came to be known. Sarhind was the only centre of any standing to impart the teachings of Mujaddid. Its luminaries were Mujaddid's sons, Khwaja Muhammad Sa'id and Khwaja Muhammad Ma'sum. Muhammad Ma'sum had great expectations of Aurangzeb when a prince, although the story that Aurangzeb was his disciple cannot be proved. Both brothers went on pilgrimage in 1656, and did not return until Aurangzeb had ascended the throne. Muhammad Ma'sum occasionally visited Aurangzeb at Court, where his own son Shaikh Saifu'd-Din had a position, but more often communicated by letter, thanking God that Sunni orthodoxy had been restored. Shaikh Muhammad Ma'sum took the credit for several puritanical administrative reforms introduced by Aurangzeb; but it clear that, in his commitment to restore Sunni orthodoxy, Aurangzeb relied not upon one man, but upon all the orthodox for support. No sudden change in state policy was possible, but harassment of ordinary people by his *Ihtisab* (moral censorship) department strengthened the Emperor's orthodox image. A number of saints and scholars quite unconnected with Mujaddid's descendants were far ahead of Muhammad Ma'sum and his successors in attempting to restore orthodoxy.

The rise of the Mujaddidis was resented by many eminent Chishtis, and their khanqahs vied with one another in exposing them as selfish opportunists. Towards the end of Aurangzeb's reign, the Chishtis obtained great influence through the untiring efforts of Shah Kalimu'llah Jahanabadi (died 1729) who, although he himself lived in Delhi, sent his disciple, Shah Nizamu'd-Din (died 1730), to the imperial camp in the Deccan. Nizamu'd-Din was advised to enrol disciples at all costs, and was even permitted to accept Hindus and Shi's as disciples without converting them to Sunnism; he settled in Aurangabad, and took the name of the town.

It is wrongly presumed that the influence of Shi'ism declined in Aurangzeb's reign. Following Akbar's policy of Deccan conquest, Aurangzeb did indeed seize the two Deccan Shi'i states, but no Shi'i is known to have lost his job or standing for religious reasons.

By the beginnings of the eighteenth century, although the political power of Islam had begun to disintegrate, India Sunni religious and ethical values had crystallized into marked attitudes. The Mujaddidi outlook, strengthened by the officials in Aurangzeb's Ihtisab department, was narrowly orthodox, legalistic, and militant, refusing to tolerate any other group. Their aim was to uproot Shi'sm, destroy Hinduism, and desecrate Hindu places of worship, if not openly then secretly. The Chishti group belonging to Shah Kalimu'llah Jahanabadi's school advocated coexistence with Hindus, Shi'is, and even with militant Sunni groups. Supported by them, and generally helped by the Qadiris and the Shattaris, were a large number of Muslims whose families had retained Hindu social practices after their ancestors' conversion, particularly in villages in Bengal and in the Deccan. The urban Muslim religious élite of Delhi and Lahore frowned upon these syncretic

practices. Nevertheless the rural classes formed the overwhelming
majority of the Muslim population, and they form it to this day.

Sikhism

HEW MCLEOD

FOR THE STRICTLY ORTHODOX SIKH the faith which by preference he
calls *Gurmat* (in contrast to the western term 'Sikhism') can be regarded
as nothing less than the product of direct revelation from God. Gurmat
means 'the Guru's doctrine'. God, the original Guru, imparted his
message to his chosen disciple Nanak who, having intuitively
apprehended the message, thereby absorbed the divine spirit and
became himself the Guru. This same divine spirit passed at Nanak's
death into the body of his successor, Guru Angad, and in this manner
dwelt successively within a series of ten personal Gurus. At the death of
the tenth Guru, Gobind Singh, the divine spirit remained present
within the sacred scripture and the community of the Gurus' followers.
He who accepts the teachings of the Gurus as recorded in the scripture
(*granth*) or expressed in the corporate will of the community (*panth*) is
truly a Sikh. In its more extreme form this interpretation holds that the
actual content of Gurmat is wholly original, owing nothing of primary
significance to the environment within which it emerged.[1]

Even if one is unable to accept a doctrine of divine inspiration,
there remains an obligation to consider the teachings of Nanak and
his successors in terms of genuine originality. Having acknowledged

[1] 'It is altogether a distinct and original faith based on the teachings of Guru
Nanak in the form of Ten Gurus, and now through Guru Granth Sahib and the Khalsa
Panth.' Gobind Singh Mansukhani, *The Quintessence of Sikhism*, Amritsar, 1958, p. I.

Guru Nanak

this measure of originality we must also pay heed to those features of Sikhism which so obviously derive from sources within contemporary Indian society. This must be done in the light of the complete range of Sikh history, from the period of Nanak to the present day. The conclusion which will follow is that Sikhism is indeed a unique phenomenon, but that this uniqueness derives more from its later development than from its earliest forms of custom and belief.

Sikhism is generally held to derive from the teachings of the first Guru, Nanak (1469–1539). In a sense this is true, for there can be no doubt that the doctrines which he taught survive within the community to this day. Moreover, there can be no doubt that a direct connection links the community of today with the group of disciples who first gathered around Nanak in the Panjab during the early years of the sixteenth century. In another sense, however, the claim is open to obvious objections. An analysis of the teachings of Nanak will demonstrate that the essential components of his thought were already current in the Indian society of his period. Nanak taught a doctrine of salvation through the divine Name. Others were already preaching this doctrine, and a comparison of their beliefs with those of the early Sikh community plainly shows that Nanak taught from within a tradition which had already developed a measure of definition.

This was the *Nirguna Sampradaya*, or Sant tradition of northern India, a devotional school commonly regarded as a part of the tradition of Vaishnava bhakti. A connection between the Sants and the Vaishnavas does indeed exist, but there are distinctive features of Sant doctrine which distinguish it from its Vaishnava antecedents. Most of these can be traced to its other major source, Tantric Yoga. The most prominent of the Sants prior to Nanak was Kabir, and it is no doubt due to the obvious similarities in their teachings that Nanak has sometimes been represented as a disciple of his predecessor.

This debt to the earlier Sant tradition must be acknowledged if there is to be any understanding of the antecedents of Nanak's thought. It is, however, necessary to add that, as far as can be judged from surviving Sant works, Nanak raised this inheritance to a level of beauty and coherence attained by none of his predecessors. From the quality of his Panjabi verses and the clarity of the message expressed in them it is easy to appreciate why this particular man should have gathered a following of sufficient strength to provide the nucleus of a continuing community.

The thought of Nanak begins with two groups of basic assumptions. The first concerns the nature of God, who in an ultimate sense is unknowable. God, the One, is without form (*nirankar*), eternal (*akal*), and ineffable (*alakh*). Considerable stress is thus laid upon divine transcendence, but this alone does not express Nanak's understanding of God. If it did there would be, for Nanak, no possibility of salvation. God is also gracious, concerned that men should possess the means of salvation and that these means should be abundantly evident to those who would diligently seek them. There is, Nanak insists, a purposeful revelation, visible to all who will but open their eyes and see. God is *sarab viapak*, 'everywhere present', immanent in all creation, both within and without every man.

The second group of assumptions concerns the nature of man. Men are by nature wilfully blind, shutting their eyes to the divine revelation which lies about them. They commonly appreciate the need for salvation, but characteristically seek it in ways which are worse than futile because they confirm and strengthen humanity's congenital blindness. The Hindu worships at the temple and the Muslim at the mosque. Misled by their religious leaders they mistakenly believe that external exercises of this kind will provide access to salvation. Instead they bind men more firmly to the transmigratory wheel of death and rebirth, to a perpetuation of suffering rather than to the attainment of bliss.

This, for Nanak, is maya. In Nanak's usage the term does not imply the ultimate unreality of the world itself, but rather the unreality of the values which is represents. The world's values are a delusion. If a man accepts them no amount of piety can save him. They must be rejected in favour of alternative values. Salvation can be obtained only through a recognition of the alternative, and through the faithful exercise of a discipline which demonstrably produces the desired result.

Nanak's teachings concerning the way to salvation are expressed in a number of key words which recur constantly in his works. God, being gracious, communicates his revelation in the form of the *shabad* (*shabda*, 'word') uttered by the guru (the 'preceptor'). Any aspect of the created world which communicates a vision or glimpse of the nature of God or of his purpose is to be regarded as an expression of the shabad. The guru who expresses, or draws attention to, this revelation is not, however, a human preceptor. It is the 'voice' of God mystically uttered within the human heart. Any means whereby spiritual perception is awakened can be regarded as the activity of the guru.

Duly awakened by the guru, the enlightened man looks around and within himself and there perceives the *hukam* (the divine 'order'). Like its English equivalent, the term hukam is used by Nanak in two senses, but it is the notion of harmony which is fundamental. Everywhere there can be perceived a divinely bestowed harmony. Salvation consists in bringing oneself within this pattern of harmony.

This requires an explicit discipline, the practice of *nam simaran* or *nam japan*. The word *nam* ('name') signifies all that constitutes the nature and being of God; and the verb *simarana* means 'to hold in remembrance'. The alternative verb *japana* means, literally, 'to repeat', and for many of the Sants a simple, mechanical repetition of a chosen name of God (for example Ram) was believed to be a sufficient method. For Nanak much more is required. The pattern which he sets forth consists of a regular, disciplined mediation upon the nam. The essence of the nam is harmony and through this discipline the faithful devotee progressively unites himself with the divine harmony. In this manner he ascends to higher and yet higher levels of spiritual attainment, passing eventually into the condition of mystical bliss wherein all disharmony is ended and, in consequence, the round of transmigration is at last terminated. The proof of this is the experience itself. Only those who have attained it can know it.

For most people a reference to Sikhism will at once evoke an impression of beards, turbans, and martial valour. It rarely suggests doctrines of salvation through patient mediation upon the divine Name. Both, however, belong to Sikhism. In order to understand how they united it is necessary to trace the history of the Sikh community since the time of Nanak.

Concerning Nanak himself relatively little can be known with assurance, apart from the content of his teachings. Hagiographic narratives abound (the *janam-sakhis*), but their considerable importance relates principally to the later period within which they evolved. It seems certain that Nanak was born in 1469, probably in the village of Talvandi in the central Panjab. During his early manhood he was evidently employed in the town of Sultanpur near the confluence of the Beas and Satluj rivers. This was followed by a period visiting pilgrimage centres within and perhaps beyond India, a period which figures with particular prominence in the janam-sakhi narratives. Eventually he settled in the village of Kartarpur above Lahore on the right bank of the Ravi river and then died, probably in 1539.

The pattern of teaching through the composition and communal singing of hymns was continued by Nanak's first four successors and reached a climax in the work of Arjan, the fifth Guru (died 1606). During the time of the third Guru, Amar Das (died 1574), a collection was made of the hymns of the first three Gurus and of other writers (Sants and Sufis) whose works accorded with the teachings of Nanak. To this collection Guru Arjan added his own compositions and those of his father, Guru Ram Das. The new compilation, recorded in a single volume in 1603–4, became the primary scripture of the community (the *Adi Granth* later known as the Guru Granth Sahib). Notable amongst Guru Arjan's own compositions is the lengthy hymn entitled *Sukhmani*, an epitome of the teachings of the Gurus.

In this respect the first four successors followed Nanak's example, faithfully reproducing his teachings in language of sustained excellence. There were, however, significant changes taking place within the community of their followers. The more important of these developments appear to have emerged during the period of the third Guru. Whereas Guru Nanak had laid exclusive emphasis upon the need for inner devotion, Guru Amar Das, faced by the problems of a growing community, introduced features which served to maintain its cohesion. Distinctively Sikh ceremonies were instituted, a rudimentary system of pastoral supervision was begun, three Hindu festival days were appointed for assemblies of the faithful, and the Guru's own town of Goindval became a recognized pilgrimage centre.

An even more significant development, one which should probably be traced right back to the period of Guru Nanak, concerns the caste constituency of the growing community. Whereas all of the Gurus, belonged to the urban-based mercantile Khatri caste, most of their followers were rural Jats. This preponderance of Jats, which continues to the present day, is of fundamental importance in the later development of the community. Many of the features which distinguish the modern community from that of Nanak's day can be traced, as we shall see, to the pressure of Jat ideals.

Signs of Jat influence became apparent during the period of the sixth Guru Hargobind (died 1644), an influence which is perhaps discernible even earlier, during the years under Guru Arjan. It was during this period that the community first entered into overt conflict with the Mughal administration. According to tradition it was Guru

Hargobind who first decided to arm his followers, a decision which he is said to have reached following the death of his father Arjan in Mughal custody.

It was during the lifetime of the tenth Guru, Gobind Singh (died 1708), that the conflict with Mughal authority assumed serious proportions. Sikh tradition ascribes to this period and to Guru Gobind Singh the features which distinguish the later community from its precursor. It is said that Guru Gobind Singh, confronted by the evident weakness of his followers, decided to transform them into a powerful force which would wage war in the cause of righteousness. This he did by inaugurating a new brotherhood, the Khalsa, in 1699.

To this decision and its fulfilment are traced almost all the distinctive features of contemporary Sikhism. All who joined the Khalsa (both men and women) were to accept baptism and swear to obey a new code of discipline. Prominent amongst the requirements of this new code were an obligation to bear the *panj kakke*, or 'Five Ks', and to refrain from various *kurahit*, or 'prohibitions'. The Five Ks comprised the *kes* (uncut hair), the *kangha* (comb), *kirpan* (dagger, or short sword), *kara* (bangle), and *kachh* (a variety of breeches which must not reach below the knee). The prohibitions included abstinence from tobacco, from meat slaughtered in the Muslim fashion (*halal*), and sexual intercourse with Muslim women. A change of name was also required of the initiate. All men who accepted baptism into the Khalsa brotherhood were thereafter to add Singh to their names, and all women were to add Kaur.

Sikh tradition also relates to the period and intention of Guru Gobind Singh another of the distinctive features of the later Sikh community. Immediately prior to his death in 1708 Guru Gobind Singh is said to have declared that with his demise the line of personal Gurus would come to an end. Thereafter the function and the authority of the Guru would vest jointly in the scripture (the *granth*, which accordingly comes to be known as the Guru Granth Sahib) and in the corporate community (the panth, or Khalsa Panth).

There can be no doubt that something did in fact happen in 1699 and no reason exists for questioning the claim that Guru Gobind Singh instituted some kind of brotherhood during his lifetime. Beyond this, however, it is still difficult to proceed with assurance, for there is evidence which suggests that particular features of the Khalsa code must have emerged subsequent to the death of Guru Gobind Singh in response to pressures independent of his intention.

Two of these pressures deserve particular emphasis. There is, first, the continuing impact of Jat ideals upon the community, which numerically the Jats dominated. During the period of the Gurus this influence would have been minimized although, as the events of Guru Hargobind's period indicate, it was by no means without effect. With the termination of the personal authority of the Guru in 1708 the pressure to incorporate features derived from Jat cultural patterns evidently became much stronger. The confused political circumstances of eighteenth-century Panjab further enhanced this Jat ascendancy, for periods of military strife would be handled with much greater success by the martial Jats than by any other group in Panjab society. Their ascendancy was by no means complete (three of the prominent leaders of this period were not Jats), but it was nevertheless extensive and it left its imprint upon the evolving community. The militant attitude of the Sikh community must be traced to the source, together with particular features such as the Five Ks.

The second of the important eighteenth-century influences also concerns the battles of that century. Because Ahmad Shah Abdali chose to represent his invasions as a Muslim crusade, the Sikh resistance developed a pronounced anti-Muslim aspect.[2] To this development can be traced the three examples of the Five Prohibitions cited above.

It was also during this critically important century and the early decades of its successor that the Sikh doctrine of the Guru emerged in its modern form. For Nanak the guru, the voice of God, spoke mystically within the human heart. Because Nanak was believed to give utterance to the divine message the title was conferred upon him, and upon his nine successors in the manner of a single flame successively igniting a series of

---

[2] Ahmad Shah Abdali of Afghanistan invaded north India nine times between 1747 and 1769.

torches. The death of Guru Gobind
Singh without surviving heirs created
a serious crisis, for ever since the time
of the fourth Guru, Ram Das, the
office had been hereditary within his
family of Sodhi Khatris. An attempt
was made to continue the pattern of
personal authority (a disciple named
Banda was widely acknowledged as
leader until his execution in 1716),
but disputes within the community
and its dispersion during the period
of persecution which followed
Banda's death eventually produced a
different pattern of leadership.

 During this period and the
subsequent years of the Afghan
invasions there emerged twelve
separate guerilla bands (the *misls*).
In order to preserve a measure of
cohesion the leaders of the misls
assembled on specified occasions
to discuss issues of common
interest. Together they constituted
the Sikh community and it was as
a community (panth) that they
deliberated.

A further development in the doctrine of the Guru came during the early nineteenth century when Maharaja Ranjit Singh, having established his dominance over his fellow *misaldars*, suppressed these confederate assemblies. The doctrine of the Guru Panth then lapsed into desuetude and in its place the theory of the Guru Granth assumed virtually exclusive authority. The presence of the Guru in the scriptures had long been acknowledged. All that was required was a shift in emphasis.

To this day the Guru Granth Sahib occupies the central position in all expressions of the Sikh faith. Decisions are commonly made by using it as an oracle, continuous readings are held in order to confer blessing or avert disaster, and the presence of a copy is mandatory for all important ceremonies. The scripture which is used in this manner in Guru Arjan's collection, the *Adi Granth*. It should be distinguished from the so-called *Dasam Granth*, a separate collection compiled during the early eighteenth century which derives from the period of Guru Gobind Singh. Although the *Dasam Granth* also possesses canonical status it is in practice little used. The bulk of the collection consists of a retelling of legends from Hindu mythology.

Another institution which deserves special notice is the Sikh temple, or gurdwara (*guraduara*, literally 'the Guru's door'). Following earlier precedents the disciples of Nanak in any particular locality would regularly gather in a room set aside for their communal hymn singing (kirtan). This room (or separate building) was called a *dharamsala*. As the community's interests expanded beyond the narrowly devotional into areas of much wider concern the function of the *dharamsala* expanded accordingly. In the process its name changed to guraduara. The gurdwaras still remain the centre and focus of the community's activities, partly because their substantial endowments provide a considerable annual income. Contemporary Sikh political activity (expressed through the Akali party) depends to a marked degree upon control of the wealthier of these institutions. The most famous of all gurdwaras, and still the primary centre of Sikh political power, is the celebrated Golden Temple in Amritsar.

Out of these five centuries of history there has emerged the modern Sikh community, a community which occupies in the life of

India today a position of prominence considerably in excess of its actual numerical strength.[3] Sikhs today are renowned for their participation in progressive farming, the armed forces, sport, and the transport industry. In all four areas the prominence belongs principally to Jat Sikhs, the caste group which still constitutes more than half of the total strength of the community. Of the other groups which have significant representations within the community, the Khatris and the Aroras, both mercantile castes, are more particularly distinguished for their work in manufacturing industries, commerce, and the professions. Other substantial constituents are a group of artisan castes, jointly known as Ramgarhia Sikhs; and converts to Sikhism from the scheduled castes (Mazhabi and Ramdasia Sikhs).

Although a measure of caste consciousness certainly persists within the community, all can join the Khalsa brotherhood and observe the common discipline.

Medieval Indian Miniature Painting

Pramod Chandra

THE PAINTING OF THE PERIOD ushered in by the rise of Islam to political supremacy in India can be divided into two broad movements. One of these exemplifies an attempt to preserve past traditions with almost superstitious tenacity. These traditions, though often emptied of meaning, retained at least the trappings of outer form which, in more propitious

---

[3] The total number of Sikhs living in India today is approaching $6^1/_2$ million, or 1.75 per cent of the country's population. Of this total number 94 per cent live in the Panjab, Haryana, Delhi, and the northern districts of Rajasthan. There are substantial pockets of Sikh emigrants in East Africa, Malaysia, and England. (More than 75 per cent of the recent entrants into the United Kingdom from India have been Sikhs.) Smaller groups are to be found in several other countries.

times, were again to quicken with life. The second movement is rooted in new artistic forms introduced primarily from Iran in the wake of the Muslim invasion. The old and the new, the 'foreign' and the 'indigenous', had gradually to come to terms with each other; and this process, in which the individual qualities of each were enhanced and brought to a new fulfilment, resulted in some of Indian painting's greatest achievements.

That the early Muslim kings of India who ruled before the Mughal emperors patronized painting has been denied by some, mostly on grounds of their religious scruples, in spite of the rather explicit statements in contemporary literature to the contrary. But this view, like many others on the painting of this period, is proving to be quite incorrect. Patient exploration and study is constantly adding to the list of illustrated manuscripts produced between the thirteenth and sixteenth centuries, even though it must be admitted that they indicate little that is distinctive, much of the work being a somewhat impoverished imitation of the various styles of contemporary Iran. A manuscript of the *Bustan* in the National Museum of India painted at Mandu for the Sultan Nasir Shah Khalji (AD 1500–10)[1] differs little but for colour from the sub-schools of Herat; significantly enough, however, an illustrated manuscript of the *Ni'mat Nama* of almost the same date (*c.* AD 1500),[2] though indebted to the contemporary style of Shiraz, shows pronounced Indian features, particularly in draughtsmanship and the rendering of female figures, and may therefore be counted as representative of a stage of artistic development when Persian influences are beginning to be assimilated by the Indian painter, a process that is of profound importance in the creation of the Mughal, and to a much lesser extent of the Rajasthani style in the sixteenth century.

The national style of the period was the western Indian style, found in one version or another over almost all of India. Surviving examples indicate that the greatest concentration was in Gujarat and that the main

---

[1] R. Ettinghausen, 'The Bustan Ms of Nasir-Shah Khalji', *Marg*, Vol. 12, No. 3 (1959), pp. 42–3.

[2] R. Skelton, 'The Ni'mat Nama: A Landmark in Malwa Painting', ibid., pp. 44–50.

Golden Temple

patronage was provided by the Jainas, though this may be accidental and occasioned by the especial care with which that community preserved its sacred books. Manuscripts with Hindu themes are known as well, and we also have illustrations done in Rajasthan, Delhi, and Jaunpur in eastern India. The style is emphatically linear, the forms flat, with sharp angular contours, the faces generally in profile but with both eyes shown, one of them protruding into empty space. The colours are few, red, green, blue, yellow, and black predominating, a monochrome patch of red often constituting the background.

Difficult though it may be to believe at first sight, the western Indian style is directly descended from the classic style of ancient India established around the fifth century AD, so brilliantly represented and preserved at Ajanta, and is the result of a progressive simplification, abstraction, and linearization, the various stages of which are clearly demonstrable. Though not immune to stylistic change, the western Indian style was nevertheless remarkably conservative, adhering closely to set formulae right up to the end of the sixteenth century, around which time it gives way under the pressure of rising new schools.

Though the conservative character of the western Indian style is generally accepted, it has nevertheless to be realized that around the middle of the fifteenth century the style does begin to show signs of real change, though it is not clear whether this is due to acquaintance with paintings of Persian derivation or due to a natural development of its own inherent tendencies. Paintings illustrating this change are rare, but are clearly represented in three fine illustrated manuscripts, the *Kalpasutra* painted at Mandu in 1439, a *Kala-kacharya-katha* of about the same date and provenance, and the *Kalpasutra* produced at Jaunpur in eastern Uttar Pradesh dated AD 1465.[3] The line flows more smoothly, the forms are fuller, and the figures begin to lose their hieratic, effigy-like character. The promise of this new style is carried to fulfilment in the splendid *Bhagavata Purana*, now unfortunately dispersed in collections all over the world, and the *Chaurapanchashika* of Bilhana in the museum at Ahmedabad.[4] A more refined version of this style is to be found in manuscripts like the *Chandayana* of Mulla Daud in the Prince of Wales Museum,[5] Bombay, which is marked by a preference for pale and cool shades of colour, of Persian inspiration, together with a delicate and fine line.

The first half of the sixteenth century, as far as painting is concerned, was a time of fervent activity. We find in existence at this time Indo-Persian styles, patronized presumably by Muslim courtly circles, a western Indian style, and new styles developing from it which have not yet been named but are represented by the group of manuscripts, including the *Bhagavata Purana* and the *Chaurapanchashika*, mentioned above.

Thus the stage was set when in AD 1556 Akbar, a grandson of Babur, the founder of the Mughal Empire in India, ascended the throne. The

---

[3] Moti Chandra and K. Khandalavala, 'A Consideration of an Illustrated Ms from Mandapadurga (Mandu) dated AD 1439', *Lalit Kala*, 6 (Oct. 1959), 8–29, and 'An Illustrated Kalpasutra Painted at Jaunpur in AD 1465', ibid., 12 (Oct. 1962), 9–15; P. Chandra, 'A Unique Kalakacarya-katha Ms in the Style of the Mandu Kalpasutra of AD 1439', *Bulletin of the American Academy of Benares*, 1 (Nov. 1967), 1–10.

[4] K. Khandalavala and Moti Chandra, *New Documents of Indian Painting*, Bombay, 1969, pp. 83–4, 79–83.

[5] Ibid., pp. 91–8.

young emperor had himself received training in painting as a child and his teacher, Khwaja 'Abd us-Samad of Shiraz together with Mir Saiyyid 'Ali of Tabriz had been leading artists in Iran before they came to India at the invitation of Humayun. Under the general supervision of these two artists and the discerning enthusiasm of Akbar, whose role as a patron was of the greatest importance, a vigorous atelier of painters drawn from all parts of the Indian Empire grew up at the imperial court. These artists brought with them elements of the various traditions to which they belonged and, in what is probably the earliest work of the Mughal School, the *Tuti Nama* of the Cleveland Museum of Art,[6] we can actually see the process by which their disparate idioms were welded to form something new—a style which represents a synthesis of the Persian and the Indian but is different from both. Very soon we have the fully formed Mughal style in the unusually large illustrations of the *Dastan i-Amir Hamza*,[7] the most ambitious undertaking of the atelier of Akbar, quite unlike Persian work in its leanings towards naturalism, and filled with sweeping movement, bright colour, and an innate sense of wonder.

The *Hamza Nama* was certainly completed by AD 1575 and an undertaking of this scale was never again attempted by the Akbari atelier. It was followed by a group of profusely illustrated historical manuscripts which share several hundred paintings between them. The earliest of these now known is an incomplete history of the house of Timur, once extending to the twenty-second year of Akbar's reign and now in the Khuda Bakhsh Library at Patna;[8] and one of the most accomplished is the *Akbar Nama* in the Victoria and Albert Museum, London.[9] The Patna manuscript can be dated about AD 1584 while the *Akbar Nama* should not be more than a decade later. The miniatures are smaller in size than those of the *Hamza Nama* and the most notable

[6] S.E. Lee and P. Chandra, 'A Newly Discovered Tuti-nama and the Continuity of the Indian Tradition of Ms. Painting', *Burlington Magazine*, 55 (Dec. 1963), 547–54.

[7] H. Glück, *Die indischen Miniaturen des Haemsae-Romanes*, Vienna, 1925.

[8] A Muqtadir, 'Note on a Unique History of Timur', *Journal of the Bihar and Orissa Research Society*, 3 (1917), 263–75.

change from the point of view of style is an ebbing of the explosive energy and movement and its gradual replacement by a studious striving for delicacy and refinement. Most of the paintings are the result of joint work by two artists, one of them the designer, generally an important painter, if not a master, and the other the artist who actually applied the colour and 'painted' the picture. To these is sometimes added a specialist in portraiture and, in rare instances, we get the name of the artist who mixes the colours, indicating the close attention paid to the manufacture and use of colour.

Stylistically belonging to the same phase as the historical manuscripts are the remarkable illustrations to the Persian adaptations of the Hindu epics, the Mahabharata and the Ramayana, the imperial copies of which are now in the collection of the Maharaja of Jaipur.[10] The Mughal painters, most of whom were Hindus, here had a subject close to their hearts, and they rose to great heights, revealing an endlessly inventive imagination and great resourcefulness in illustrating the myths.

The closing phases of the style of Akbar are marked by the growth of a very personal and intimate idiom, shown in a series of illustrations to works of classical Persian poetry, notably the *Khamsa* of Nizami in the British Museum, a *Khamsa* of Amir Khusrau Dihlavi in the Walters Art Gallery, Baltimore, a *Diwan* of Hafiz in the Reza Library at Rampur, and other poetical manuscripts.[11]

The outstanding painters of the reign of Akbar, according to the perceptive court chronicler Abu'l Fazl 'Allami, were Daswant and Basawan. Of Daswant's work the greatest part is preserved in the Jaipur Mahabharata, and, though another painter is associated with him

[9] E. Wellesz, 'An Akbar Namah Ms.', *Burlington Magazine*, 80 (1942), 135–41.

[10] T.H. Hendley, *Memorials of the Jeypore Exhibition*, Vol. 4, London, 1884.

[11] F.R. Martin, *Miniature Painting and Painters of Persia, India, and Turkey*, London, 1912, Pls. 178–81; E. GrŸbe, *Classical Style in Islamic Painting*, Venice, 1968; and S.C. Welch, 'Miniatures from a Ms. Of the Diwan of Hafiz', *Marg*, Vol. 11, No. 3 (1958), pp. 56–62.

in these paintings, his genius is manifest. Basawan's paintings are more broadly distributed and we have in him a painter of extraordinary accomplishment, who builds primarily in colour, prefers full and voluminous forms, and shows a great understanding of human emotions and psychology.

The painting of Jahangir's reign (AD 1605–27) departs markedly from the style of the Akbar period, though many elements that come to the fore had been previously anticipated. The tradition of book illustration is gradually abandoned and there is a pronounced emphasis on portraiture. The great darbar pictures, thronged with courtiers and retainers, are essentially an agglomeration of a large number of portraits. The compositions of these paintings are also much more restrained, being calm and formal. The colours are subdued and harmonious, as is the movement, and the exquisitely detailed brushwork is a marvel to behold. A large number of studies of birds and animals were also produced for the Emperor, who was passionately interested in natural life, and who never ceased to observe, describe, measure, and record the things rare and curious with which the natural world abounds.

To Jahangir, painting is the favourite art; he prides himself on his connoisseurship, and greatly honours his favourite painters. Abu'l Hasan, the son of Aqa Riza, who migrated to the Mughal Court from Herat, is most admired; Ustad Mansur is singled out for praise as a painter of animals and birds; and Bishandas is said to be unequalled in his age for taking likenesses.

With Shah Jahan, whose main interest was architecture, but who was also a keen connoisseur of painting, the Jahangiri traditions are continued, but in a modified way. The compositions become static and symmetrical, the colour heavier, the texture and ornament more sumptuous. The freshness of drawing, the alert and sensitive observation of people and things, is overlaid by a weary maturity, resulting not in the representation of living beings but in effigies with masked countenances. The output of the imperial atelier also appears to decline so that there are far fewer works available, and of these the *Shah Jahan Nama* in the collection of Her Majesty Queen Elizabeth,[12] looted during the sack of Lucknow by British troops, is the finest and most representative example of the style.

During the reign of Aurangzeb (AD 1658–1707) patronage seems increasingly to shift away from the court; works which can be identified as products of the imperial atelier are extremely few and continue the style of Shah Jahan. This would at least indicate a lack of interest, though Aurangzeb's antipathy to the arts has been greatly exaggerated. The fairly large number of paintings assigned to his reign were probably executed for patrons other than the Emperor, this leading to an inevitable decline, for Mughal painting was essentially a carefully nurtured court art, and its removal from the natural habitat led to its impoverishment and debasement. There was a brief revival during the reign of Muhammad Shah (AD 1719–48), but the rapid disintegration of the Mughal Empire sealed the fate of the arts which were intimately associated with it. Artists dispersed to the various provincial centres where the great nobles were establishing kingdoms of their own, and there, on occasion, the new environment induced a brief spasm of life. The decay, however, was irreversible, and was reinforced by the change in taste, progressively corrupted by ill-understood Western influences. Thus when the Mughal style finally passed into oblivion it was natural for it to be replaced by the so-called Company School, catering specifically to the patronage of the British ruling class in India and to the Indian gentry whose traditional tastes had been already subverted.

The Rajasthani style of painting, spread mainly over the various states of Rajasthan and adjacent areas, came into being at approximately the same time as the Mughal School, but represents a direct and natural evolution from the western Indian style, and from painting in the style of the Bombay Asiatic society's Mahabharata, rather than a revolutionary transformation of those traditions, as was the case with the Mughal style. The subject matter here is essentially Hindu, its primary concern the Krishna myth, which was the central element in the rapid expansion of

---

[12] L. Ashton (ed.), *Art of India and Pakistan*, London, 1949, Pl. 138.

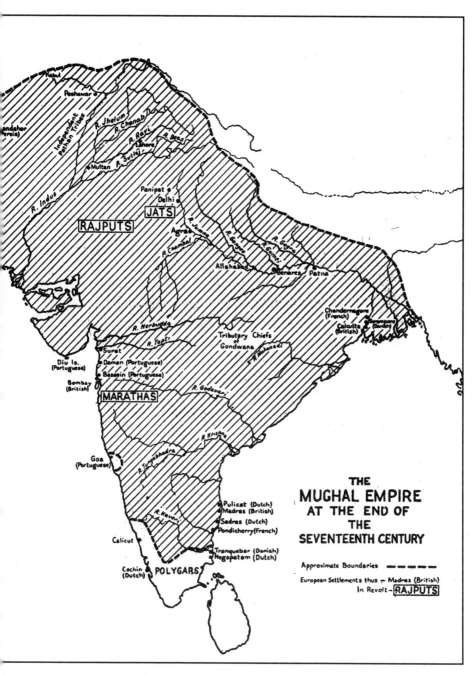

Mughal Empire at the end of the 17th century

devotional cults at this time. The style, in marked contrast to the naturalistic preferences of Mughal painting, remains abstract and hieratic, and its language, though mystical and symbolic, must have immediately evoked a sympathetic response in the heart of the Hindu viewer.

The Rajasthani style developed several distinct schools, their boundaries seemingly coinciding with the various states of Rajasthan, notably Mewar, Bundi, Kotah, Marwar, Kishangarh, Jaipur (Amber), Bikaner (which is something of an exception to the rule in being quite heavily indebted to the Mughal School), and yet others whose outlines are slowly beginning to emerge. The School of Mewar is among the most important, producing pictures of considerable power and emotional intensity during the seventeenth century, the early phase between 1600 and 1650 marked by the dominance of the School of Sahibdin, a painter whose name has been fortunately preserved. The fervour of the early years begins to subside towards the close of the seventeenth century, and eighteenth-century paintings, though often full of charm, never capture the earlier mood. The School of Bundi, sharing slightly more with the Mughal School than does the School of Mewar, comes into being about the end of the sixteenth century and is distinguished by a more refined line and a love for vivid, rhythmic movement which survives well into the eighteenth and even the nineteenth century in the spectacular scenes of sport and hunt painted in the neighbouring state of Kotah. The vitality of many Rajasthani schools, even in the nineteenth century, when the Mughal style had collapsed and shifting patronage under Western influence made survival difficult, is really quite remarkable.

The School of Kishangarh, filled with lyrical mysticism, is one of great charm and finesse, owing much to Mughal technique of the eighteenth century. It is, however, much more consciously stylized, and, in its best works, quite transcends the inane secularism of the late Mughal style from which it was derived.

The Pahari style is yet another important school of miniature painting, so called because of its prevalence in the former principalities of the Himalayan foothills, stretching roughly from Jammu to Garhwal. Two broad phases have been distinguished. The earliest Pahari paintings are marked by bold colour, vigorous drawing, and what can be called a primitive and intense expression, analogous to the mood of some early Rajasthani painting of the first half of the seventeenth century, though the Pahari examples are later in date and executed on a much more sophisticated and accomplished level. The themes are Hindu, and shared in common with Rajasthani painting. The name most commonly used for this kind of work is the 'Basohli' style, after a state of that name, but paintings in a similar idiom are found in other hill states also. The later phase of the Pahari style that comes into its own about the third quarter of the eighteenth century is similarly called the 'Kangra' style after a state of that name, though it too is found in other hill centres.

More poetic in mood, though similar in technique to the Mughal School, the Deccani style again evolves as a combination of foreign (Persian and Turkish) and somewhat strongly indigenous elements inherited seemingly through the artistic traditions of the Vijayanagara Empire. The various kingdoms of the Deccan plateau evolved idioms with their own distinctive flavour from the middle of the sixteenth to the nineteenth century. Of these, the Bijapur version, particularly under the patronage of the remarkable Ibrahim 'Adil Shah II (1580–1627) is marked by a most poetic quality. Important work was also done in the powerful sultanates of Golconda and Ahmednagar. Contemporary with the Mughal School, the Deccani styles were in close contact with it, and their development too follows a parallel course. In the eighteenth century, Hyderabad, the capital of the Asaf Jahi Dynasty, became a very vigorous centre of painting, a large volume of work similar in mood to the output of provincial Mughal centres being produced there.

The history of Indian painting from the thirteenth to the nineteenth century is filled with many riches and what has been said above provides only the faintest indications of its wealth.

PART THREE

Challenge and Response—
The Coming of the West

The Mughals
and the British

Percival Spear

Though the British did not themselves overthrow the Mughals, but stepped, region by region, into their empty political shoes, they found everywhere traces of Mughal rule and unquestionably made much use of them in their reconstruction. A glance at the foregoing is enough to show that the British were by no means so original in many of their contributions to India as one has been tempted to think. The British achievement must be judged in conjunction with that of its Mughal predecessors, as the Mughals themselves must not be credited with what they took over from their past.

The concept of the emperorship as a semi-sacred office apart part from the old religions was a Mughal innovation. At first the British spurned this. One could hardly imagine a less sacred institution than the East India Company, or a less mystical person than the governor-general. This common-sense attitude strengthened with success until it received a rude shock when the Mutiny revealed the depth of sentiment still surrounding the Mughal *padshah* and Maratha Peshwa. The assumption of government by the Crown and the personal attitude taken by Queen Victoria towards India were in fact leaves taken out of the Mughal book. The assumption of the imperial title in 1876 was a corollary of the move of 1858, not in itself anything new.

There is a close relationship between the British and the Mughal revenue arrangements. From Bengal to Gujarat, as the British spread over the country, they found either Todar Mal's★ *bandobast* in decline, or beheld its relics in the form of custom or what was done 'before the troubles'. They took over the Mughal system of exact measurement of the land, of distinguishing soils and crops in estimating production, and of using various kinds of agents in collection. At first they were flexible than the Mughals in such matters as remissions on account of floods and famine and in dealing with defaulters, with much resulting hardship. The harsh dealings at the time of the Bengal famine of 1770[1] and the overassessment in the early days of the Delhi territory are examples. With experience they improved. Their assessments became more accurate and scientific, their revenue demand more lenient as well as more predictable than that of their predecessors. On the whole their achievement was notable, for they built up a rural administration not only stable but generally equable and equitable. There were, however, two significant departures from Mughal practice. One was the action of Cornwallis, Pitt, and Dundas in creating the Permanent Settlement of Bengal in 1793 (which extended to Bihar, Orissa, and parts of the Madras Presidency). This converted the zamindars into something like English landlords and their peasants virtually into tenants-at-will, giving them the unearned increment of land which was then far from completely cultivated. Zamindari had long been recognized as a form of property; it was the British who turned it into landed property.[2] The consequence was the creation of a landed class which as a whole was loyal but not progressive, tenacious but not enterprising. This work was already being undone when the British left India. The other departure

★ Akbar's revenue minister—pub.

[1] See W.W. Hunter, *Annals of Rural Bengal*, London, 1897, p. 39. Thirty-five per cent of the peasantry died. Less than 5 per cent of the revenue was remitted in 1769/ 70: it was increased by 10 per cent in 1770/1.

[2] See Irfan Habib, *The Agrarian System of Mughal India*, London, 1962, Ch. V.

was the system of selling up defaulters in the land revenue, instead of bullying them as the Mughal officials did and then leaving them in possession. This produced a displacement of classes, tending to replace old rural families by absentee city-dwellers, more interested in rents than tenants.

The Mughal *mansabdari* system as an effective executive service was in collapse before the British began to rule. It cannot seriously be maintained that the British restored it or borrowed from it. But it is significant that they found that they could not do without an equivalent. Their administration did not settle down until they had organized a service recruited with some eye to ability, trained to some extent for the duties it had to perform, inculcated with a high sense of duty, and disciplined both financially and morally.

The British had two separate services, the civil and military, as compared to the undivided Mughal one, and the civil had several subsections. The foreign ascendancy was progressively reduced until even the highest of the services, the India Civil Service, was half-Indian. Here indeed was a contribution of value to contemporary India. The services were handed over intact to the new administration as going concerns. They were loyal to authority and to each other. They were highly capable, they possessed a high morale, they were aloof from politics, and they possessed a degree of self-reliance and readiness to act in emergencies which was unusual in such bodies. Though shorn of their European cadres the services possessed enough Indian members who had been sufficiently integrated to shoulder the burden of independent administration.

A further Mughal bequest to the British was official ostentation, arrogance, and greed. These epithets were freely applied by ambassadors, travellers, and merchants to the 'omrahs' in the Mughal heyday and to nawabs in general in the eighteenth century. It was not inadvisedly that the merchant officials who returned from Clive's Bengal and Benfield's Madras with fortunes were called 'Nabobs' in England. The early Company's officials, or many of them, undoubtedly shared in the Mughal ostentation and greed. But neither lasted long, the one swept away by the economies of a utilitarian age and the other by the reforms of Cornwallis and his successors. The most corrupt and colourful of services became in the nineteenth century the most dutiful and sedate; our only regret must be that in shedding their colour the services also lost some degree of imagination.

The Mughal policy of tolerance was extended and amplified by the British. But while it was more complete it was also more frigid, for the Mughals, while occasionally demolishing temples, would also endow others, give grants to Hindu as well as Muslim divines, and patronize Hindu festivals. The religious neutrality of the government, as pressured by Christian groups in Britain, forbade all this and left the people with a feeling of aloofness and disdain.

When we turn to the Mughal cultural heritage, we come to a parting of the ways with the British. Influence there was, but it was peripheral and fleeting. The British remained faithful to their own style of building, limiting their Mughal loans to the ornate marble bathroom with sunken bath (up-country) and to Bengali style annexes for the 'zenana'. They patronized the miniature painters to some extent and used them widely for studies of buildings, plants, and animals; they were even influenced in their own painting by Indian techniques. But this died away as European contacts increased and photography came in. The taste for Persian literature did not survive the generations of Warren Hastings, Metcalfe, and Elphinstone.

It is now possible to consider the rest of the British contribution in its own right, as it were. The observer who visits India today will still find many visible traces of the British. Houses, public buildings, and memorials strew the land. But he will not see much of these for long. The houses were mostly brick-built and are subject to decay and change; most of the public buildings are quite undistinguished. Few of the more pretentious possess much merit and some of those that possess it are copies from England, like Barrackpore House in Calcutta. The British brought with them the classical vogue of eighteenth-century England which produced a number of graceful churches and houses in Calcutta and elsewhere. Thereafter Gothic came in, with its memorials in the Calcutta and Lahore cathedrals and 'P.W.D.' churches. The Gothic fashion extended to bungalows, but though there was some graceful imitation of the classic style, the Gothic never took root in India. Then came Lord Curzon, who intended a British Taj Mahal and achieved the Calcutta Victoria Memorial. In its ostentation, its obtuseness, and its solidity it was not an unfitting symbol of the current imperialism. The final British effort was New Delhi, where Lutyens and Baker disagreed in producing something of high merit and symbolic beyond their intentions. For the central complex as it now stands is an epitome, not of imperial power, but of bureaucracy. A rocky eminence, approached by a processional way, is crowned by two secretariat blocks, with the legislature dropped on one side as an apparent afterthought (as indeed it was), and the central feature of the President's (ex-Viceroy's) house pushed (unintentionally) too far back to be dominant.

In considering the British impact as a whole it is necessary to distinguish between the various functions which they performed. They

Hockey—a game introduced by the British

dominated the country for a century and a half as its rulers; they acted
as agents for the entry of ideas and techniques from the West; and they
possessed characteristics of their own which they implanted on the
country. The first impact is the more obvious, the second the more
profound, and the third the most engaging. Taking the last first, we may
note, as characteristics of the British as a people, marked individualism,
a love of sport and games, class-consciousness, and the habit of working
in groups. Some of these traits, like class consciousness and love of
sport, dovetailed into existing social habits. But in the realm of sport the
British have added to the Indian stock by contributing their own
games. In hockey India once led the world, but it are three others,
football in Bengal, tennis and cricket everywhere, which have attained
the level of addiction and become part of the country's contemporary
life. British individualism has worked by example rather than precept; it
has been an impalpable influence in promoting independence in a
society weighted with the restrictions of caste, the authority of parents
and the joint family, and the reverence for age. The cooperative or
group mode of action has taken root in the vogue of the committee,
from the Congress down to the tennis club.

As for the British political impact, let us first consider the judicial
system and the rule of law which went with it. The judicial system
began with Mayor's Courts in the settlements which were, however,
only intended for the settlers themselves. Later the Supreme Court was
set up in Calcutta (1774), which created confusion by applying British
law to Indian cases. With the acquisition of Bengal the Company at first
took over the Mughal courts; in fact in that respect they were then
Mughal agents. A long period of trial and error may be said to have
culminated with the completion of the Indian Penal Code. By that time
India had a complete judicial system from High Courts downwards,
which is functioning smoothly today. It was the first official sphere in
which Indians won distinction, and perhaps for that reason is specially
cherished. The law administered was Hindu and Muslim on the personal
plane, and Muslim tempered with British humanism in the criminal
sphere. The effect of thus bypassing the British penal system in the early

years of the nineteenth century was to make it more humane than the contemporary British system. Since then a great body of commercial and public law has been added, drawing on British precedents.

The idea of a secular law, related to justice but apart from the great religions, has been implanted in the Indian mind. It is to the judge, not to the pandit or the *mulla*, that people look for justice. The courts stand out as a secular embodiment of the concept of right. They form in fact a pillar of the secular state.

A second characteristic of the courts has been their independence, not only from religious interference, but notably from the state executive. They have continued this course in both India and Pakistan, with general approval. This independence of the judiciary on political issues, which England may claim to have won in the seventeenth century, was something new to Indian experience.

There remains the rule of law, which both emphasizes the independence of the courts and provides a safeguard against executive tyranny. The idea that the government could be sued as of right instead of being petitioned as of grace or mercy, was something quite new. If the government itself could be sued with impunity, why not the big man of the district, the zamindar, the princeling, the wealthy entrepreneur? The whole legal process did much to implant the idea of individual civil rights in the popular mind.

A further British contribution was the introduction of the idea that the positive promotion of public welfare was a normal duty of government. Classical Hindu and Muslim ideas of government called for non-interference. The early Company's officials took over this view and maintained it into the nineteenth century. But pressures, religious, rational, and utilitarian, mounted in Britain which led Tory Ellenborough to write in 1828 to the Governor-General Lord William Bentinck: 'We have a great moral duty to perform.' The India debates of Hastings's time and the eloquence of Burke had enforced the principle of responsibility of the government for good administration. With Bentinck the further step was taken of positive promotion of public welfare. The first steps in this direction were the negative ones of the prohibition of sati (suttee),

St John's Church, Calcutta

the suppression of *thuggee*, and the discouragement of infanticide. But they were followed by the new education policy, the introduction of English, irrigation projects and the building of roads and railways, and health measures. Self-interest may have entered into some of these measures, and in many respects it may be held that they did not go nearly far enough. Nevertheless the principle was there, a principle which nationalists often used as a rod with which to beat the foreign government and cheerfully accepted afterwards. Was it not in the name of this principle that Gandhi launched his attack on the salt tax? With Nehru the new government accepted in principle, and to some extent realized in practice, the idea of a welfare state.

The principle of welfare can take many forms. One of these in the British case was the development of self-government. For this in itself no originality can be claimed, for it is not to be supposed that Indians in general have in the political sphere desired anything else through the centuries of foreign domination. But representative and parliamentary government was something new, and it is this which the British, in the later stages of their rule, introduced into the country and which has taken root. The British rulers in India were themselves inclined to the Mughal idea of the state; these innovations were almost entirely due to pressure from outside. The first ideas of the ultimate independence of a modernized India appeared in the 1820s and 1830s with men like Mountstuart Elphinstone and Macaulay, but little was done to implement them for another eighty years. Representation of Indian opinion was introduced in a tentative way, to reach its logical development with the Morley–Minto reforms in 1909. The advent of responsible self-government on the parliamentary model was a twentieth-century development, beginning as late as 1921 with the inauguration of the Montagu–Chelmsford reforms. Nevertheless it immediately took root; this type of government became a fixed Indian demand and has been sedulously maintained since independence.

Along with parliamentary government we must link nationalism. This is perhaps one of the most remarkable examples of the British impact, for the British neither designed, nor formally introduced, nor advocated it. Nationalism was 'caught' by the new Indian intellectuals, especially in Bengal, by the joint effect of observing the habits of the British and studying their literature. Mother India, a new secular goddess, was created. The feeling was recruited on the intellectual plane by the study of Continental as well as English writers, especially Mazzini, and on the emotional by its linkage with religion. To Mahatma Gandhi belongs the credit of bringing it to the people at large, and presenting it as a religious but not a sectarian cult. Indian nationalism has a distinctive ethos of its own, but it is a fact of the present day and it owes its existence to the British impact.

The concept of welfare has many forms. In the 1830s it included the education and language policy of the Indian Government. Briefly, English was substituted for Persian as the language of government and the higher courts, the local languages being used in the lower. English also became the medium of instruction in the higher government educational institutions, and the content of learning included contemporary Western knowledge. Western science and history therefore came into the curriculum, and the whole range of Western ideas and attitudes was conveyed through English and European literature. Admittedly the motivation of the policy was mixed, as was that of the Indian attitude towards it. But, if a supply of English-knowing subordinates was one motive on the British side, so also was the desire to throw open Western intellectual treasures to the East. While on the Indian side many learnt English as a passport to a career, there was an active group led by the reformer Ram Mohan Roy which desired the spread of Western knowledge for its own sake.

The role of the British as agents covers much of the British material achievements and also much ideological merchandise. In the former realm the British were the agents for the developing science of the West with its inductive logic and experimental methods. The first visible sign of this importation was the Calcutta Medical College established by Bentinck, where dedicated Hindu students broke caste in the name of the new knowledge and the new methods. These new principles came in their theoretical form through the colleges and in their concrete form at first through engineering and then through the new industrialism. The growth of the mechanized cotton industry in the later nineteenth century was symbolic of practical India's acceptance of Western techniques, as the growth of private arts colleges was symbolic of Indian acceptance of Western ideas. The word acceptance should not be interpreted as wholesale adoption to the exclusion of Indian ideas. It would be more accurate to say that these things were entertained alongside their Indian counterparts. The critical process of assimilation had still to come, but it was recognized that these things had come to stay in the country and in future had to be reckoned with as part of its heritage.

On the ideological side must be placed the whole range of ideas and values which come from the West. Officials, non-officials, and missionaries carried them in very varied forms, but these forms were all expressions of fundamental concepts rooted in the West as a whole. None of these things were really new to India viewed in her totality; they were new to contemporary India because they had been overlaid by custom through long stretches of Indian history. Intellectually the concept of the critical reason, more particularly a product of the Enlightenment, was introduced under the cloak of criticism of Indian customs, institutions, and ideas. The cry of 'superstition' and 'abomination of heathenism' were Anglicized versions of Voltaire's 'écrasez l'infâme' and further back of Greek scepticism. When these things roused echoes in Indian minds it was the European tradition as a whole rather than the British in particular that they were recording.

From the same basis of European values came the emphasis on universal human rights and duties, on the rights of the individual as a person, and his responsibility for and to society as a whole. These things came in the British forms of evangelical and radical humanism, of the radical rights of man, and of Whig contractual civil rights. But they had their root more immediately in French thought and more ultimately in the whole classical Christian tradition. To this source must be ascribed social criticism of such things as sati, infanticide, Hindu widowhood, caste, and popular religious cults. Equally from the same source must be derived the positive aspect of these ideas, the equality of all not only before God but also before the law, the personality and citizenship of women as well as men, the principles of democracy. The part of the British in introducing these things was very great. But in this respect they are to be judged, not so much by the things they sponsored, as by the fidelity of the sponsorship. As in the material sphere, we cannot say that these things would not have come without them; we can only say that they would have come at a different time and in a different way.

Hindu Religious and Social Reform in British India

J. T. F. Jordens

Introduction

Viewing the millennia of Indian history, one can hardly think of a greater contrast than the one that exists between eighteenth-century and twentieth-century India. On the one hand we have a stagnating traditional culture and society at very low ebb, in fact in a state of decadence not witnessed before, a decadence condemned by most modern Indians from Ram Mohan Roy onwards. On the other hand, we have a still traditional society in the throes and the creative excitement of modernizing itself, of emerging as a new nation, remaining thoroughly its own and rooted in its culture, yet taking its place in the contemporary world. The nineteenth century was the pivotal century that saw the initiation of this process, that brought about an enormous transformation in the religious, social, economic, political, and cultural spheres.

Social and religious reformers were, naturally, not a new phenomenon in Hinduism; in fact in some ways the very nature of Hinduism is to be continuously adaptive and reformist. Yet the nineteenth-century reform movement was in general distinguished from previous Hindu reform by a cluster of new characteristics. It became closely wedded to a political movement, and consequently sought to influence political authority, administration, and legislation. This political movement became very soon an all-India nationalist movement, and reform acquired a nationalist flavour and an all-India extension.

The reformers themselves had no doubts as to the main stimulants of this new spirit. The British administration, English education, and European literature brought to India a constellation of fresh ideas which constituted a challenge to the new intellectuals. Rationalism as the basis for ethical thinking, the idea of human progress and evolution, the possibility of 'scientifically' engineering social change, the concept of natural rights connected with individualism, were all alien to traditional society. An equally strong influence was exerted by the ideas and the work of the Christian missionaries.

I. The First Stage: Up to 1880

In the first decades of the nineteenth century, India had already produced a small new social group, the English-educated intelligentsia, mostly closely associated with British administration or British trade. It was amongst these

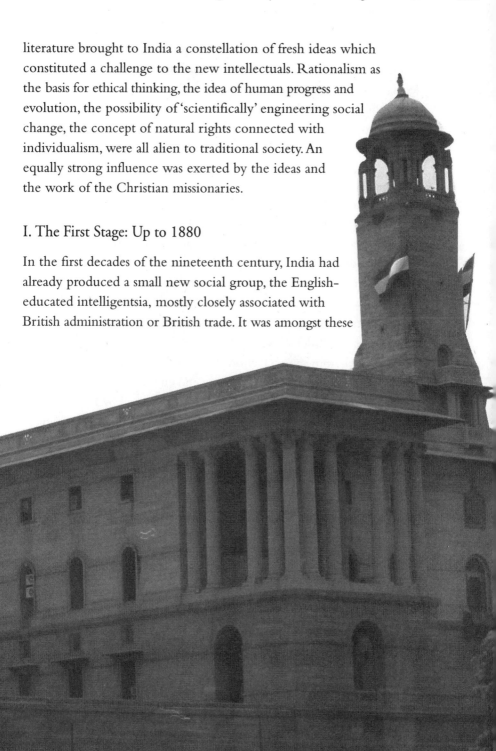

people that several ideas of reform first arose. They were primarily trying to deal with a personal problem that affected their own lives very deeply: constant contact with Britishers and European ideas made them look upon some social and religious characteristics of their own society with horror and disgust. There was not as yet any concern for the mass of the people, or any desire to transform the structure at large.

Bengal

Bengal was the first to undergo significant British influence and to produce the new English-educated group. By the early 1800s we notice already a crystallization of different reactions to Western influence, and there emerge three distinct groups, the radicals, the reformers, and the conservatives. Ram Mohan Roy (1772–1833) was the first great modern reformer, and has for good reason been called 'The Father of Modern India'.

In the religious sphere Ram Mohan's main target of attack was the Hindu system of idolatry, its mythology and cult. He proposed as an alternative a deistic type of theism, strongly influenced by European deism and the ideology of the Unitarians with whom he had close links.

As a social reformer, Ram Mohan's interest was mainly in the appalling condition of women in Hindu society, an interest that was to dominate the social reform movement for many decades. He is rightly famous for his long and successful campaign for the abolition of sati, the self-immolation of widows on the funeral pyres of their husbands, and he fought incessantly against child marriage and for female education.

Ram Mohan's method was primarily propaganda, leading on to agitation. His propaganda was carried out by streams of tracts from his pen, all related to his reforming ideas. This was reinforced by journalism: he was a pioneer in the birth of the vernacular press, mainly through his Bengali and Persian weeklies. He also strongly promoted English-type education as the main instrument for reform. The crowning achievement of Ram Mohan's organizational efforts was the foundation of the Brahmo Sabha (later known as Brahmo Samaj) in 1828. This was a religious body 'to teach and to practise the worship of One God'. It had a temple of its own, where congregational worship took place, free from idolatry and superstition, modelled mostly on Unitarian worship. During Ram Mohan's lifetime and for a decade afterwards, it was but a small body of men gathering regularly for religious services, but later under new leaders it gained greater significance.

Ram Mohan never broke with Hinduism, and in his public life he was careful not to offend the orthodox: he felt reform had to be carried out from within the Hindu community. This view was repudiated by the young radicals of the time, led by the brilliant Eurasian teacher Henry Derozio (1809–31), whose movement came to be known as 'Young Bengal'. Their religion was rationalism, and they bitterly attacked orthodoxy in all its aspects. Not only was their talk revolutionary, but their actions often matched their convictions: some threw away their sacred thread, ate beef, and openly flaunted their contempt for Hinduism, and for 'half-liberals' like Ram Mohan. Orthodox society was up in arms and acted swiftly to dismiss Derozio from Hindu College and put pressure on the other young men. It was a massive campaign in which many suffered severely even from their families. Derozio's premature death in 1831 weakened Young Bengal, and by the 1840s it was dead as a movement: the youth of its members, their lack of clear ideology and leadership, their isolation from real society, were handicaps too great to allow them to survive as a group the onslaught of the orthodox. But many individuals of this group, matured by age, trained in the hard school of rational thought and fired with burning nationalism, became outstanding figures in government posts and in the hectic political and cultural life of Bengal.

After Ram Mohan Roy's death the Brahmo Samaj was in the doldrums for a decade, and then Debendranath Tagore (1817–1905) took over its leadership and gave it a new direction. He changed the Samaj from a loose society into an organization with members formally initiated by a ceremony. He drew up a declaration of faith, established a theological school, sent out the first Brahmo missionaries, and created a new liturgy, the 'Brahma Rites'. He himself was inclined towards the contemplative and the bhakti aspect of Hinduism, and averse to Ram Mohan's rationalism. With a stress on devotion, ethical duties, and the near-Vedic but non-idolatrous Brahma rites, the Samaj moved closer to the mainstream of Hinduism, as it grew quickly in numbers. Its main preoccupation was with religious not social reform, and it avoided offending orthodoxy too much.

But with Keshub Chandra Sen (1838–84) a new wind started to blow in the Samaj. Soon after his accession to the Society, Debendranath elevated him to leadership next to himself. Keshub was an impatient iconoclastic reformer, repudiating all Hindu cult, rejecting caste and the seclusion of women. In religion he had a new 'universalistic' tendency, with strong leaning towards Christianity. Soon the Samaj split in two; on the one hand Debendranath and the older members, cautious in reform, Hindu in religion, formed the Adi Brahmo Samaj; on the other Keshub and his young men, impatient and cosmopolitan, established the new Brahmo Samaj of India. Sen's Samaj was the most popular. Universalism was stressed by the introduction of selected texts from the great religions, and on the other hand the connection with Hinduism and with Bengal was strengthened by the adoption of modes of worship characteristic of the followers of Chaitanya, such as the public devotionalism of the *samkirtan*. In the social sphere too Keshub forged ahead, and in 1871, after visiting England, he founded the Indian Reform Association, which organized female education, workers' education, charity, and temperance bodies. Keshub achieved a great success in the passing of the Marriage Act (1872) which legalized Brahmo marriages. This, however, was perhaps the main factor in effectively separating the Brahmos from the Hindu community, thus impeding greatly their effectiveness as a leaven of society.

It was perhaps the influence of Ramakrishna that made Keshub become increasingly obsessed with his own religious development. When in 1878 he allowed his thirteen-year-old daughter to marry a prince with Hindu rites, it was the occasion for the majority of Brahmos to break away, forming the Sadharan Brahmo Samaj. Of the three Samajs it was the Sadharan which persisted and remained a force for reform in Bengal.

During this time Bengal also produced the scholar Ishvarachandra Vidyasagar (1820–91) who took up the widow remarriage movement, the first social reform cause that was taken up all over the country, and who saw it to a successful conclusion.

Maharashtra

From 1840 on we find in Maharashtra ample evidence of a growing religious and social reform awareness. There were already in many places local reform groups and societies, many of which were started by students of the Elphinstone Institution founded in 1827. In this early stage two personalities already stand out. Gopal Hari Deshmukh (1823–92), known as Lokahitawadi, was English-educated and destined for a legal career. His writings in Marathi contained bitter attacks against the social iniquities of traditional society, the caste system, and the condition of women. He also denounced loudly that typical feature of Maharashtra, the absolute intellectual and moral dominance of brahmans over Hindu life. His friend and collaborator Jotiba Govind Phule (1827–90), of low caste, took up this fight against brahmanic oppression in his voluminous prose and poetic works, and gave it a concrete form in his organization for the uplift of the low castes, the Satyashodhak Samaj. Among many theoretical reformers, Phule was a very practical man: he started girls' schools, schools for untouchables, and a foundling home for widows' children. His passionate and practical concern was for the poor, the low-caste workers, the peasants. In his work we find the beginnings of the later political anti-brahman movement of Maharashtra, and also of the trade unions.

In 1867 Maharashtra brought forth its own organization of religious and social reform, the Prarthana Samaj. It was a visit of Keshub Chandra

Sen as a Brahmo Samaj missionary that inspired the Maharashtrians to found their own society.

Despite similarities to Bengal, the movement in Maharashtra was also in certain aspects quite different from its Bengali counterpart. The Maharashtrians saw reform as a gradual process of transformation of values and institutions. There was no need to revolutionize the social fabric or the Hindu religion. As a result they concentrated on the propagation of their ideas through education and writing on the one hand, and they got down to the practical task of social work on the other.

The Prarthana Samaj, as an organization, never had a great influence. But its members, like M.G. Ranade, R.G. Bhandarkar, and K.T. Telang, were among the great leaders of nineteenth-century Maharashtra and they became the founders of the Social Reform Movement in later years.

North India

Northern India in the meantime produced a real Hindu Luther, whose reform work was to have the deepest and most lasting effect. Dayananda Saraswati's (1824–83) formative years were very different from those of most other reformers, for whom English education was a major element in their development. Dayananda, from a Gujarati brahman family, ran away from home in his youth to become an ascetic. For seventeen years he wandered around India, putting himself to school under different teachers, and observing Hinduism with a closeness no other reformer ever achieved. In 1863 he became a wandering preacher, and five years later he added the establishment of schools to his activities. In 1875 he published his major work, the *Satyarth Prakash* and founded his reform society, the Arya Samaj.

Dayananda's theological vision was one that emerged neither from a personal mysticism nor from Western ideas, but from the intimate observation of the corrupt Hinduism of his day. He attacked polytheism,

Victoria Memorial

idolatry, and the many superstitious beliefs and rites connected with them, and the stranglehold of the brahmans on sacred lore and religious practice. He had the vision of a primeval monotheism, above the paraphernalia and hostilities of all human creeds. This religion, he felt, was in fact the original Vedic religion, which was contained in the four Vedas but had become corrupted over the centuries.

In his reform of ritual, Dayananda was inspired by the same spirit. Though he purged them of their idolatrous and superstitious impurities, he kept the basic rites of Hinduism: the five daily sacrifices and the sixteen sacraments. To these he added the new reformist type of communal worship, including the singing of hymns, sermons, and lectures, besides the new *homa* sacrifice.

The contemporary caste system was nothing but the utter degeneration of the original Vedic varna system: society was then divided in four classes according to the deeds and qualities of each individual person, and women had equal rights with men. That was the system, Dayananda felt, to which India should return, and the main instruments of reform would have to be three: schools would rear the children in the new spirit, completely isolated from contemporary society; government action would reclassify people according to qualities and merit; and a *shuddhi* campaign would bring Christians and Muslims back to the Hindu fold.

The beginnings of the Arya Samaj were tentative. Although many aspects of Dayananda's social platform and the iconoclastic side of his religious programme appealed to many, the intellectuals of Bombay and Calcutta, influenced as they were by their own provincial attitudes towards religious reform, found Dayananda's Vedic creed not at all palatable. But after a few years the Samaj scored explosive success in the Panjab, and from then on it became the most broadly based movement of all.

II. The Second Stage: 1880–1900

From 1880 two important tendencies which had been stirring in the previous decades occupied the Indian scene: nationalism and political action. From now on individuals and groups openly identified themselves with an Indian nation, a new concept in Indian history; and this élite group, consciously nationalist, conceived its function as being primarily one of political agitation and reform. This predominance of nationalism and politics now began to exert influence on the ideas of religious and social reform which had previously prevailed. Nationalism itself developed two patterns, a religious one and a secular one, and each school assigned a different place to social reform.

Two early outstanding examples of the new religious nationalism are Bankim and Tilak. It is very striking how the religious nationalism of both in fact had deep provincial roots, and may be seen as Bengali and Maharashtrian nationalism respectively, only half-heartedly projected on to an all-India scale. Bankim Chandra Chatterjee (1838–94) found Bengal divided between the traditionalist orthodox and the progressive reformers, both of whom he saw as unable to create a real revival, the ones slaves to rigid tradition, the others blind admirers of the West. Bankim felt that real revival could only be achieved by changing the national character through an internal reform of Hinduism. His novels awoke in the Bengalis, first the middle class, and later the masses, a self-confidence and pride in their language and their religion.

Bal Gangadhar Tilak (1857–1920) was as Maharashtrian in his nationalism as Bankim was Bengali. He too wanted the Indians to become strong again, proud and united in nationalism, and he too saw Hinduism as the very basis of this new spirit. To promote this spirit he published books and articles, exalting the antiquity and greatness of Hinduism, and preaching activism in his *Gita Rahasya*. But he did more: he inaugurated new Hindu festivals, the Ganapati festival and the Shivaji festival, thus reaching the populace with his ideas of Hindu nationalistic activism, instilling in them a pride in their glorious Maharashtrian past. Although he was not himself against social change, he was against social reform inspired by Western ideas.

It was in the 1880s that the social reform movement at last became organized on a national basis. It was a Bombay Parsi, Behramji Malabari (1853–1912), who launched the issue that set social reform on its way to becoming consciously national: the campaign for the legal checking of infant marriage by an Age of Consent Bill. Malabari's campaign was different from earlier ones in that it was the work of a determined and skilful journalist who was primarily intent on putting the concrete and harrowing reality before the people in such a way that it could not be ignored. The Age of Consent Bill controversy put social reform on the national map and achieved the indissoluble wedding of social reform with the nationalist movement.

When the Indian National Congress was founded in 1885 the question came up immediately whether or not the Congress should include social reform in its deliberations. The question was debated for a couple of years, while the Age of Consent Bill controversy was raging, and it was finally decided to exclude social questions from Congress deliberations, but to form a separate body, The National Social Conference, to meet each year immediately after the Congress meeting. M.G. Ranade (1852–1901) was the key theorist and organizer of this Conference. The first important way in which the Conference broke with the existing provincial social reform bodies, was in its affirmation of a secular ideology: thus it had the same secular roots as the Congress, emphasizing that individual conscience and humanism were the basic motives of reform. The Conference was not an active instigator of reform; its role was that of a national focus of local reform work: local work was given national recognition, and the reformers discussed their aims and methods in this forum, and passed resolutions of an all-India nature.

While during the last two decades of the nineteenth century the evolution described above was going on on the national stage, the provincial reform groups continued their own growth.

Maharashtra

In Maharashtra all major towns started their own local Reform Associations, the activity and growth of which depended much on the individual leaders. An outstanding personality was the widow Pandita Ramabai (1858–1922) who founded in 1890 the Sharada Sadan, a home for high class widows in Poona. She was closely assisted by Dhondu Kheshave (later Maharshi) Karve, who married a widow himself and revived the Widows Remarriage Association of Poona. He too established a home for widows, and promoted female education. The Prarthana Samaj continued its work, and sponsored reform mainly through educational work directed at women and low-caste workers, elementary schools, and orphanages.

Madras

Madras at this time was only just beginning to interest itself in social reform. The rigidity of the caste structure and the slower political awakening in this province were certainly important causes of this delay. In 1892 the Madras Hindu Social Reform Association came into being, led mostly by radical reformers. They, however, were a small high-caste group, and their ambition was mostly turned inwards upon the members, who individually took a number of reformist pledges.

Bengal

In Bengal, where social change had advanced rapidly, social reform went into a depression. The Sadharan Brahmo Samaj was very active in philanthropic work on behalf of the underprivileged and the lower classes, but it was not engaged in social reform as such.

Nevertheless, Bengal did produce a religious figure of immense influence: Ramakrishna (1834–86). A simple temple priest at the temple of Kali at Dakshineshwari near Calcutta, he achieved fame as a great mystic. His doctrine, arrived at by experimentation with other religions, was simply that 'all religions are true', but that for everyone the religion he was born in was the best possible one. In a Shankarite way he did not condemn idolatry, as it met the religious needs of simple people. In the last years of his life he attracted around himself a group of young educated Bengalis who were captivated by his personality and his doctrines. The leader of these was Narendranath Datta (1862–1902), who became Vivekananda, the founder of the Ramakrishna Mission and of a new order of monks.

North India

In northern India, the Panjab and the North-Western Province, social reform was organized in a unique way. General bodies had little impact here: it was the Arya Samaj and the caste organizations that dominated the scene. The Arya Samaj, though it experienced a split between orthodox and liberals in 1893, grew as no reform body every grew: by the end of the century its members were fast approaching 100,000. Their educational work was advancing steadily and they soon rivalled the Christian missionaries in the number of their schools. The Arya Samaj began effectively to reach out to the masses and started the process of changing Hindu society from within.

It was in the north that the first new caste organizations arose. Here the caste system had some characteristics which distinguished it from other regions and made reform through caste possible: the dominance of the brahmans was comparatively weak, the majority of people belonged to intermediate contiguous castes, and the lowest groups were not so depressed as in other areas. Castes were traditionally well organized and held effective power over their members.

In 1887 the Kayastha Conference was formed in Lucknow, comprising the group of subcastes whose traditional occupation was that of writer. The early split of the organization into a reformist and an orthodox section testifies to the eager reformist ideas of a good number of its leaders. Another important organization was that of the Vaishyas, established in 1891. In this period the caste organizations kept away from politics, but in the twentieth century they assumed in several areas of India very great political importance, in fact frequently dominating the political game.

III. The Third Stage: from 1900

The first two decades of the twentieth century saw Indian politics engaged in the great debate between the moderates and the extremists, and in their struggle for control of the Congress. That story is told in another chapter. The development of the social reform movement, however, was intimately connected with that debate and that struggle. The main objections of the extremists against the moderate leadership were two: that in aims and methods the moderates were completely

British-oriented and therefore slow and unpatriotic; and that they did not reach down to the mass of the people. The extremists advocated a militancy based on national and religious identification and wanted involvement of the masses.

However, most of the revivalists, except Tilak, were themselves very much committed to social reform in many spheres of life. The differences lay in inspiration, in motivation, and in the model of society they aspired for. The revivalists succeeded in demonstrating that a purely nationalistic motive and a Hindu model could be the inspiration for whatever reform the reformer envisaged. But they proved more than that: they showed that Hindu nationalism and an ideal Hindu society had a mass appeal that was absent in Western-type reform.

Vivekananda (1863–1902), the great disciple of Ramakrishna, was strongly influenced by very different streams of thought. First there was his Western education and close contact with Keshub's Brahmo Samaj. Then followed the influence of his master Ramakrishna, the Hindu mystic. After the master's death Vivekananda wandered around India, and then he spent several years in America and Europe. The influnece of Ramakrishna on him was very great; it gave him an overriding pride in the theoreitcal and practical achievements of Hinduism. He saw the deficiencies of Hinduism more clearly than many, and he denounced them more vehemently: the tyranny of the brahmans, the degeneration of caste, the stultification of ritual, the physical and moral cowardice. Yet he castigated the reformers mercilessly for their literature of abuse, their 'ornamental' reforms, their arrogance borrowed from a veneer of Western education. The reform he preached passionately was to be evolutionary, not breaking with the past, inspired by the Hindu religious conviction that man is God, reaching out to the root of all evils, the condition of the poor. Such reform would lead to the *punya bhumi*, the holy land of India, where the nobility of man and his spirituality would both be fully developed.

His message, however, was not worked out into a programme, and he did not have a political base; therefore he did not become a national leader. However, his leadership found scope in the Ramakrishna Mission, which in this century has become an important agency of religious reform and social service, especially in Bengal.

The long life of Aurobindo Ghose (1872–1950) was full of contrasts. His education was completely English: from the age of seven he spent fourteen years in England. In an early pamphlet, *Bhavani Mandir*, Aurobindo shows how strongly he had been influenced by Bankim's ideas. We have here the idea of a religious order devoted to the Mother, and to political and social action to regenerate India. From his very early days he also accused the Congress of failing to reach the masses, and proclaimed that it was through the religion of the Mother that the masses could be effectively reached. These ideas came to their full efflorescence during the years when he collaborated with B.C. Pal in the editorship of *Bande Mataram*. His term in jail in 1908, where he studied the *Gita* and experimented in yoga and forms of mysticism, completely redirected his life. He retired to Pondicherry, where he established an ashram. Here he built his own original philosophy of integral non-dualism and achieved the reputation of a great mystic and a saint. He acquired a number of Indian and European followers, but the Pondicherry ashram was very much a circle of initiates in an esoteric gnostic religion without any significant influence on Indian life.

Lala Lajpat Rai (1856–1928), born in the Panjab, was the son of a Hindu father with leanings to Islam, who was a follower of Syed Ahmad Khan, and an orthodox Sikh mother. He was brought up on Islamic teachings, but soon he rejected his upbringing and strongly identified himself with Hinduism. After a time as a member of the

Brahmo Samaj, he joined the Arya Samaj. In 1885 he founded with Hans Raj the Dayananda Anglo-Vedic College at Lahore, and became involved in Arya leadership; at the time of the split in 1898, Lajpat became the leader of the liberal branch. In the last decade of the nineteenth century his initial interest in Congress politics faded, but he came back into the political sphere from 1900 onwards, became a very powerful extremist leader, and was accused by the non-political Aryas of drawing the Samaj into politics against the desire of Dayananda.

Lajpat Rai's writings and actions clearly demonstrate the man and his ideas: Arya ideology wedded to extremist nationalist politics. During the famines of 1896–7 and 1899–1900, he was extremely active in relief operations, largely financed by his own funds, and in 'rescuing' thousands of orphans from Christian missionaries. At the 1900 Lahore Congress he moved the resolution to devote at least half a day of each annual session to the discussion of industrial and educational problems. He was also largely responsible for the new interest of the Arya Samaj in the low castes, and in 1920 he was elected president of the first All-India Trade Union Congress. In October 1928, although his health was failing, he led a procession against the Simon Commission and was struck in a *lathi* charge. This aggravated his condition and he died a fortnight later.

North India

In northern India the Arya Samaj gave the lead. Until 1900 the Samaj had preached caste reform but had not really expected anybody but ardent Aryas to act upon it, and its membership was in fact mostly restricted to the educated classes. From 1900 onwards the Samaj, the two factions collaborating, started a campaign to reform the caste system. The method was nothing short of revolutionary: the low-caste groups were recruited and their status was ceremonially raised to that of the twice-born with rights of interdining and intermarriage. The success of Christian missionaries in converting these low castes was definitely an important factor in the action of the Samaj. In fact the movement for conversion of low castes grew out of the shuddhi movement for conversion of Christians and Muslims, the child of Dayananda's fierce Hindu nationalism, and gradually involved the Samaj more and more in communal agitation and in collaboration with the communal orthodoxy of the Mahasabha. Both by its successful syncretism of social reform and Hindu nationalism and by its successful reaching out to the mass of the people, the Arya Samaj proved the most impressive and influential religious and social reform movement of the era.

Maharashtra

Maharashtra had its own approach: revivalism here did not coalesce with social reform, probably because of the hostility of Tilak and the influence of Ranade. But social reform in the twentieth century expressed its new spirit by an increased concern for the mass of the people. In Maharashtra a great number of societies arose, not unified like the Arya Samaj, but in a way more practical and down to earth in their approach. Only the most important can be mentioned here. The Social Science League, started in 1911 in Bombay by Chandavarkar, active to this day, pioneered in its concern for the working classes by initiating night schools, technical schools, libraries, recreational facilities, and co-operative credit societies. The Seva Sadan, on the other hand, established by Malabari, specialized in the care of women of all castes, providing educational, welfare, and medical services. Maharshi Karve put the crown on his work for women's uplift by inaugurating a women's university.

The Servants of India Society, founded by G.K. Gokhale in 1915, was a society for an élite of dedicated individuals, who were rigorously trained and paid a subsistence salary only. Its membership remained small, its influence as an institution limited, but the work of its members in social reform was very considerable, again in the practical field of famine relief, union organization, co-operatives, and uplift of tribals and depressed classes. The Prarthana Samaj, similarly limited in influence as a body, also entered this field by its most effective Depressed Classes Mission of India, founded in 1906. By 1913 it ran thirty educational institutions and has rightly been called 'a forerunner to Gandhian programmes for the Harijans'. The non-brahman movement of Jotiba Phule, mentioned previously, languished after his death, but was revived in the 1900s by the Maharaja of Kolhapur State. Later on this non-brahman movement was to become a formidable political force in south India. The later movement in Maharashtra for the emancipation of the untouchables, led by Dr Ambedkar, was primarily political in nature.

Madras

After 1900 the slow-starting movement in Madras got under way. Revivalist thought in south India had received a powerful stimulus from Vivekananda's visit and the writings and speeches of Annie Besant, the leader of the Theosophical Society. At first Mrs Besant was an anti-reformist religious revivalist, but around the end of the nineteenth century one of the many changes in her attitudes was on the way, and in 1904 she founded the Madras Hindu Association 'to promote Hindu social and religious advancement on national lines in harmony with the spirit of Hindu civilization'. Her great influence both in Madras and on a national scale supported the new alliance of revivalism and social reform. Madras thus became in tune with the national tendency. The great social problem of the south was the tremendous gap between the high and the low castes, and the utter degradation of the latter. Their rise in status and in power during the twentieth century was spectacular, but not as a direct result of the work of the social reform movement as such. More effective factors were first the great advance in social services for depressed classes and workers, conducted by a variety of organizations, Christian missions, the Theosophical Society, the Depressed Classes Mission, and the Ramakrishna Mission. In fact it has been stated with good reason that before the First World War Madras may have led the rest of India in this field.

Bengal

The situation in Bengal was very different from that in the other provinces. On the one hand Bengal possessed by far the most 'socially reformed' group: the Brahmos and the Western-educated gravitating around them. On the other hand, the social movement as such had become practically non-existent.

A good deal of practical social work was increasingly undertaken, mostly by the Sadharan Brahmo Samaj, but it did not grow out into social reform crusades nor did it take organizational forms.

Conclusion

By the 1920s the Indian religious and social reform movement had lost its peculiar identity as an important and distinct phenomenon of Indian life. Many factors contributed to this. One of them was the appearance on the national stage of Gandhi, who was to dominate and often confuse it with his new ideas on politics, religion, and society. Politics itself developed in a different way, and from now on we see a much closer association of concern for social reform with political awareness and action, and a conviction that the state through legislation must take responsibility for the reform of society. Nehru's concept of the Welfare state embodied this ideal at its best. Another important factor was that agitation for social reform dispersed itself more and more into the practical business of organizing social service in different special fields, such as the education and upliftment of women by the All-India Women's Conference, village development projects, the organization of the depressed classes, and the foundation of labour unions.

The Nationalist Movement

H.F. OWEN

DURING THE SEVENTY OR SO years from the foundation of the first nationalist associations until the achievement of independence, the Indian nationalist movement changed its character in various ways, under the influence of the traditional past and the more recent British past, and also as a result of the new ideas and methods that marked its development. Modifying slightly the periodization which Michael Brecher has distinguished in the history of the nationalist movement,[1] one might divide the history of the movement into (i) the 1870s–1890s: the period of Moderate pre-eminence; (2) the 1890s–1914: the struggle for supremacy within the movement between the Moderates and Extremists; and (3) 1914–1947: the period of agitational politics and Gandhi's leadership. Broadly speaking, in the first of these periods the nationalist movement was essentially British in its intellectual origins; in the second it drew both on indigenous symbols and ideas and upon Western (including British) ideologies and examples; and, in the third period, the movement drew upon widening circles of Indian and imported inspiration while becoming increasingly inventive, particularly under the impetus of Gandhi's creative genius.

Any nationalist movement in a colonial situation is bound to have both a negative and a positive aspect. The negative aspect is the

---

[1] M. Brecher, *The New States of Asia: A Political Analysis*, London, 1963, p. 22.

determination to expel the foreign rulers and achieve self-government; the positive aspect is the concept of the sort of nation which should emerge from the struggle for independence. In negative terms the Moderates aimed at moving slowly towards self-government for India, with the 'white' colonies of the British Empire as their model. The moderate Indian Association emerged in 1876 in Calcutta and spread across northern India with the express goal of stimulating 'the sense of nationalism amongst the people';[2] and from its earliest sessions in 1885 and 1886 the Indian National Congress pointed to Canadian and Australian self-government as the models for India.[3] In terms of the sort of nation they wished to see emerge, the Moderates worked actively for a liberal, secular, democratic India through education and social and religious reform. In this they were carrying forward the social and intellectual reform movements of Ram Mohan Roy, Ranade, and others, aiming, in Gokhale's words, at the selective 'assimilation of all that is best in the life and thought and character of the West'.[4] The Moderates set up associations, such as the Poona Sarvajanik Sabha in 1870, to work for the improvement of the whole of Indian society,[5] seeking educational and other social reforms through their membership of legislative bodies and organizations such as the National Social Conference. They hoped to achieve their ends through the introduction of representative democratic political reforms by the National Congress, and by such methods as public meetings, deputations, and the presentation of memorials—all modelled directly upon British constitutional politics.

[2] Cited in J.C. Bagal, *History of the Indian Association, 1876–1951*, Calcutta, [1953], p. 8.

[3] *Proceedings of the First Indian National Congress held at Calcutta 1886*, Calcutta, 1887, p. 99.

[4] Quoted in T.V. Parvate, *Gopal Krishna Gokhale: A Narrative and Interpretative Review of His Life, Career and Contemporary Events*, Ahmedabad, 1959, p. 164.

[5] See J.C. Masselos, 'Liberal Consciousness, Leadership and Political Organization in Bombay and Poona, 1867–1895' (unpublished Ph.D. thesis, Univ. of Bombay, 1964), p. 286.

The Extremists (who might more happily be termed 'militants', if the other term had not been sanctioned through use by the Extremists themselves and by their opponents or rivals) became increasingly assertive from the 1890s onward, and demanded self-government more rapidly than the Moderates did, and without the latter's concern for gradual preparation. The Extremists' aims in terms of the sort of India they wanted are not so clear cut as those of the Moderates, but they extolled India's pre-British past, particularly its Hindu past, as the model for the present and future, and they deplored what they regarded as the Moderates' over-hasty, subservient, and damaging acceptance of British and other Western models as suitable for reforming Indian religion, society, or polity. Aurobindo, for example, spoke rather vaguely of self-government for India as 'the fulfilment of the ancient life of India under modern conditions' and 'the final fulfilment of the Vedantic ideal in politics'.[6] In this, the Extremists were the political counterpart to the Hindu revivalist movements of the last third of the nineteenth century, represented by such organizations as the Sanatana Dharma Mahamandal, the Arya Samaj, the Theosophical Society, and the Ramakrishna Mission. Both Hindu revivalism and Extremist nationalism were hybrids, springing from Western and indigenous sources. Their indigenous origins were obvious enough—the conscious turning back to the Vedas, the *Gita*, and Vedanta; the defence of Hindu ideas and worship against the criticism of missionaries and liberals; the movements to reclaim Hindu converts to Islam and Christianity initiated in the 1890s; the public festivals in honour of the Hindu god, Ganesh, and the Hindu hero king Shivaji; and the invocation of the Mother Goddess as an embodiment of both Bengal and India, to be cherished and restored, and as witness to

[6] Cited in H. and U. Mukherjee, *Sri Aurobindo's Political Thought (1893–1908)*, Calcutta, 1957, p. 40.

the oaths of patriotic conspiracy. But the very turning back to an idealized national cultural past for inspiration was in the mainstream of nineteenth-century European romanticism and its offspring, nationalism. The Extremist nationalists used largely Western techniques—trying to mobilize the support of public opinion through newspapers and public meetings, employing passive resistance in its various phases,[7] and occasional terrorist tactics. The hybrid amalgam was epitomized in Tilak's famous epigram: 'Swaraj is my birthright and I will have it.' The term Swaraj ('self-rule') was hallowed by its association with the area of the Maratha confederacy which remained self-governing longest; but the whole notion that self-government (now broadened to include the whole of India) is somehow the individual's and the nation's right has a particularly Western ring to it.

The Maharashtrian Extremists of western India were mainly from the Chitpavan Brahman community, which inherited traditions of political leadership and resistance to invaders. It has been argued that they shared a cultural consensus with the lower castes of the region[8] which enabled them to recruit widespread support, but they were also anxious to preserve their social dominance. In the Panjab, on the other hand, the Arya Samaj, which greatly influenced the character of Extremist nationalism there, shared much of the Moderates' rather Western-style concern for reform and the purification of Indian society and religion— notably by assimilating the untouchables in the higher castes. In Bengal, again, the traditions of the high-caste *bhadrolok* who predominated among the Extremists were essentially élitist, making difficult the recruitment of lower-caste, not to mention Muslim, participants. The Extremist nationalists' influence was concentrated in these three regions, and it was partly because of this and their failure to unify or at least to

[7] See Sri Aurobindo, *The Doctrine of Passive Resistance*, Calcutta, 1948; B.G. Tilak, 'Tenets of the New Party' (1907) in *All about Lok. Tilak*, Madras, 1922, pp. 492–505; regarding Western models, see C.M. Case, *Non-Violent Coercion; a Study in Methods of Social Pressure*, New York, 1923, e.g. pp. 326–8.

[8] R. Kumar, *Western India in the Nineteenth Century: A Study in the Social History of Maharashtra*, London and Canberra, 1968, pp. 6–11, 31–2, 319–20, 332.

federate these regional movements that they failed in their attempt to capture Congress. Following their ejection from Congress in 1907, nationalist activity declined markedly.

In 1914 there began a revival of nationalist activity, which led on to the triumph of agitational politics which marks the third period of the movement. Mrs Annie Besant inaugurated this transformation, drawing on both her personal knowledge of radical methods of agitation in Britain and upon her understanding of Indian history and Hindu traditions, acquired as the head of the Theosophical Society. Under her leadership, in conjunction with Tilak, between 1914 and 1918 agitational nationalism began for the first time to spread from the cities into the countryside on a nationwide scale.[9] Under Gandhi's leadership this process gathered momentum.

Gandhi himself learned much from the West—methods of civil disobedience and passive resistance from Thoreau, for instance, and the concepts of the dignity of labour and social reform—as did Jawaharlal Nehru and other younger leaders in their attachment to socialism and large-scale industrialization. But there was also a deliberate turning back to the indigenous and the traditional. Gandhi advocated *swadeshi* ('one's own country'), by which he meant the use of indigenous and local institutions as well as Indian-made goods,[10] and fostered the use of the traditional Indian spinning-wheel, the *charkha*; he invoked Hindu and Jain concepts such as *ahimsa* (non-violence) and *tapasya* (self-inflicted suffering); and called for *hartals* or the cessation of business activity, a traditional means of persuading the authorities to modify what the protesters regard as oppression.[11] Through his celibacy (*brahmacharya*)

[9] See the writer's 'Towards Nation-wide Agitation and Organization: The Home Rule Leagues, 1915–18' in D.A. Low (ed.), *Soundings in Modern South Asian History*, London and Berkeley, Cal., 1968.

[10] See 'Swadeshi' (14 Feb. 1916) in *Speeches and Writings of Mahatma Gandhi*, Madras, 1933, pp. 336–44; *Young India*, 3 Dec. 1919, p. 8.

[11] See A.L. Basham, 'Traditional Influences on the Thought of Mahatma Gandhi', in R. Kumar (ed.), *Essays on Gandhian Politics: The Rowlatt Satyagraha of 1919*, Oxford 1971, pp. 17–42; N.K. Bose, Studies in Gandhism, Calcutta, 1962, esp. 'Conflict and its Resolution in Hindu Civilization', pp. 69–115.

and asceticism Gandhi was invoking extraordinary, super-physical powers in which tens of millions of his countrymen believed deeply.[12] Much of Gandhi's success in attracting a vast following was due to this use of concepts such as *moksha*, symbols and parables drawn from the stories of Rama and Prahlada, of institutions (even the Muslim Khilafat), and of techniques like the *hartal* which were already part of the consciousness of various Indian groups.

As one of the most creative figures in modern history, Gandhi combined his own ideas and responses with influences from many sources to form a social psychology and a programme of action for remedying situations of conflict. He was probably less concerned with the 'negative' nationalist goal of evicting the British than with the positive question of the sort of India he wished to see emerge. He was more concerned to inculcate his technique of *satyagraha* as the means of solving social and political conflict in India, and eventually in the rest of the world.[13] Erik H. Erikson[14] has suggested, comparing him with Freud, that Gandhi offered a cure for the neuroses which threaten to destroy society through the technique of *satyagraha* (literally 'holding firmly to truth'). In this technique of non-violent resistance, or even non-violent coercion, important differences which prove unamenable to compromise or arbitration are solved by one of the opponents refusing to comply with the other's wishes and accepting the consequences, even if this involves physical injury or deprivation of liberty: such sufferings patiently endured will ultimately, possibly assisted by the non-violent pressure of public opinion, bring about a change of heart in the enemy.

During this third period of Indian nationalism, Gandhi led three great extended campaigns involving increasingly large numbers of people drawn from virtually all sections of society—in 1919 and, after a lull, 1920–2; in 1930 and 1931–2; and again in 1940 and 1942. He also led

---

[12] See A.L. Basham, *The Wonder that was India*, London, 1956, pp. 244–6.

[13] See the writer's 'Non-Co-operation, 1920–22' in S.N. Ray, (ed.), *Gandhi, India and the World*, Philadelphia, Pa., 1970, pp. 171–2.

[14] *Gandhi's Truth: On the Origins of Militant Nonviolence*, London, 1970.

or guided *satyagraha* campaigns, which were at first more localized but had widespread effects—such as those in Champaran and Gujarat in 1917–18, which demonstrated his technique and attracted lieutenants and adherents who were to participate in the first nationwide campaign in 1919. The campaigns at Vykom in 1924–5 and Bardoli in 1928 focused national attention upon such matters as how to improve the lot of depressed social groups and how to refuse to pay taxes.

Gandhi's success was also based upon concern for the material problems and deprivations of millions of his fellow-countrymen: his first campaigns were on issues of rural exactions and taxes and workers' wages. His advocacy of the *charkha* and *khadi* (hand-spun, hand-woven cloth) was aimed at supplementing the incomes of poor people, particularly in the countryside, and forcing better-off groups to identify themselves with them; his manufacture of salt in illicit circumvention of the tax on this dietary staple was the most flamboyant example of his concern to increase material and social welfare, which included improvement in the status of women and untouchables; and even his adoption of the loin cloth in 1921 marked his identification with the poorest Indians rather than his asceticism.[15]

Even though Gandhi bestrides the decades from 1919 like a colossus, other leaders with other policies also made their mark on Indian nationalism. During the 1920s, after the subsidence of the Non-Cooperation agitation, the Swarajists, under the leadership of Motilal Nehru, Srinivasa Iyengar, Kelkar, and Vithalbhai Patel, contested successfully with the Moderate nationalists or Liberals for entry into the legislatures: they entered with a policy of non-cooperation with the Government from within but stayed to cooperate in parliamentary politics. In this many influences may be discerned—Gandhian moral indignation at British rule; Tilak's responsive cooperation; and even Moderate appreciation of British institutions; as well as concern to protect and further the élite social and economic groups from which the Swarajist members in the various provinces were mainly

[15] See *Hindu*, 23 Sept. 1921, p. 5.

drawn.[16] In the mid-1930s Congress again contested the elections, going on to form the Government in seven of the ten provinces, and in 1945–6 it stood for election, emerging as the dominant party at the centre. Already at its Karachi session in 1931 Congress had passed its resolution on Fundamental Rights and Economic and Social Changes, which, as well as including a declaration of rights and freedoms, posited the public ownership or control of basic industries and communications. This resolution owed some elements to Gandhi, such as total prohibition, the abolition of untouchability, and the reduction of land revenue, but its underlying socialistic tone and its passage at that time were primarily the work of Jawaharlal Nehru and the nascent Congress Socialists—and their inspiration was largely non-Indian, notably the American and French bills of rights, and European socialism, underscored by the example of Russian Communism.

II

In terms of its negative goal of evicting the British, the history of the Indian nationalist movement is a 'success story'. To what extent, though, was the Indian nationalist movement responsible for the departure of the British? The British were apparently unmoved by early nationalist demands for progress to self-rule and by the various devices by which these demands were pressed. As early as the revision of the Partition of Bengal in 1912, however, it was revealed that a determined agitation— even though largely confined to one region of India—could make the British respond to the wishes of articulate groups of Indians organized in nationalist bodies. Again, in the memorandum which the Viceroy, Lord Hardinge, sent home in October 1915, he and at least some of the provincial executives and the member of his Council showed themselves responsive to the Indians' arguments for political reform.[17] The Home

[16] See D.E.U. Baker, 'The Break-down of Nationalist Unity and the Formation of the Swaraj Parties, India, 1922 to 1924', in *University Studies in History*, Vol. 5, No. 4 (1970), esp. pp. 86–7.

[17] See Memorandum by His Excellency the Viceroy, Oct. 1915, in Hardinge Papers, Cambridge University Library.

Rule agitation at the time of the First World War, reinforced by the reform proposals produced by various branches of the nationalist movement and jointly by the Congress and Muslim League, forced the Secretary of State to concede that Indian legislators' 'authority and responsibility' must be increased,[18] which led on to the Montagu–Chelmsford Reforms, and the attempts by the British governments in India to find allies among the Moderates, now comprising the Liberal Party, all of which fostered the development of parliamentary institutions in India. Gandhi's agitation of 1920–1 seems to have prepared the Viceroy, Lord Reading, for a major concession of power,[19] and the agitations of the later 1920s and early 1930s encouraged the British Government to put to one side the Indian Statutory Commission's report and call the Round Table Conferences, thus reopening the whole question of the amount of power to be devolved.

Following the British Conservative Party's rejection of the 'die-hard' opposition to Indian reform, led by Churchill, at its December 1934 conference,[20] the Government of India Act of 1935 provided for provincial responsible government on the basis of greatly enlarged electorates. It was ironic that it was Churchill, under the pressure of the threatening 'Quit India' agitation in the wartime circumstances of 1942, who sent his Lord Privy Seal—significantly a Labour man—to offer the Indian nationalist leaders independence at the end of the war, recognizing wryly that Britain was defending 'India in order, if successful, to be turned out'. The ultimate timing of the departure was affected by other factors as well as Indian nationalist pressures. Britain was exhausted by the war, financially and militarily, and this weakened her determination to hold on imperially.

[18] Sir A. Chamberlain to the Viceroy, Lord Chelmsford, 29 Mar. 1917 and 2 May 1917, in Government of India, Home Dept. Political file A, July 1917, Nos. 299–313.

[19] See D.A. Low, 'The Government of India and the First Non-Co-operation Movement—1920–1922', *Journal of Asian Studies*, Vol. 25, No. 2 (Feb. 1966), p. 249.

[20] See S.C. Ghosh, 'Decision-Making and Power in the British Conservative Party: A Case-Study of the Indian Problem, 1929–34', *Political Studies*, Vol. 13, No. 2 (June 1965), pp. 198–212; D.A. Low, 'Sir Tej Bahadur Sapru and the First Round-Table Conference', in D.A. Low (ed.), *Soundings in Modern South Asian History*, p. 296.

Attlee and his Labour Party colleagues, the last and most unfettered of a line of liberal-minded politicians committed to political advance for India—in this case to the hilt—were elected to power at the critical moment. But at the same time the British were encouraged in their *exeunt* by the memory of the bitterness and extent of the wartime nationalist agitation in India, by the spectre of mutiny foreshadowed in the Indian National Army, by the disturbances surrounding the INA trials and the subsequent mutinies in Karachi, Bombay, and elsewhere.

III

India is a parliamentary democracy in the sense that the central and state governments of the day are responsible to the Parliament or state legislatures and through them to the adult population, who at election time have a true choice between candidates of various parties. The seed of Indian democracy was planted by the Western, and particularly the British, education introduced in the nineteenth century, but that India has grown into the world's largest democracy is due largely to the lengthy experience of the nationalist movement and its interaction with British governments.

Numbers of Congress Moderates had found their way into the legislatures in the elections on very restricted franchises (described as 'selection') under the 1892 and 1909 Councils Acts: here they learnt to operate the limited parliamentary institutions available and to press for more. Having withdrawn from Congress to form the Liberal parties in 1918, they were returned as one of the largest and certainly most articulate groups in the expanded legislatures under the Montagu–Chelmsford reforms in 1921, in the absence of Congressmen as a result of the Non-cooperation campaign. In these councils they were able to achieve reforms and to influence the executive, which reinforced the notion of the government and the bureaucracy being answerable, and in certain areas of policy under 'dyarchy' even responsible, to elected representatives. The activities of the Liberals, along with other elected members of the councils such as the non-brahmans in Madras and

Bombay, also demonstrated that the legislatures were repositories of power, and so made numbers of Congressmen anxious to obtain election, both to further nationalist goals and to gain the fruits of power and influence for the social groups from which they came. Even when the numbers of elected Liberal members of the legislatures were reduced by Congress competitors at elections in the 1920s and 1930s, the Liberals continued to be important in Indian political and nationalist life, as nominated if not elected legislators; as members of the Viceroy's or governors' executives and as their advisers; as members of important constitutional inquiries such as the Muddiman Committee, the committees associated with the Simon Commission and the Round Table Conferences; as commissioners and investigators; and as negotiators between Congress and the British. Men such as V.S. Srinivasa Sastri, P. Sivaswami Iyer, R.P. Paranjpye, and M.R. Jayakar played important roles for much of this period, and a Liberal like T.B. Sapru not only seems to have played an important part in drafting Congress constitutional documents such as the Lucknow Pact of 1916 and the Nehru Report of 1927 but also continued this role in drawing up independent India's constitution.

Those Congressmen who were elected as Swarajists in 1923 and 1926 received training in operating institutions of a parliamentary type. They found that they had to learn to operate them even in order to obstruct and protest. This constitutional tradition was reinforced in Congress when Congressmen stood successfully for election in 1937 and in 1945–6, and the experience gained in running responsible provincial governments between 1937 and 1947 stood many members of the later Congress ruling party in good stead after independence.

Under the 1935 Act the provincial governments followed the Westminster prime ministerial model rather than presidential models; it was this which Congress politicians learnt to operate and which they introduced at the centre and retained in the provinces at India's independence. An irresponsible executive was identified with foreign rule, and responsible parliamentary government was aspired to as the hallmark of self-government. In certain ways the British model was quite clearly modified or even transformed by Indian practice before

independence. One of the chief examples of this was in the dominance
of the system by one party virtually for the first forty years after
independence. The dominance of the particular party in question, the
Congress Party, was the natural result of its role as, in a sense, the
embodiment of the Indian nation during the nationalist struggle, and of
the organization, prestige, leaders, and membership it inherited from
that struggle.

Two factors important in maintaining the conditions in which
democracy can flourish are a civil service that is impartial, intelligent,
apolitical, and uncorrupt, at least in its upper levels, and an army which
is independent and at the same time subordinate to the political wing.
The nationalist period helped to bequeath such a bureaucracy and
army to India. While Gandhi had called for government servants to
desert their imperialist masters, the nationalist movement made little
attempt to undermine the position of the law, the civil service, or the
army as such, and on the other hand through agitation and participation
in government it contributed to their Indianization.

Salt Satyagraha

India's federal structure is inherited from the British, who devised it as a workable means of ruling and as a structure within which power could be devolved in the parts while retaining control at the centre, drawing on the models of the United States or the 'white' dominions. It also marks a recognition of the facts of human political geography in India. But in addition it bears influences from the nationalist period; Gandhi reorganized Congress into linguistic provincial units in 1921, and through linguistic reorganization the Indian states have approximated increasingly towards the structure of the dominant party. The strength of the central government vis-à-vis the states, epitomized in the role of the President and in matters such as finance, development investment, tariffs, and imports, may be seen as the administrative reflection of the strong Working Committee or High Command in Congress.

India is a secular state—or rather, in so far as Indian governments assist all the religious groups in the country, it is more accurately described as 'pluralistic'. This owes much to the persistence of the Moderate aim of a secular state, but was modified by Gandhi's insistence that morality and politics were one and by his appeals to the convictions of various religious groups. It was modified, too, by the Hindu communal movements of the 1920s and 1930s, such as the *sangathan* and *Ùuddhi* movement, the Rashtriya Swayamsevak Sangh, and the Hindu Mahasabha, in some ways the descendants of the Hindu assertiveness of Extremist nationalism; and by Congress's blunting of their appeal to Hindus by resisting the Muslim minority's demands for safeguards. The resulting dominance of the Hindu majority community inside and outside Congress was reinforced in the newly independent India by the flight of some of the best Muslim talent to Pakistan, so that there has been a continuing problem of ensuring that Muslims are treated equally with the other communities,[21] and feel themselves to be treated equally. At the same time, the Moderates' goal of secularism was pursued through

[21] Of recruits to the Indian Administrative Service between 1948 and 1960, for example, nearly 90 per cent were Hindu and only 1.9 per cent Muslim. See R. Braibanti and J.J. Spengler (eds), *Administration and Economic Development in India*, Durham, N.C., 1963, pp. 53–4.

the 1930s and 1940s by nationalists, such as Jawaharlal Nehru, attracted by the notions of social egalitarianism and economic development which were gaining ground in the West.

The nationalists promoted too the other elements that are essential to Western liberal democracy—freedom of speech, freedom of association, and freedom of the press—which accord well with Indian religious notions of the relativity of truth and characterize the spirit of modern India. The modern Indian provision of special facilities to underprivileged or 'backward' groups, which include a wide range of castes and tribes, flows in a straight line from the Moderates' and Arya Samajists' work for social reform through Gandhian social uplift and Nehru's concern for greater social equality.

The nationalist movement therefore did much to form modern India, and it may be asked why its consequences were so very different for Pakistan which is not secular but Islamic, and which has experimented both with presidential democracy and military autocracy. In fact considerable areas of West Pakistan in particular had hardly been affected by British education and large parts of the population were relatively untouched by the nationalist movement, many Muslims having deliberately held aloof from it and from active or at least independent participation in the legislatures. The Muslim League, which achieved Pakistan, had only developed into a well-organized party in the seven years or so before partition, and had little experience of running parliamentary or other large-scale political institutions. Even in the principal Muslim majority regions, Bengal and the Panjab, the Muslim League had little experience of running government. That Pakistan was a romantic and impractical solution to the Muslims' very real fears and problems—at least for many Muslims in the subcontinent—is indicated by the fact that half as many Muslims remained in post-independence India as in Pakistan before the breakaway of Bangladesh. The abandonment of secularism and the concept of Pakistan as an Islamic state provided little guide to how the state should be ruled, as the long agony of drawing up a constitution demonstrated, and, once Pakistan had been achieved, the need for co-operation between Muslim politicians, many of them able men, disappeared. Jinnah set the country on a presidential path, but before this institution, novel to the subcontinent, could be developed he and then his successor, Liaqat Ali Khan, died. Inheriting, like its Indian counterpart, the same traditions, the Pakistani army was at first reluctant to interfere, but on the breakdown of democratic and constitutional forms it was drawn into the process of governing.

IV

The political sociology of the independent states of the subcontinent has continued to change since independence[22]—particularly under the impact of universal franchise and economic development—but many of the social groups which have been active in politics since independence had established themselves over the preceding sixty years. Their energies had been mobilized frequently but not invariably by the nationalist movement. Research in progress on the United Provinces, for instance, shows that while the nationalist movement there was almost dormant for most of the later part of the nineteenth century, local government boards were arenas of increasing political activity, particularly along lines of rivalry between Muslims and rising Hindu groups.[23] Sooner or later, however, most groups which had stood outside the nationalist

[22] See e.g. R. Kothari and R. Maru, 'Caste and Secularism in India: Case Study of a Caste Federation', *Journal of Asian Studies*, Vol. 25, No. 1 (Nov. 1965), pp. 33–50; L.I. and S.H. Rudolph, *The Modernity of Tradition: Political Development of India*, Chicago and London, 1967; M. Rashiduzzaman, 'The Awami League in the Political Development of Pakistan', *Asian Survey*, Vol. 10, No. 7 (July 1970), pp. 574–87.

[23] L. Brennan, 'Land Policy and Social Change in Rohilkhand, 1801–1911' (unpublished M.A. thesis, University of Western Australia, 1968); F. Robinson, 'Municipal Government and Muslim Separatism in the United Provinces, 1883–1916' (unpublished paper, European Conference on Modern South Asia, Copenhagen, 1970); cf. C. Bayly, 'Local Control in Indian Towns: The Case of Allahabad, 1880–1920', *Modern Asian Studies*, Vol. 5, part 4 (Oct. 1971), pp. 289–311.

movement found that they could not afford to remain aloof from it—
as in the case of the Hindus and Muslims of the United Provinces
(now Uttar Pradesh), when Congress and the Muslim League sought
to arrange electoral concessions on behalf of those communities in
1916.[24] Either they decided that they would benefit from joining
Congress; or else the nationalist movement set out to woo and
accommodate them.

The first groups to be mobilized in the nationalist associations
and *sabhas* and in Congress in the 1870s and 1880s comprised
Western-educated Indians, mainly men engaged in the professions or
in the service of government or business firms, as well as students
aspiring to such jobs. They came almost entirely from the castes and
communities with traditions of administration and learning, notably
brahman castes, writer castes (Kayasthas and Prabhus), Parsis, and, to a
much lesser extent, Muslim groups associated with trade. Initially, they
were to be found largely in the Western port-cities and Poona.[25]
During the 1890s and the early years of the twentieth century,
however, the Extremists drew increasing numbers of less successful
members of these Western-educated groups into political agitation, in
the up-country towns in Maharashtra and Bengal, and in the Panjab
as well. In addition, Tilak in western India and Lajpat Rai in the
Panjab succeeded in involving members of some peasant castes and
urban labouring groups.

The Home Rule movement of the First World War period
carried agitational politics to many new regions—to the Tamil,
Telugu, Malayalam, and Kannada-speaking regions of the Madras
Presidency, to Gujarat, Sind, the United Provinces, and Delhi, and to
Bihar—and it caught up new social groups, notably commercial men

[24] See the writer's 'Negotiating the Lucknow Pact, 1916', *Journal of Asian Studies*,
Vol. 31, No. 3 (May 1972), pp. 561–87.

[25] See Masselos, 'Liberal Consciousness, Leadership and Political Organisation in
Bombay and Poona, 1867–1895'; B.T. McCully, *English Education and the Origins of
Indian Nationalism*, New York, 1940, esp. pp. 225–9, 281–387.

and their caste-fellows in Bombay, Gujarat, and Sind, and members of agricultural castes in the rural towns and villages of Gujarat, Maharashtra, and northern India. At the same time, the Home Rule agitation contributed to political mobilization in ways that its leaders had not intended. Non-brahmans in western and southern India were provoked into opposing the Home Rule movement, which they saw as likely to benefit only those high-caste groups already predominant in the nationalist movement. These non-brahmans were members of peasant castes in Maharashtra and the Karnatak[26] and landowners and traders in the south.[27] The Home Rule movement responded to these developments in turn by setting out, with some success, to enlist the help of members of these non-braman groups in nationalist activities.

Gandhi's local political movements and first all-India movements in the period 1917–22 mobilized a wide range of groups in various parts of British India. These include peasant-proprietors, notably in Andhra and the Panjab, as well as members of the Patidar and Anavla brahman castes in Gujarat on a much larger scale than in the Home Rule movement; and also rural tenants in parts of the United Provinces and Bihar and in the Midnapore district of Bengal and Kamrup district in Assam. The response in urban areas was widespread, but

[26] See A. T. Tansley, 'The Non-Brahman Movement in Western and Central India, 1917–23' (unpublished M.A. thesis, University of Western Australia, 1969), pp. 53–74; Maureen L.P. Patterson, 'Caste and Political Leadership in Maharashtra', *Economic Weekly* (Bombay), 6 (25 Sept. 1954), 1065–6.

[27] E. F. Irschick, *Politics and Social Conflict in South India; The Non-Brahman Movement and Tamil Separatism, 1916–1929*, Berkeley, Cal., 1969, pp. 48, 51, 61–2.

varied in terms of the social groups it involved. One can point specifically to less–Westernized businessmen, such as Marwaris in Calcutta, central India, and towns in Madras Presidency, Banias, Bhatias, and Jains in western India, and local money-lending and commercial castes in Delhi and the Panjab cities and towns; to artisans and urban proletarian groups, such as transport operatives and market labourers in the major Indian cities and in the towns of the Panjab, Gujarat, Sind, and the United Provinces, and increasingly in the later part of the period mill-operatives in cotton-milling centres; and to groups which had long been active in nationalist politics but now were so on a larger scale than ever before, professional men and college students. Conspicuously, too, the Khilafat movement drew into the agitation large numbers of Muslims from virtually every socio-economic background and geographic region, though in many cases their political activity was later to be diverted into separatist channels.[28]

One should not assume that people caught up in one Gandhian agitation remained fully active politically thereafter. Nevertheless, once people had been involved in *hartals* or demonstrations they were linked to the network of nationalist communications and leadership, and it was easier to enlist them again later.[29] Furthermore, in the periods between his great agitational campaigns of 1919–22, 1929–32, and 1940–2, Gandhi continued to win support through his constructive programmes which Congress took up, and through smaller-scale agitations. During the 1920s, for instance, through the Vykom and Bardoli satyagrahas and through Gandhi's campaign for women's rights and the promotion of *khadi*, he and his lieutenants

[28] This period is starting to receive close attention from scholars, see e.g. R. Kumar (ed.), *Essays on Gandhian Politics: The Rowlatt Satyagraha of 1919*, Oxford, 1971.

[29] On the importance of communications for nationalism, see K. W. Deutsch, *Nationalism and Social Communication: An Inquiry into the Foundations of Nationality*, Cambridge, Mass. 1966.

drew groups of untouchables and women into the political sphere. It has been argued, too, that the ideas of social equality and justice injected into Congress by Jawaharlal Nehru and the Socialists from 1930 onwards helped to retain for the nationalist movement the adherence of the underprivileged, notably working-class and peasant groups.[30] Indeed it seems that the activities of the Socialists and of the Kisan Sabhas (peasant associations) attracted such people in larger numbers as time went on.

This process was reinforced by the constitutional political activity of Congress in lengthy periods in the mid-1920s, 1930s, and 1940s, following the major Gandhian agitations. During these periods Congress participated, along with other parties, in the elections for the provincial and central legislatures—as it did at all times in those for local government bodies—and the mounting competition for seats, accompanying extensions of the franchise, brought increasing circles of society into the political process.

As Congress expanded its organizational machinery and achieved electoral success, it became increasingly attractive to groups which had stood aloof from the nationalist movement or opposed it. Notably the non-brahmans of western India joined Congress in forming governments in Bombay from the 1937 elections onwards[31] and the non-brahmans of south India likewise in the 1950s.[32] One group of whom this was not true was, of course, the Muslims. Some Muslims were attracted by the growing success and influence of Congress, and its secular ideology, but the legacy of extremist nationalism and the Hindu communal movements of the 1920s and 1930s stiffened Congress resistance to concessions and safeguards for the Muslim

[30] See R. Kumar, 'The Political Process in India', *South Asia*, 1 (Aug. 1971), 106.

[31] See Tansley, 'The Non-Brahman Movement in Western and Central India, 1917–23', pp. 216–17.

[32] See L.I. and S.H. Rudolph, *The Modernity of Tradition: Political Development in India*, pp. 55–61.

minority. This gave Muslims ample cause for apprehension, and enabled the Muslim League to draw Muslims into the separatist movement in the 1940s.

V

The Indian nationalist movement has had a lasting effect not only upon the successor states in the subcontinent but upon many other countries as well.

As the first great modern anti-colonial movement in the non-Western world, it encouraged nationalist movements in other Asian colonies—in Indonesia, Burma, Indo-China, and Ceylon. In the later 1920s the Indonesian nationalist movement looked explicitly to Gandhi's ideas and the model of Gandhian non-cooperation, even though Sukarno came to criticize what he regarded as Gandhi's concern with abstractions.[33]

Nationalist movements in Africa, particularly in British colonies, also looked explicitly to India, as well as to other successful nationalist movements in Asia. Uganda, Zambia, and Malawi each had its 'Congress', which sought to represent the whole nation; Africans in South Africa have their African National Congress. And the Ghanaian national movement, for example, was to have its share of imprisonment before self-government was won in 1957.[34]

India's successful movement for self-determination also had a practical implication for independence movements elsewhere. Once

[33] B. Dahm, *Sukarnos Kampf um Indonesiens Unabhngigkeit:Werdegang und Ideen eines asiatischen Nationalisten*, Schriften des Instituts fŸr Asienkunde in Hamburg, Band XVIII, 1966, pp. 52, 80, 83, 125. For Indian influences on Burmese nationalism, see D.E. Smith, *Religion and Politics in Burma*, Ithaca, N.Y., 1958, pp. 193, 217–21, 300–3, 319, 412–18. ForVietnamese nationalists' invocation of Indian models, see D.G.E. Hall, *A History of South-East Asia*, London, 1964, p. 719;J. Buttinger, *Vietnam:A Dragon Embattled*, London, 1967,Vol. 2, pp. 728, 1077, n. 27. For Ceylon, see C. Jeffries, *Ceylon—the Path to Independence*, London, 1962, pp. 37, 89, 102, 110, 113–14.

[34] See T. Hodgkin, *Nationalism in Colonial Africa*, London, 1956, pp. 146–8; R. Emerson and M. Kilson (eds), *The Political Awakening of Africa*, Englewood Cliffs, N.J., 1965, pp. 3, 8, 16, 49, 52–3, 71.

India was independent, the *raison d'être* for much of the rest of the British Empire[35] ceased to exist. It took British statesmen some years to recognize this, but, as they did so, they became more willing to let it go, and this in turn accelerated the whole process of decolonization.

The Indian national movement has provided an inspiration to other movements for political and social reform, particularly in the democracies of the West, and these movements have turned to Gandhi's techniques for models. In the black civil rights movement in the United States, as early as 1942 the leaders of the March on Washington Movement, aiming at equal treatment in wartime employment for both blacks and whites, considered the use of Gandhi's methods of civil disobedience.[36] In 1950 Martin Luther King was greatly attracted by what he heard of Gandhi, and in his campaigns for black rights, beginning with the successful Montgomery bus boycott in 1956, he deliberately modelled his strategy upon Gandhi's methods.[37]

VI

In the context of South Asia's history, the contribution of the Indian nationalist movement may prove to be long- or short-lived. The participants in the movement and their leaders were human, and as such fallible: the observer may not admire or approve of everything they did, and those who try to apply their methods to other situations of conflict or discontent may sometimes do so inadequately. But the Indian nationalist movement has earned its place in history alongside

[35] See R. Robinson and J. Gallagher, with Alice Denny, *Africa and the Victorians: The Official Mind of Imperialism*, London, 1963, pp. 76, 86, 93, 114, 117–18, 123, 133, 162, 190–3, 199–202, 255, 283–91, 306, 464.

[36] H. Garfunkel, *When Negroes March: The March on Washington Movement in the Organisational Politics of the F.E.P.C.*, Glencoe, Ill., 1959, pp. 133, 135.

[37] See L.D. Reddick, *Crusader without Violence: A Biography of Martin Luther King, Jr.*, New York, 1959, esp. pp. 80–1, 133–55, 208; Coretta S. King, *My Life with Martin Luther King, Jr.*, London, 1970, pp. 176–8, 192, 202, 218, 353–4.

the greatest developments in human organization and men's thought, most of all because of the moral stature of its greatest leader, Gandhi.

Modern Literature

Krishna Kripalani

THE PRESENT LINGUISTIC POSITION OF India has been summed up in the Constitution, which has scheduled fifteen major languages of the country: the eleven Indo-Aryan languages consisting of Sanskrit with its tenfold progeny: Assamese, Bengali, Gujarati, Hindi, Kashmiri, Marathi, Oriya, Panjabi, Sindhi, and Urdu; and the four Dravidian languages: Kannada, Malayalam, Tamil, and Telugu. To these fifteen, the Sahitya Akademi (National Academy of Letters, India) has for its own purposes added five more: Maithili, the language of north-east Bihar, which has a rich heritage of medieval literature, Rajasthani the language of Rajasthan, rich in ballads, Dogri the language of the Jammu region in the State of Jammu and Kashmir, Manipuri the language of Manipur in eastern India, and English. Sixteen of these twenty languages are the speeches of specific regions; Sanskrit and English cut across all regional boundaries, while the people speaking Urdu and Sindhi are scattered over different regions. All of them are the mother tongues of large or small communities, with the exception of Sanskrit, which is no longer a spoken tongue in India, although nearly 5000 persons entered it as their mother tongue in the 1961 Census.

Although the importance of a language is not necessarily to be measured by the number of persons speaking it, the relative strength of numbers is not without its significance. From this point of view Hindi may be deemed the leading language of modern India, covering as it

does the major part of north India with a population of about 150 million. This wide sweep of Hindi is, however, not without its limitations, and might be viewed more as a process than as an accomplished and uncontroverted fact.

There is, besides High Hindi and High Urdu, a large indeterminate zone where the common speech is an unpretentious middle path between the two, known as Hindustani. This was the speech which Mahatma Gandhi cherished as the *lingua franca* of modern India, hoping that it would be accepted as a common heritage by Hindus and Muslims alike. But, like many of his other dreams, the hope survives as a historical memory. Today Urdu is the official language of Pakistan and a national language of India.

One of the most characteristics aspects of modern Indian literature is thus its multiple character. It has been said that Indian literature is one, though written in many languages—a faint echo of the famous Vedic verse: 'Truth is one though sages call it by various names.'

English had the historical advantage of coming to India at a time when Sanskrit and Persian had long played out their roles as languages of enlightenment and had become mere custodians of past glory and refuges of orthodoxy. India has had many dark ages in the long course of her history, but the latter half of the eighteenth century was perhaps the darkest. Political chaos had combined with intellectual lethargy to proliferate a wilderness of cankerous growth in which, if culture survived at all it was as a few isolated oases in a vast desert.

The English language was thus voluntarily, and even enthusiastically, learnt by the young intelligentsia of Bengal, and later of other parts of India, fretting under the load of an inhibiting and meaningless discipline which the traditional learning had come to be. No doubt even at that time, the orthodox were not lacking who denounced with righteous fervour the British Government's decision to 'impose' English on Indians, though they were no less ambitious to learn the language for themselves. This bitterness (with its anomaly of denouncing English while acquiring it) has survived and has been considerably reinforced; it has been made not a little virulent by political passions—until English has been dislodged from its position as the official language and has been retained on sufferance as the associate language, while continuing in fact to perform the same service, more or less.

This service was twofold. Politically, English developed and strengthened the consciousness of national oneness more effectively and more profoundly than had ever happened before in Indian history. It also linked this consciousness with the aspiration to realize the national destiny in the context of democratic freedom. Intellectually it shook the intelligentsia out of a mental torpor which had well nigh paralysed all initiative and spirit of inquiry. The intelligentsia fostered under the new regime took to English readily, impressed by the wonderland of scientific knowledge and technique which it revealed, and charmed by a literature that seemed the more stimulating because it was so different from their own. All this would have come in any case in the course of time, as it has come to other peoples, but historical circumstances made the English language the agent of this revolutionary ferment in India and gave it a unique historical role in the development of modern India and its literatures. It would be ungracious, if not churlish, to disown this debt.

Strangely enough, knowledge of the English language and the attraction of English literature (and through it, later, of other Western literatures), instead of impeding the development of Indian languages, have proved a powerful stimulus. The new era of modern Indian literatures may be said to have begun in 1800, when Fort William College was established in Calcutta and The Baptist Mission Press in Serampore, near Calcutta. The College was founded by the East India Company to provide instruction to British civil servants in the laws, customs, religions, languages, and literatures of India in order to cope with the increasing demands of a fast-growing administrative machinery. The Press, the first to be set up in north India and still one of the best, was founded by the Baptist Mission mainly with the object of propagating Christian literature among the 'heathen' population. Whatever their original objects, the actual working of these two institutions produced results far beyond their scope. The credit for this must largely go to Dr John Gilchrist, a professor of the College, his learned and indefatigable associate William Carey, and an able and devoted band of Indian scholars. Textbooks for the teaching of Bengali, Hindi, Urdu and other Indian languages, as well as for imparting the various branches of knowledge, had to be literally manufactured, for there was little written prose available in the Indian languages, and what was available was hardly adequate for the purpose. Reading material was translated from the Sanskrit classics as well as from foreign literature, and dictionaries and grammars were compiled. William Carey, who was also one of the founders of the Baptist Mission Press, himself wrote a Bengali grammar and compiled an English–Bengali dictionary as well as two selections of dialogues and stories. He was also the author of *A Grammar of the Karnataka Language*.

The first printing press in India was set up by the Jesuit missionaries in Goa in 1566 and books in Tamil and other Dravidian languages began to be printed in the second half of the sixteenth century. Many foreign missionaries learnt the languages of the people. They not only translated the Bible and wrote Christian *Puranas* but also rendered considerable service to the languages by compiling the first modern grammars and dictionaries. The pioneer labour of the German missionary Ziegenbalg and his Italian successor Beschi in Tamil and of Father Leonardo Cinnoma in Kannada, as well as of many others in Telugu and Malayalam, is still recalled with gratitude in the history of these literatures. But, although the printing press came to South India much earlier and the foreign missionary enterprise functioned much longer and more zealously than in Bengal, the impact of Western learning as such was comparatively slow and the resurgence of literary activity bore fruit in its modern form much later than in Bengal.

Bengali type was first designed and cast by Charles Wilkins, the distinguished Sanskrit scholar (and collaborator of Sir William Jones, who founded the Asiatic Society of Bengal in 1784), and was first used in Halhed's Bengali Grammar in 1778.

The establishment of Hindu College in 1817 and the replacing of Persian by English as the language of the law and the increasing use of Bengali were other landmarks which encouraged the introduction of modern education and the development of the language of the people. It was, however, Raja Ram Mohan Roy (1772–1833) who laid the real foundation of modern Bengali prose, as indeed he did of the Indian renaissance in general. Though essentially a religious and social reformer, the learning, versatility, and zeal of this extraordinary man blazed new trails in almost every field of Indian life and culture. The form which he gave to Bengali prose, necessarily somewhat crude and tentative, revealed its rich potentiality in the hands of Ishvarachandra Vidyasagar (1820–91) and Akshaykumar Datta (1820–86), both of whom were, like their great predecessor, primarily social reformers and educationists. Because they were men of serious purpose who had much to say, they had little use for the flamboyance and rhetoric natural to a language derived from Sanskrit, and they chiselled a prose that was both chaste and vigorous.

Path finders rather than creative artists, they standardized the medium which their younger contemporary, Bankim Chandra Chatterjee (1838–94), turned with superb gusto and skill into a creative tool for his novels and stories. He is known as the father of the modern novel in India and his influence on his contemporaries and successors,

Leaders of the Indian Nationalist Movement—Bose, Gandhi, Tilak, and Nehru

in Bengal and other parts of India, was profound and extensive. Novels, both historical and social—the two forms in which he excelled—had been written before him in Bengali by Bhudev Mukherji and Peary Chand Mitra. Mitra's *Alaler Gharer Dulal* is in fact the first specimen of original fiction of social realism with free use of the colloquial idiom, and anticipated, however crudely, the later development of the novel. But it was Bankim Chandra who established the novel as a major literary form in India. He had his limitations, he was too romantic, effusive, and didactic, and was in no sense a peer of his great Russian contemporaries, Tolstoy and Dostoevsky. There have been better novelists in India since his day, but they all stand on his shoulders.

Though the first harvest was reaped in Bengali prose, it was in the soil of poetry that this cross-fertilization with the West bore its richest fruit. Michael Madhusudan Dutt (1824–73) was the pioneer who, turning his back on the native tradition, made the first conscious and successful experiment to naturalize the European forms into Bengali poetry by his epic in blank verse, *Meghnadbadh*, based on a *Ramayana* episode unorthodoxly interpreted, as well as by a number of sonnets.

It was Tagore who naturalized the Western spirit into Indian literature and thereby made it truly modern in an adult sense. He did this not by any conscious or forced adaptation of foreign models but by his creative response to the impulse of the age, with the result that the *Upanishads* and Kalidasa, Vaishnava lyricism, and the rustic vigour of the folk idiom, are so well blended with Western influences in his poetry that generations of critics will continue to wrangle over his specific debt to each of them. In him modern Indian literature came of age—not only in poetry but in prose as well. Novel, short story, drama, essay, and literary criticism, they all attained maturity in his hands. Though Indian literature in its latest phase has outgrown his influence, as indeed it should, Tagore was the most vital creative force in the cultural renaissance of India and represents its finest achievement.

As poetry in Michael Madhusudan's hands and the novel in Bankim's, the modern drama too owed its inspiration to the Western model. The tradition of classical Sanskrit drama had long been lost and had not in any case percolated into the popular pattern of culture. But there is hardly a people who do no love to watch a visual representation of their life and lore, and so there arose a kind of composite folk drama— *Kathakali* in Kerala, *Yakshagana* in Karnataka, *Ankiya Nat* in Assam, *Tamasha* in Maharashtra, *Yatra* in Bengal, *Ras-lila* in Braj and Manipuri, etc.—in which Puranic themes were interpreted on an improvised stage with the help of declamation, mime, song, and dance, and this was popular all over India. Whatever its other virtues, it was not drama proper. It was a composite entertainment, in the sense in which the word is understood today, more melodrama than drama, which is essentially an urban growth and a cultivated and sophisticated art, requiring considerable organization and resources.

Calcutta being the first cosmopolitan city in India to grow under the new regime, it was natural that it should witness the birth of the modern drama. It has still a lively stage tradition. Curiously enough, the first stage play in Bengali produced in Calcutta was by a Russian adventurer-cum-Indologist, Lebedev, in 1795. It was an adaptation of a little-known English comedy, *The Disguise*, by Richard Paul Jodrell, oddly mixed with English and Hindustani dialogue to suit the needs of a mixed audience. The main dialogue was, however, in Bengali and the actors and actresses were likewise Bengali.

Many years passed before a serious attempt was made to build an authentic stage, mainly under private patronage. The first original play in Bengali was *Kulin Kulasarvasva*, a social satire against the practice of polygamy among *Kulin* brahmans, written by Pandit Ramnarayan. Ramnarayan's second play, *Ratnavali*, based on a Sanskrit classic, provoked Madhusudan Dutt to try his hand at this medium. His impetuous genius turned out a number of plays in quick succession, some based on old legends and some social satires.

His place was taken by Dinabandhu Mitra (1829–74), a born dramatist whose very first play, *Nil Darpan* (published in 1860), exposing the atrocities of the British indigo planters, created a sensation, both literary and political. The Revd. J. Long, a noble-hearted missionary who had the audacity to publish the play in English, was fined and imprisoned by the authorities. Dinabandhu wrote many more plays and was followed by a succession of playwrights among whom were Rabindranath Tagore's elder brother Jyotirindranath, Manomohan Basu, and, later, the more famous Girischandra Ghosh and Dwijendralal Roy. Girischandra was actor, producer, and playwright, and it is to his indefatigable zeal that the public theatre in Calcutta is largely indebted. But though both he and Dwijendralal achieved phenomenal popularity in their day, their popular appeal was due more to the patriotic and melodramatic elements in their plays than to any abiding literary merit. On the other hand, Rabindranath Tagore's plays, though they had considerable literary merit and were marked by originality and depth of thought, were too symbolic or ethereal to catch the popular imagination. And so he too failed to create a firm tradition in this field, with the result that of all literary forms in modern Indian literature the drama remains the least developed.

Bengali had the advantage of bearing the first impact to the introduction of English education and Western learning in India. Being a sensitive and emotional people, the Bengalis reacted to this with whole-hearted and passionate warmth. But the general pattern of literary resurgence was more or less the same in all Indian languages, each responding in its own manner, some sooner and some later.

Of the numerous languages of India perhaps Marathi was, after Bengali, the most vigorous in its response to the spirit of the new age, partly because of its robust intellectual tradition, reinforced by memories of the erstwhile glory of the Maratha Empire, and partly because Bombay, like Calcutta, provided a cosmopolitan modern environment. Among the stalwarts who laid the foundation of its modern literature may be mentioned the poet Keshavsut, the novelist Hari Narayan Apte, and Agarkar, Tilak, Chiplunkar as the builders of prose. Apte's novels stimulated the development of the novel in some other languages too, particularly in the neighbouring Kannada. Kirloskar and Deval did for the Marathi stage what Girischandra had done for the Bengali.

Narmad's poetry blazed the trail in Gujarati, while Govardhanram's *Sarasvatichandra* made a landmark in Gujarati fiction. Hindi had to face the difficult task of cutting a new broad channel into which the waters of its many tributaries could flow and which could be perennially fed from the vast reservoir of Sanskrit. This feat was performed by 'Bharatendu' Harischandra and Mahavirprasad Dwivedi.

The problem of Urdu was different. Its form derived from the same basic structure as Hindi, the common speech known as *Khari Boli*, had been standardized much earlier. Flourishing under court patronage, it had made phenomenal progress and was the most important Indian language to prosper in the eighteenth century. But it luxuriated in its own affluence and remained aloof from the vital currents that were sweeping the country forward in the nineteenth century. It is not without a certain significance that its greatest poet, Ghalib, was still composing doleful—though magnificent—ghazals redolent of Persian rose gardens when Michael Madhusudan, Bankim, and Dinabandhu were cutting new paths for Indian literature.

The development of modern Assamese and Oriya, the two eastern neighbours of Bengali, was also late in coming and was preceded by valuable spadework done by the Christian missions. Lakshmikanta Bezbarua and Padmanath Gohain Barua in Assamese, and Fakirmohan Senapati and Radhanath Ray in Oriya were the early pioneers in their respective fields.

Kashmiri, Panjabi, and Sindhi had an even more retarded development, partly on account of the political conditions and partly because of the cultural glamour of Urdu in regions predominantly Muslim. All the more credit to the pioneers who held aloft the banner of their mother tongue when it hardly paid to do so: Mahjur and Master Zinda Kaul in Kashmiri, Sardar Puran Singh and Bhai Vir Singh in Panjabi, and Mirza Kalich Beg and Dewin Kauromal in Sindhi.

What is surprising is the rather late and tardy resurgence in the four Dravidian languages, which had had a longer and a richer literary past than the northern languages as well as an earlier and closer contact with the Christian missions. The past has weighed more heavily on the South than on the North in India and nowhere more heavily than on Tamilnadu. However, in course of time, the creative spirit in these languages too responded to the impulse of the age, in as rich a flowering as in the other languages of India, led by Puttanna, 'Sri', and Kailasham in Kannada, by Kerala Varma and Chandu Menon in Malayalam, by Bharati and Kalki in Tamil, and Viresalingam and Guruzada Appa Rao in Telugu. It is worth observing that the youngest of the Dravidian languages, Malayalam, has responded to the new age more dynamically than the oldest, Tamil, which even now looks too wistfully to the past.

Main Trends

The development of modern Indian literature has been marked by certain characteristics, some of which it shares with modern literatures the world over, while others are incidental to the special circumstances attending its birth. One of the latter is a certain dichotomy in the mental attitudes of the writers, some welcoming the new impulse, some resenting it—a dichotomy no less discernible in the make-up of the individual writer, whose one eye looks wistfully backwards, the other longingly ahead. There has always been in all countries and ages a conflict between the orthodox and the unorthodox, but in India, because the new impulse was identified with an alien culture and foreign domination, the clash of loyalties has been sharper. The very impact of Western thought, with its emphasis on democracy and self-expression, stimulated a nationalist consciousness which resented the foreign imposition and searched for the roots of self-respect and pride in its own heritage. Tagore's novel *Gora* is a masterly interpretation of this built-in conflict in the very nature of Indian renaissance, a conflict which still persists and has coloured not only our literature but almost every aspect of our life.

The first outstanding Bengali poet of the nineteenth century (and the last in the old tradition), Ishwar Chandra Gupta (1812–59), whose remarkable journal, *Samvad Prabhakar*, was the training ground of many distinguished writers and who wrote the first literary biographies of his predecessor poets, was a doughty champion of the native heritage and poured his biting ridicule on everything that savoured of the new, irrespective of whether it was good or bad. Even the great Bankim

Chandra, himself a leading herald of the new, looked more and more wistfully to the past as he grew older. Tilak in Marathi and Bharati in Tamil were even more aggressive in their native pride and had their counterparts in all Indian languages.

This pride in India's past grew more lyrical under the stress of political aspirations and provided increasing fuel to the movement for national freedom. Whilst it thus served a useful purpose, it had its unhealthy and reactionary aspect in so far as it encouraged an exaggerated self-righteousness and distorted the historical perspective. Even so chaste a spirit as Mahatma Gandhi could fall under its spell and utter with passionate sincerity the dismal half-truth that the British association had ruined India not only economically but intellectually, morally, and spiritually.

On the other hand, it is well to recall the testimony of Romesh Chunder Dutt, the distinguished scholar and historian who was himself one of the builders of the nineteenth-century renaissance, as recorded in the first edition of his *The Literature of Bengal*, published in 1877.

The conquest of Bengal by the English [wrote India's first modern historian] was not only a political revolution but ushered in a greater revolution in thoughts and ideas, in religion and society. We cannot describe the great change better than by stating that English conquest and English education may be supposed to have removed Bengal from the moral atmosphere of Asia to that of Europe. All the great events which have influenced European thought within the last one hundred years have also told, however feeble their effect may be, on the formation of the intellect of modern Bengal. The independence of America, the French Revolution, the war of Italian independence, the teachings of history, the vigour and freedom of English literature and English thought, the great effort of the French intellect in the eighteenth century, the results of German labour in the field of philosophy and ancient history—Positivism, Utilitarianism, Darwinism—all these have influenced and shaped the intellect of modern Bengal. ... In habits, in tastes, in feeling, freedom and vigour and partiarchal institutions, our literature therefore has undergone a corresponding change.

In so far as this somewhat effusive acknowledgement of India's debt
to the West contains the core of a fair analysis, it was true in 1877 of a
very limited intelligentsia in the city of Calcutta. It was hardly true of
the rest of Bengal and India. Nevertheless, it was this limited intelligentsia
that was the main vanguard of the moral and intellectual upsurge of the
nineteenth century.

From the beginning of the twentieth century Indian literature was
increasingly coloured by political aspiration, passionately voiced in the
songs and poems of the Tamil poet Bharati and the Bengali poet Kazi
Nazrul Islam. The spiritual note of Indian poetry which had attained a
poignant and rapturous pitch in the medieval Vaishnava outpourings
became fainter and fainter and was drowned by more earthly pains and
longings. Tagore's *Gitanjali* is the swan song of this great tradition.

Tagore's influence, after the award of the Nobel Prize in 1913,
crossed the frontiers of Bengal and was for some time a source of

exhilaration, if not always of inspiration, to his contemporaries all over India, from Master Zinda Kaul in Kashmir to Kumaran Asan in Kerala. The influence was, however, superficial, since most of them knew him only through the English translations. The influence was more fruitful in the case of Assamese, Oriya, Gujarati, and Hindi, where the young poets took the trouble to learn Bengali, mainly to read him in the original. The *Chhayavad* or Romantic school in Hindi poetry, led by Nirala, Pant, and others, which was a potent stimulus in the development of modern Hindi literature, was directly inspired by it. Tagore's main impact was, however, indirect, inasmuch as it gave confidence to Indian writers that they could achieve in their mother tongue what had been achieved in Sanskrit or European languages.

But Tagore's influence, such as it was, was soon overshadowed by the impact of Gandhi, Marx, and Freud, a strange trinity. Though none of these three was a man of letters proper, they released intellectual and

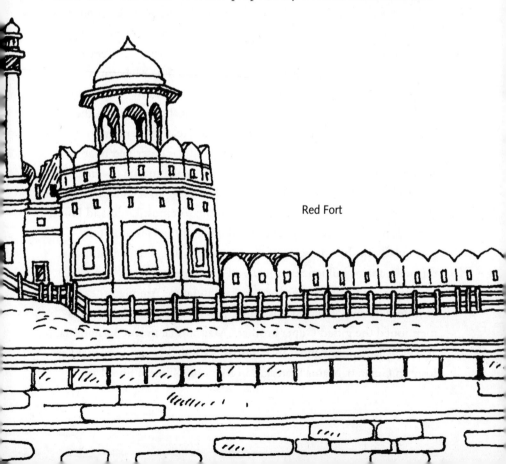

Red Fort

moral passions and introduced new techniques of thought and behaviour which had a profound effect on young writers all over India. Gandhi impact, confined to India, was both widespread and deep, though it was deeper on some languages than on others, much deeper, for instance, on Gujarati and Hindi than on Bengali. Gandhi transfigured the image of India and turned national idealism from its futile adulation of the past to face the reality of India as she was, poor, starving, and helpless, but with an untapped potential of unlimited possibilities.

Both Vivekananda and Tagore had said the same thing before, but it was Gandhi more than anyone else who made this image vivid and real and gave a new insight to the Indian intelligentsia, enlarging their sympathies and adding a new dimension to their imagination. Indian writers learnt to discover their own country, not in ancient Banaras and Madurai but in the slums of Calcutta and Bombay, and in the innumerable 'dunghills scattered over the land', as Gandhi described the Indian villages in their poverty and squalor. He thus provided a powerful ethical stimulus to the literary trend, which had already begun, from romanticism to realism, from the highflown and artificial 'literary' style to the vigour and raciness of the spoken idiom. The Mahatma's insistence on non-violence and on simplicity and purity in personal life touched a responsive chord in the inherent idealism of Indian thought and thus served as an indirect inspiration to creative literature.

The eminent Hindi novelist Premchand has described in an autobiographical essay how, inspired by the Mahatma, he resigned from government service and settled down in a village to see life in the raw and to write about it. His later career as the foremost Urdu and Hindi novelist, his imaginative insight into the life of the common folk, particularly in the villages, and his simple and direct delineation of it formed a major influence on many of his contemporaries and reflect the impact of Ganhi on modern Indian literature. Among other writers of note who responded to this impact, each in his own fashion, may be mentioned the gifted Gupta brothers, Maithilisharan and Siyaramsharan, as well as Jainendra Kumar in Hindi, Kaka Kalelkar and Umashankar Joshi in Gujarati, Mama Warerkar in Marathi, Nilmani Phookan in

Assamese, Kalindicharan Panigrahi in Oriya, Annadashankar Ray in
Bengali, Bharati in Tamil, Vallathol in Malayalam, and many more in
these and other languages.

The eruption of Marxism in the early 1930s is a phenomenon
which India shares with many other countries. The infection caught by
Indian literature was, however, neither virulent nor on the whole
unhealthy. Gandhi had already given a new orientation to the popular
imagination by looking for God, not in the temple but in the *daridra-
narayana*, hungry outcaste. This moral vaccination had a twofold reaction:
on the one hand, ethical sensibility moved leftwards and it became almost
virtuous to be radical; on the other hand, class hatred was softened if not
rendered comparatively innocuous. This would explain how a Vallathol
could invoke Lenin with as much gusto as the lyrical fervour with which
he sang of Mary Magdalene and Gandhi, and why Premchand, who
ended his autobiographical testament with an affirmation of the Vaishnava
faith that not a blade of grass stirs but as God wills it, came to be hailed
by the 'Progressives' as the Gorky of India. On the other side is the example
of the works of Bengali writers with professed Marxist leanings—Manek
Bandyopadhyay's *Putul Nacher Itikatha* is a fine illustration—who are not
ashamed to delineate bourgeois types in their fiction with real sympathy
and understanding. 'Progressive' writers in Urdu and Panjabi, who are a
dominant influence in these literatures, are less sensitive, and indulge with
naïve gusto in mockery and hatred. They make up for this lack of
sensibility, however, with an added dash of virility.

The literary impact of the current explosive, in Bengal, in Kerala,
and in some other parts of India, of class hatred and violence, and of
an organized campaign to desecrate and destroy all vestiges of
inherited cultural values in the name of a Maoist 'cultural revolution',
is a phenomenon too recent for a proper assessment. To some extent
this rebellious and desperate mood is part of a worldwide eruption.
How far it will turn out to be a lasting or vital literary inspiration it is
hard to predict. Already its excesses are causing a general revulsion.

Freud, like the Vedas, is hardly ever read by Indian writers, but as
the pious justify every folly in the name of scripture, so there is no

dearth of writers who imagine that they are probing the depths of the human psyche by smelling sex everywhere. Nevertheless, the impact of Freud, however naïvely interpreted, has helped to loosen many inhibitions from which the earlier writers, brought up in the climate of nineteenth-century puritanism, had suffered.

To these two foreign and non-literary stimuli, Marxist dialectics and Freudian probings, must be added a literary one proper, though equally an importation, namely the new formalist experiments which have achieved both popularity and prestige in the West. These experiments, known under various high-sounding names associated with such writers as Ezra Pound, T.S. Eliot, James Joyce, Jean-Paul Sartre, and others, are mainly in form and technique and have little to do with any particular faith or ideology, although they may reflect a significant mental attitude. A writer may be very daring in form but conservative or even reactionary in religious or political faith, or vice versa. Bishnu De and Buddhadeva Bose in Bengali, Ajneya and Shamsher Bahadur in Hindi, Mardhekar and Vinda Karandikar in Marathi, and a host of other parallels in Indian languages share a common iconoclastic zeal in form but are faithful of their respective orthodoxies in faith.

On the whole, the impact on Indian writing of the mixed interaction of these three imported influences has been a salutary one, despite some wild aberrations. It has given a much-needed jolt to the smugness of the traditional attitude, with its age-old tendency to sentimental piety and glorification of the past. The revolt began in Bengal, although Bengal was already the home of unorthodoxy in literary form, Tagore and his contemporaries having long blasted 'the castle of conformism'. But the adulation of Tagore was itself becoming an orthodoxy, which provoked in the early 1920s a group of young gifted writers known as the Kallol group to proclaim their revolt. The revolt of the new, as Tagore pointed out, is very often its audacity only, and these writers soon discovered that Tagore could outmodern them whenever he cared to. Nevertheless, the revolt yielded a rich harvest, in both poetry and prose, in the work of Jivanananda Das, Premendra Mitra, Buddhadeva Bose, Manek Bandyopadhyay, Subhas Mukhopadhyay, and others. This movement has been paralleled in almost all Indian languages and has been particularly fruitful in the lyric and its counterpart in prose, the short story. While valiant champions of the older tradition have continued to hold their own, like Viswanadha Satyanarayana in Telugu, Mahadevi Varma in Hindi, and many more in the various languages, it is the spirit of nonconformism that gives variety and colour to much of modern writing in India.

But poetry hardly suits the temper of the modern industrial society and if it continues to be written in India in such profusion and with such exuberance, it is partly because the tradition of poetry being sung or chanted is very old and deep-rooted there, and partly because a certain prestige clings to poetry as 'purer' literature than any other. Even so, poetry as a form of narrative has lost its ancient vogue and has willy-nilly yielded the place of honour to the novel and the short story, which are today the most popular as well as the best cultivated forms of literature. In Bengal both these forms attained an early maturity in the hands of Tagore and have since made phenomenal progress under his younger contemporaries and successors, among whom Sarat Chandra Chatterjee achieved a popularity, both in Bengal and outside, which equalled, if not surpassed, that of Tagore. Though not so spectacularly popular, the novels and stories of Bibhuti Bhushan Bannerji (whose *Pather Panchali* in its screen version has since received wide publicity), Tarashankar Bannerji, Manek Bandyopadhyay, Satinath Bhaduri, 'Bonophul', Achintya Sengupta, Prabodh Sanyal, and many have maintained a high standard. Whether the treatment is romantic, realistic, or impressionist, whether the exploration is historical, regional, tribal, or psychological, the bias Marxian or Freudian, they have continued the tradition of humanism and of sympathy for the fallen bequeathed by Tagore and Sarat Chandra.

Among notable contemporaries in other Indian languages who have handled the art of fiction with originality and skill may be mentioned Biren Bhattacharya and Abdul Malik in Assamese, Pannalal Patel and Barshak in Gujarati, Jainendra Kumar and Yashpal in Hindi, Masti and Karanth in Kannada, Akhtar Mohiuddin and Sufi Ghulam

Mohammad in Kashmiri, Thakizhi (whose *Chemmin* has been published in several foreign editions) and Bashir in Malayalam, Khandekar and Gadgil in Marathi, the Mohanty brothers in Oriya, Nanak Singh and Duggal in Panjabi, Mi. Pa. Somasundaram and Ka. Na. Subramanyam in Tamil, Bapiraju and Padmaraju in Telugu, and Kishan Chunder and Bedi in Urdu. These names are merely illustrative and can be matched by many more. They represent not only a medley of techniques and attitudes but also uneven levels of creative achievement and conflicting trends. But India is a land of contrasts, not only economically but culturally as well.

The position of Sanskrit itself is an apt illustration. Deemed a 'dead' language because it is no longer a spoken tongue, it is nevertheless not only a very vital source language on which almost all Indian languages, except Urdu, draw for their vocabulary, but also a living fount of literary

Rashtrapati Bhawan

inspiration to Indian writers, an honour rivalled only by English. Perhaps there has not been a single writer of outstanding distinction in the modern period (Urdu writers excepted) who has not drawn freely on the wealth of both Sanskrit and English literatures, though some have taken more from the one than the other. Some ultra-moderns, like Sudhin Datta in Bengali, are indeed a curious complex of Sanskrit, Baudelaire, and Eliot, as some leftists like Rahula Sankrityayana are of Sanskrit, Tibetan, and Marx.

The position of English is in some respects unique in India. On the one hand it is resented by the ultra-nationalist sentiment as a relic of erstwhile foreign imposition and is allowed to continue officially on sufferance; on the other it is still the main medium of higher education in most of the universities, especially in the sciences and technology which are the backbone of

modern education, and the one link among the intelligentsia all over India. The fact that Jawaharlal Nehru when he was the Prime Minister of India and Dr S. Radhakrishnan the then President of India could converse with each other in English only and employed it as their main literary vehicle, and also the fact that the collected works of Mahatma Gandhi are being published (under the auspices of the Government of India) in English are themselves a commentary on the current usefulness of this language in India as 'a link language', to quote Jawaharlal Nehru's description of it in the Indian Parliament. It may also be noted that more books continue to be published in English than in any Indian language in India.

But apart from its utilitarian value as a language of higher education in the sciences and a 'link language', a fair number of Indian writers, including such eminent thinkers steeped in Indian thought as Vivekananda, Ranade, Gokhale, Aurobindo, and Radhakrishnan, have volutarily adopted it was their literary medium. Even the bulk of Mahatma Gandhi's writings are in English. This phenomenon is as old as modern Indian literature itself. There has been, from Derozio in the 1820s to R.K. Narayan today, an unbroken tradition of some gifted Indians choosing to write in English. Many of them, like the Dutt sisters, Toru and Aru, their versatile uncle Romesh Chunder, Manomohan Ghosh, Sarojini Naidu, and, among contemporaries, Mulk Raj Anand, Raja Rao, Bhabani Bhattacharya, and many others, have achieved distinction.

Some English novels of R.K. Narayan, a born story-teller with an eye for observation and the gift of gentle irony, are superior in intrinsic literary merit to a great deal of mediocre stuff that passes for literature in some Indian languages. On the other hand, it cannot be denied that, as far as creative writing is concerned, no Indian writer in English has reached anywhere near the heights attained by some of the great writers in the Indian languages.

What modern Indian literature sadly lacks is a well-proportioned and many-sided development. Against its achievement in poetry and fiction must be set its poverty in drama, in critical apparatus, and the literature of knowledge in general. Though Indian life is full of drama which is being well exploited in fiction, in scenarios for the screen, and even in plays for the radio, drama proper has failed to keep pace with the best in poetry and fiction, either in quality or output, the reason probably being that drama has little scope for growth independently of the stage and there is almost no professional stage worth the name in the cities of India, despite some brave endeavours in Calcutta and Bombay, and recently in Delhi.

There is, indeed, no dearth of books published on literary research and criticism. But much of it, unfortunately, is laborious and unimaginative pedantry, flogging the dead horse of Sanskrit aesthetics or indiscriminately applying borrowed cannons and 'isms' from abroad, irrespective of the context of Indian life and tradition, or, worse still, unashamedly boosting regional or national claims. Happily, despite this clamour of pedantry, patriotic piety, and political bias, good literature continues to be written and, as it justifies itself, it helps to sharpen the reader's sensibility. Since the time of Tagore, a growing minority of intelligent critics well versed in the literary traditions of their own country and of the West have bravely maintained a more wholesome approach that is neither overwhelmed by the burden of the past nor overawed by the glamour of the latest fashion. This healthy trend should gain in strength with a growing realization that, in the republic of letters as in that of men, a sensitive and well-trained critical apparatus and its judicious and fearless exercise are the *sine qua non* of happy results.

One would imagine that the achievement of Indian independence in 1947, which came in the wake of the Allied victory and was followed by the collapse of colonialism in the neighbouring countries of South East Asia, would have released an upsurge of creative energy. No doubt it did, but unfortunately it was soon submerged in the great agony of the partition, with its inhuman slaughter of the innocents and the uprooting of millions of people from their homeland, followed by the martyrdom of Mahatma Gandhi. These tragedies, along with Pakistan's invasion of Kashmir and its activities in Bangladesh, did indeed provoke a spate of poignant writing, particularly in the languages of the regions most affected, Bengali, Hindi, Kashmiri, Panjabi, Sindhi, and Urdu. But poignant or passionate writing does not by itself make great literature.

If no great literature has yet emerged out of this chain of convulsions, it must be recalled that half a century had to elapse after Napoleon's invasion of Russia before *War and Peace* was written. Meanwhile, Indian literature is richer today in volume, range, and variety than it ever was in the past, even if no great peaks are visible, such as once marked its landscape. The writers are exploring new fields and there is hardly a branch of literature in which experiments, some feeble, some vigorous, are not being made. Translations from one Indian language into another, as well as from many foreign languages, help to widen the writer's horizon and to stimulate his urge to experiment and to emulate. The Union and State Governments are increasingly aware of the role of literature in society and do what they can to encourage good writing, both directly and through the National and State Academies and Book Trusts.

Contributors

A.L. BASHAM (1914–86) was Director, Royal Asiatic Society of Great Britain and Ireland.

THOMAS BURROW (1909–86) was F.B.A. Boden Professor of Sanskrit and Fellow of Balliol College, University of Oxford.

PRAMOD CHANDRA is Professor Emeritus, University of Bombay, India.

S.N. DAS GUPTA (1885–1952) was formerly Lecturer in Philosophy, University of Cambridge and Professor of Mental and Moral Science, University of Calcutta.

N.A. JAIRAZBHOY is Emeritus Professor, University of California, Los Angeles.

J.T.F. JORDENS was formerly Dean, Faculty of Asian Studies, Australian National University, Canberra, Australia.

KRISHNA KRIPALANI (1907–92) was Secretary, Sahitya Akademi.

B.B. LAL was formerly the Director General of the Archaeological Survey of India.

HEW MCLEOD is Emeritus Professor of History, University of Otago.

H.F. OWEN was Lecturer in History, University of Western Australia, Perth, Australia.

SARVEPALLI RADHAKRISHNAN (1888–1975) was formerly Professor of Philosophy, University of Calcutta; Professor of Eastern Religions, University of Oxford; and Vice Chancellor, Banares Hindu University. He also served as the Vice President and the President of India.

P.S. RAWSON was formerly Dean, School of Art and Design, Goldsmith's College, University of London.

S.A.A. RIZVI was formerly Reader in South Asian Civilization, Australian National University, Canberra, Australia.

MARTIN S. BRIGGS (b.1882) was formerly Lecturer, London University School of Architecture.

BHIKSHU SANGHARAKSHITA founded the Friends of the Western Buddhist Order.

PERCIVAL SPEAR (1901–82) taught History at St Stephen's College, University of Delhi.

ROMILA THAPAR is Emeritus Professor of History, Jawaharlal Nehru University, Delhi, Honorary Fellow of Lady Margaret Hall, Oxford, and Corresponding Fellow of the British Academy.

A.N. UPADHYE was formerly Professor of Jainalogy and Prakrit, University of Mysore, India.

A.K. WARDER is Professor Emeritus of Sanskrit, University of Toronto.

Acknowledgements

The Publisher would like to thank all the institutions and individuals listed below for giving permission to use copyrighted photographs and illustrations in the book:

American Institute of Indian Studies page: 155

Archeological Survey of India pages: 15, 18–19, 26, 27, 34, 57, 61, 79, 82, 91, 96

Dilip K. Chakrabarti and Nayana Chakrabarti pages: 39, 45, 84, 86–7, 111, 118, 125, 130

Khushwant Singh pages: 262–3

Anurag Srivastava pages: 31, 64, 100, 104–5, 167, 176–7, 178, 193, 197, 236–7

B.P.S. Walia page: 213